SIGNAL—"WHO ARE YOU?"   ANSWER—"PA'-NI."

PAWNEE HERO STORIES
and FOLK-TALES

with notes on
The Origin, Customs and Character
of the Pawnee People

GEORGE BIRD GRINNELL

Introduction by
Maurice Frink

University of Nebraska Press, Lincoln

1961

Library of Congress catalog card number 61–10153
International Standard Book Number 0–8032–0896–0 (cloth)
International Standard Book Number 0–8032–5080–0 (paper)

MANUFACTURED IN THE UNITED STATES OF AMERICA

First Bison Book printing October, 1961

Most recent printing shown by first digit below:
6   7   8   9   10

INTRODUCTION TO THE
BISON BOOK EDITION

The Pawnee Indians possessed a religion more highly developed in some respects than that of any other Plains tribe. The Pawnees had brought their beliefs into a logical system. They venerated a supreme being named Tirawa, who ruled the Universe. Lesser beings, associated by the Pawnees with the stars and animals, guarded and helped the people. As Tirawa was the father, so the corn which they raised and on which their subsistence depended was the mother. Around them the Pawnee religion centered, rich in symbolism and poetic imagination, with ceremonies that were a potent force in holding together the tribe, giving its scattered bands a cohesion which was proudly manifest in the Pawnees' name for themselves: Men of men.

So what? one may ask. Who cares to what deities a vanished people prayed? What does it matter today that once there were Indians who believed in a supernatural being called Tirawa, that they saw him in the rains and the lightning, and heard the first thunder of spring as his sign that planting time was come?

It matters because the people who were the possessors of our land are becoming a part of us. Their dark skins are growing lighter as their blood slowly mingles with ours. This process of integration, which is proceeding at a steady pace, will strengthen us to the extent that the good stays on top—to the extent that we derive value from assimilation of the higher qualities of a people whom some of us have found it too easy to consider a lesser race.

The Indian contribution to our culture is by no means limited to our folklore and to our place names. It appears in our art and music and literature; and even in such mundane matters as food (think of the traditional Thanksgiving menu) and clothing and equipment (the moccasin, the canoe, the snowshoe). But in our fast-moving civilization the Indian, in the process of acculturation, is rapidly losing his "Indian-ness," and there is an urgent necessity to make sure that the traditions and values, tangible and intangible, of his culture are preserved. For this reason alone, quite apart from its intrinsic interest, the republication of George Bird Grinnell's first book about the Indians is to be commended. It reminds us that

Indian hero stories and folk-tales are not just quaint relics of the past: they are a part of us all, a common heritage.

The old-time Pawnees, for all their ferocity in war and their cruelty to enemies, possessed many qualities worthy of emulation, qualities whose absorption strengthens us. They were generous, home-loving, and industrious in tilling their fields and hunting the all-important buffalo. It was their tragedy that their homeland lay in the main path of the whiteman's westward migration routes, and so they succumbed early to some of the eroding effects of contact with frontier civilization. But they (and we) are fortunate that there came among them, just before it was too late, a white chronicler with the sympathy and the skill to set down an account of their religion, their mythology, and their brave service in a cause they might have been expected to oppose, the white man's subjugation of the hostiles.

The chronicler, George Bird Grinnell, was born in the year of the California gold rush. Disciplined by attendance at a military school and with his perceptions sharpened by travel abroad, he matriculated at Yale, from which he received his A.B. in 1870. (In 1880 he took his Ph.D., and was awarded a Litt.D. in 1921.) On his graduation he became an assistant in osteology at the

Peabody Museum, New Haven, and soon thereafter spent six months in the unmapped West as a bone-hunter on an expedition led by O. C. Marsh, pioneer paleontologist, who was collecting vertebrate fossils for the Peabody. This expedition marked the beginning of Grinnell's long career, during which he added vastly to our knowledge of the natural resources and animal life of the American West as well as of its primitive peoples.

The Marsh expedition of 1870 was guided by two Pawnee braves picturesquely named Duellist and Best-of-All. Also with the party was the organizer and commander of the Pawnee Scouts, Major Frank North. Grinnell's first contact with the Pawnees awoke in him such interest that in 1872 he returned to live for a time with the tribe. The detailed and exciting description of a buffalo hunt in which he participated during this summer may be found in this book beginning on page 270.

In 1874 Grinnell was one of a corps of Yale scientists invited by Lieutenant Colonel George Armstrong Custer to accompany a military expedition into the relatively unexplored Black Hills of South Dakota. On this expedition Grinnell first met such frontiersmen as Lonesome Charlie Reynolds, who was to die with Custer on the

Little Big Horn, Luther North, the brother of Frank, and others of their heroic breed.

In 1875 Grinnell accompanied a reconnaissance party led by Colonel William Ludlow, Chief Engineer, Department of Dakota, to northwestern Wyoming and the Yellowstone country, which three years before had become our first national park. The reports prepared by Grinnell on birds and mammals of that area are still authoritative. Subsequently, he was a leader in securing legislation which protected Yellowstone from despoliation.

Although he was invited to go along on Custer's last campaign against the Sioux in 1876, other responsibilities prevented Grinnell's sharing the fate that overtook Custer at the Little Big Horn. Grinnell, incidentally, was one of those who believed that Custer would have been saved if Reno, instead of retreating in the face of resistance, had pushed his opening charge against the Sioux village.

During these and later years, Grinnell divided his time between New York, where he did his writing and where his business and journalistic interests were located, and the West, where he studied its natural and human history in the field. He knew intimately the Indians of many tribes, in particular the Pawnees, the Blackfeet, and Cheyennes. His many years' study of the latter culminated in publication of his classic and definitive *The Fighting Cheyennes,* in 1915, and the two-volume *The Cheyenne Indians,* in 1923.

He wrote a score of books, and was editor or co-author of eight or ten others. But this was only part of his accomplishments. In his obituary in *The New York Times,* April 12, 1938, thirty lines of the column-and-a-half article were devoted to a mere listing of scholarly and scientific organizations of which he was an active member. While still an assistant at the Peabody Museum, he became natural history editor of *Forest and Stream,* beginning an association which lasted until 1911 and included thirty years as editor and president of the company. Grinnell was a pupil of Lucy Audubon, wife of the great naturalist, and in 1886, through *Forest and Stream,* he formed an association for the protection of birds. Thus the first Audubon Society was born. He was a member of the advisory board for the Federal Migratory Bird Law, and a Fellow of the American Ornithological Union.

On a hunting trip in 1885 with James Willard Schultz to the St. Mary's Lake region in Montana, Grinnell discovered a glacier to which, over his protest, his name was given. Schultz later wrote of him: "He was one of the most indefatigable and daring mountain climbers that I ever knew. ... No one could wish for a better camp companion. He was always ready to do his share of the work, and never have I seen him in an angry mood, unless it may have been at some refractory, stubborn pack horse, but you all know how that is." An article by Grinnell in the *Century Magazine* for September, 1891, drew public attention to the region and resulted in the creation in 1910 of Glacier National Park. Fusillade Mountain in the Park was named by Grinnell because on one occasion he and his companion hunters "fired a regular fusillade" at a herd of mountain goats without scoring a hit.

For many years chairman of the National Parks Council, Grinnell succeeded Herbert Hoover as president of the National Parks Association. He was one of the founders of the Boone and Crockett Club, which a group of sportsmen and conservationists organized in 1887 at the home of Theodore Roosevelt. In 1895 club members formed the New York Zoological Society, and Grinnell selected the site for its zoo in the Bronx.

He wrote extensively on duck and big game hunting. Teddy Roosevelt was one of his collaborators on this subject. For his work in the field of conservation, Grinnell in 1925 was awarded the Theodore Roosevelt Gold Medal of Honor. President Calvin Coolidge, in his White House presentation of the medal to Grinnell, said of him: "Few have done as much as you, and none has done more, to preserve vast areas of picturesque wilderness for the eyes of posterity in the simple majesty in which you and your fellow pioneers first beheld them. In Yellowstone Park you prevented the exploitation and therefore the destruction of the natural beauty. The Glacier National Park is peculiarly your monument."

"Fellow pioneer"—I have a feeling that this might have been the designation by which Grinnell, although he was also scientist, editor, author, and explorer, would prefer to be remembered. In all his work he was a goer-before, an upstream man, an opener of doors. So long as books are read, his will be studied because they are authentic firsthand accounts of the settlement of our West. He was there. He saw it happen. He was a part of what he saw. And he wrote of it all with clarity and honesty, with the scholar's precision and the pioneer's affection for a passing era.

I have no way of knowing how real the following hero stories and folk-tales may be to the few remaining Pawnees. But the fact that similar beliefs still persist among some Indians was indicated in a recent conversation I had with a young Crow from Montana. We were in a museum looking at a map which illustrates the anthropologists' theory of the peopling of the North American continent by migration of Asians across the Bering Strait. The young Crow studied the map, then turned away. "We don't believe that," he said. "We believe Old Man Coyote put the Indians here because he wanted them to have this country."

Grinnell, I think, would have heard him with approval. Perhaps the reader, too, will find himself in sympathy with such sentiments when he has read the stories Grinnell has recorded. At the very least he will be grateful to Grinnell for their preservation.

MAURICE FRINK

Executive Director
State Historical Society of Colorado

PAWNEE HERO STORIES
AND FOLK-TALES

TO THE MEMORY OF

MAJOR FRANK NORTH

—Pa'-ni Le-shar—

THIS RECORD OF HIS PEOPLE IS INSCRIBED.

NOTE.

LAST spring I visited the Pawnee Agency in the Indian Territory. On the day after my arrival, I rode over to the house of Eagle Chief, whom, under his warrior name, White Eagle, I had known for many years. Entering the door, I found myself in the presence of the Chief, who, after quickly putting his hand over his mouth in his astonishment, greeted me with a cordial deep-voiced *Lau*. Then we sat down and filled the pipe and talked. Through all our talk I could see that he was curious to know the object of my visit. At last he said, "My son I am glad that you have come to us once more. My mind is big when I look at you and talk to you. It is good that you are here. Why have you come again to the Pawnee village? What brings you here at this time?"

I answered, "Father, we have come down here to

visit the people and to talk to them; to ask them about how things used to be in the olden times, to hear their stories, to get their history, and then to put all these things down in a book, so that in the years to come, after the tribe have all become like white people, the old things of the Pawnees shall not be forgotten."

The Chief meditated for a while and then said, "It is good and it is time. Already the old things are being lost, and those who knew the secrets are many of them dead. If we had known how to write, we would have put all these things down, and they would not have been forgotten, but we could not write, and these stories were handed down from one to another. The old men told their grandchildren, and they told their grandchildren, and so the secrets and the stories and the doings of long ago have been handed down. It may be that they have changed as they passed from father to son, and it is well that they should be put down, so that our children, when they are like the white people, can know what were their fathers' ways."

Most of the material contained in this little book was collected on that visit.

CONTENTS.

HERO STORIES.

FOLK-TALES.

NOTES ON THE PAWNEES.

THE PAWNEES AND THEIR STORIES.

ONCE the Pawnees were a great people. They were very numerous. They were undisputed masters of a vast territory. They had everything that heart could wish. Their corn and their buffalo gave them food, clothing and shelter; they had weapons for war and for the chase. They roamed over the country without let or hindrance. In peace they were light-hearted and contented; in war cunning, fierce and successful. Their name was a terror to their enemies. This was in the past. Now they are few in number, poor, a prey to disease, a vanishing race.

My acquaintance with the tribe began in 1870. From that time to the present I have had frequent intercourse with them; have lived in their villages; and been with them on their buffalo hunts. During the weeks and months spent in camp and village, I

have listened to many stories of Pawnee heroes and
to folk-tales of the miraculous doings of the olden
time. In my intercourse with the tribe, extending
over a period of nearly twenty years, I have been
deeply impressed by the high qualities of the Pawnee character; and the more familiar I have become
with this people, the more strongly have I felt that
a permanent record should be made of the tales
which reflect that character. Unless thus collected
now, much of this lore must inevitably be forgotten.

For the Pawnees are passing away. When I first
joined them on their buffalo hunts from their old
home on the Loup Fork in Nebraska, the tribe
numbered three thousand; last March in the Indian
Territory I found but eight hundred. And more
rapidly than the dwindling of the people are their
traditions lapsing from memory under the changed
conditions of the tribe's life. The lore, which sprang
up as an indigenous growth of the wide-stretching
prairie and the wilderness where the wild Pawnee
warrior hunted free, finds scanty nurture in the un-
congenial soil of fields tilled by Pawnee followers of
the plow. With the new modes of living come new
views of life, new motives, new sympathies—in a
word, civilization. To earn a living by toil, to wrest

subsistence from the earth, this is the problem confronting the Pawnees to-day, the task which is engaging the sinew and purpose of the tribe. In the transition stage, the memory of the old days, of old manners and rites and ceremonies and of old heroes, is with the elders of the race, those ancient braves whose lives bridge the past and the present. When I visited the Agency last March, it was to write down from the lips of these old men such material as I could collect. When they shall die much of the unwritten lore will perish too, for with them will cease that sympathetic and perfect credence, which alone gives to folk-lore vitality and lastingness. What is written in this volume then belongs distinctly to the wild Indian.

The task that I have set for myself is that of a recorder. No attempt has been made to give a literary color to the hero stories and folk-tales here written out. I have scrupulously avoided putting into them anything of my own. The stories are told to the reader as they were told to me. They are not elaborated. I have tried to show how Indians think and speak, rather than to make their stories more entertaining by dressing them up to suit the civilized taste. My object in giving these narratives in their

present shape is to make a book which shall be true
to life, and shall faithfully reflect the Pawnee character, as the story tellers have themselves painted it.
In a very few cases I have added some words ex-
plaining matters so well understood by those familiar with the Indians as to need no explanation. If
these tales have any ethnological value, it will be
enhanced by their being given in the precise form
in which they were told by those to whom they have
been handed down from generation to generation;
but quite apart from this is another point which is
entitled to consideration.

The entire ignorance concerning Indians, which
prevails among the general public, can be dispelled
only by letting that public understand something of
the ways of life of the wild Indian, something of the
subjects about which he thinks and talks, as well as
of how he looks at these subjects, and what he has
to say about them.

The late Mrs. Jackson's charming story, "Ra-
mona," did much to bring the more intelligent class
of readers in touch with the Indians, and to awaken
sympathy for them by pointing out the unnumbered
wrongs perpetrated on this race by the Government.
Mrs. Jackson's book was a story, a novel; wonder-

fully well told and full of truth and feeling; but while it may have been a relation of facts, it did not profess to treat of actual persons. It is looked upon by many readers as a mere romance. It is a book about which I was once asked, skeptically, "Did you ever see any Indians like those?" In the Pawnee stories here set down there is no romance nor coloring. The Indians themselves are talking, and whatever the faults and weak points of these tales—and some of them are sufficiently obvious—they at least give the reader a true conception of Indians as they have actually lived. They are stories of Indians by Indians. There is about them nothing of the white man; and the intelligent person, who is sufficiently interested in the subject to read this book through, will gain from it a new insight into Indian character.

The Indian of Cooper — with his bravery, his endurance, his acuteness, his high qualities of honesty, generosity, courtesy and hospitality—has been laughed at for half a century. Yet every man who has mingled much with the Indians in their homes has known individuals who might have sat for the portraits which Cooper drew of some of his aboriginal heroes. There are good men among Indians,

just as among the whites. The prevalent notion of
the Indian has been formed from the worst class of
this people, the lazy, filthy beggars who haunt the
settlements of the West, who to their own vices have
added new ones picked up from their surroundings,
and who are hopelessly degraded. These are not
typical Indians, and it is unjust to judge a whole
race from such degenerate specimens. There is still
another notion of the Indian fondly cherished by
many worthy people, whose sympathies have been
wrought upon by the cruelty and injustice with
which we have treated this race. These good people
look upon all Indians as simple children of nature,
who would do no wrong if they had not been con-
taminated by contact with vicious whites. It is unnecessary to say that this notion of the Indian is also
incorrect.

The Indian is neither a fiend nor a saint. There
are good ones and bad ones. As a rule, perhaps they
try to act up to their ideas of what is right, but the
standard of a race of barbarians cannot be the same
as that of a civilized people, and in judging of their
character we must make allowances for this difference. The standard of right and wrong among
civilized people is a growth, the product of the ex-

perience of thousands of years. The Indian races
have not been through a like experience. They have
regarded as virtues some things which seem to us
the worst of crimes. The Indian differs from the
white man in education and manner of life, and so,
of course, in his modes of thought. He has not
been taught the lesson of self-control, which his surroundings oblige each civilized man to begin to learn
as a child. He has known until recent times no law
save that of strength. He has been taught that war
is the noblest of pursuits—the only one worthy of
man. And that war has consisted in making forays
upon his enemies, taking their possessions, and, if
possible, their lives and their scalps. His warfare
consisted in surprises rather than open combat. A
scalp taken was a trophy of victory; and the scalp
of a woman was almost as eagerly sought as that of
a brave or of a chief. It was an evidence of injury
inflicted on the enemy. To steal horses from the
enemy was an achievement creditable and also prof-
itable.

We commonly speak of the raids of war parties as
horse stealing expeditions, but this is wholly mis-
leading, because to the civilized understanding the
phrase horse stealing carries with it an idea of dis-

honesty. No such meaning attaches to the Indian equivalent of this phrase. They take horses by stratagem or secretly, by the usual, and to them legitimate, methods of warfare. To speak of their stealing horses, using that verb in the sense which we commonly give it, would be like saying that an army stole the cannon which it captured in an engagement with the enemy. Captured horses were the legitimate spoils of war. The wealth of the Indians was in their horses. They had no fortified places, no ships of war, no cannon, no works of art. Their only valuable possessions were their horses. These were the only property that could be carried off. Therefore, when an expedition was made against a hostile tribe, scalps and horses were naturally its object. Horses, being their only valuable possessions, constituted their medium of exchange, so far as they had any. Did a man wish to purchase an ornament, or an article of dress which took his fancy, he gave a horse for it. If he bought a wife he paid for her in horses. The most valuable present that could be made was a good horse; and horses were often given by the well-to-do to their friends and relations who had been sick or unfortunate. On the other hand, when, as was sometimes the case, a conquered tribe was condemned to pay a war indemnity, they paid it in horses. It is related that when the Skidi broke their treaty with the other bands, and were afterward conquered by them, they were obliged to pay such a fine.

This view of Indian warfare being understood, the motive of the hero stories here given, and of many of the folk-tales, becomes plain.

The Pawnees are essentially a religious people. They worship *Ti-ra'-wa*, who is in and of everything. Unlike many of the Indian tribes of the West, they do not adore any material thing. They regard certain places as sacred, but these are so only because blessed by the Divine presence. The Pawnee Deity is not personified. He is intangible, quite as much so as the God of the Christians. The sacred character of *Ti-ra'-wa* extends to animal nature. The fishes which swim in the rivers, the birds of the air and the beasts which roam over the prairie, have sometimes intelligence, knowledge and power far beyond those of man. But they are not gods. Their miraculous attributes are given them by the Ruler, whose servants they are, and who often makes them the medium of his communications to man. They are his messengers—his angels—and their powers are always used for good. Prayers are made to them; sometimes for direct help in time of need, but more often for intercession. Often in the folk-tales it will be seen that when the blessing asked for is some small thing, a prayer is made to the animals (*Na-hu'rac*), but if the petitioners are asking for some great thing, something which is very difficult to grant, then the prayer is made to "One Above," to "The Ruler," that is, to the Supreme Being.

Nothing of importance was ever undertaken without a prayer for help, for success. All the serious undertakings of the year, whose success would affect the general welfare, were preceded by religious ceremonies, when all the tribe took part, and prayers were made and sacrifices offered to *Ti-ra'-wa;* and in all lesser enterprises, the individuals who were interested humbled themselves and implored the Divine assistance. A party starting off on the war-path prayed for success and made a burnt offering. Prayer and sacrifice always marked the beginning of the feast, and often its end. Success in their undertakings was acknowledged by grateful offerings to the Ruler. The victorious warrior sometimes sacrificed the scalp torn from the head of his enemy, and this was burned with elaborate ceremonies by the

High Priest. He who brought back from a foray many horses, gave one to the priest as a thank-offering to the Ruler. One of the well-known Seven Brothers said to me, "It is our aim, after we have been helped, to give thanks."

The feeling of these Indians toward their God is one of humility and reverence. They do not love him, but they look to him for help at all times. The young are exhorted to humble themselves before him, to pray to him, to look to One Above, to ask help from the Ruler. In the stories which are included in this book the allusions constantly made to *Ti-ra'-wa*—the Supreme Power—the prayers offered and the humility and self-abnegation so often expressed, show faith, profound religious feelings, and great elevation of thought.

Among tribal names of North American Indians, none is more familiar to us than Pawnee; yet of no tribe is less known. Frequent allusions to them occur in the writings of early travelers in the West; but only one satisfactory attempt has been made to write a connected history of this family. In the *Magazine of American History* for 1880 Mr. John B. Dunbar published a most interesting account of this tribe, but his sketch is mainly historical, and does not profess to treat exhaustively of the lives and modes of thought of this people. It is, however, a history of very great importance and value and in preparing the historical matter which is included in this volume, I have not hesitated to draw on Mr. Dunbar's papers, which must form the basis of any subsequent account of the Pawnees, and which should be read by all who are interested in this people.

I owe much of my interest in and knowledge of the Pawnees to my long intimacy with the late Major Frank North, who from his extended intercourse and close connection with this people—a connection which lasted more than thirty years—was unquestionably better informed about them than any other white man has ever been; and with Capt L. H. North, his brother, who was for many years associated with Major North in command of the Pawnee Scouts.

In gathering the material here presented I have been assisted also by James R. Murie, a nephew of Comanche Chief; by Ralph J. Weeks, a half-brother of Lone Chief; by Harry Kuhns, by Eagle Chief and Bear Chief, Skidis; by Good Chief and Curly

Chief, Kit-ke-hahk-is; by Secret Pipe Chief and Frank White, Chau-is, and by many others of my Pawnee friends, to all of whom my acknowledgments are due.

In the pronunciation of the few Pawnee words used in these stories, the vowel sounds, as nearly as I can give them, are as follows: *a* as in father, *e* as the *a* in ale, *i* as *e* in cede, *u* long as *oo* in pool, *ŭ* short as in us, *au* as *ou* in house. These sounds depend somewhat on the letters which follow the vowels, and the spelling does not always conform to the rule laid down. The last two syllables in the word Pita-hau-erat, for example, are pronounced *ērăt* or *idot*. The sounds of *d*, *l*, *n* and *r* are difficult to express by English letters; *r* sometimes has its own sound quite distinctly, at others more the sound of *d*; *n* often has a *d* sound, and *l* a sound of *n*. It will be noted that throughout this volume I have used the familiar English word Pawnee instead of the evidently more correct *Pa'-ni*.

Finally I have refrained from commenting on the stories, though there is abundant opportunity for comment.

G. B. G.

July, 1889.

HERO STORIES.

COMANCHE CHIEF.

The Peace-Maker.

I.

MANY years ago there lived in the Ski'-di village a young man, about sixteen years old. His name was *Kut-a'wi-kutz* (the hawk). At this time the Pawnees wore their hair in the ancient fashion, cut as the Osages wear theirs; the whole head was shaved except a roach running back from the forehead beyond the scalp lock.

A war party went off to the south and he joined them as a servant. They went a long way and a long way, traveling far, but they got no horses and came back. Afterward another party started off on the warpath, and he went with it. They traveled many days, going to the southwest, and at length they came to a camp, and hid themselves to wait until it was dark. It was a camp of the Comanches.

When night had come they all went into the camp to steal horses. This young man went to a lodge near which stood three horses, two spotted horses and one gray. They were tied near the door of the lodge, and from this he thought they must be fast, for the Indians usually tie up their best horses close to the lodge door, where they will be under their eyes as much as possible. He went to the lodge to cut the ropes, and just as he was about to do so he thought he heard some one inside. He stepped up close to the lodge, and looked in through a little opening between the door and the lodge, and saw a small fire burning, and on the other side of the fire was sitting a young girl, combing her long hair. The young man looked around the lodge to see who else was there, and saw only an old man and an old woman, and the fire-maker. He cut the ropes of the two spotted horses standing outside, led the horses out of the camp, and met his companion. To him he said, "Now, brother, you take these horses and go to the hill where we were hiding to-day, and wait for me there. I have seen another fine spotted horse that I want to get; I will go back for it and will meet you before morning at that place."

He went back, as if to get the spotted horse, but

returned to the lodge where the girl was. He went all around it, and looked at it carefully. He saw that there were feathers on the lodge, and rows of animals hoofs hanging down the sides, which rattled in the wind, and to one of the lodge-poles was tied a buffalo tail, which hung down. Then he went back to the door and looked in at the girl again. She had braided her hair and was sitting there by the fire. He stayed there a long time that night looking at her. Toward morning he went to look for his companion. When he met him he told him that some one had taken the spotted horse before he got to it; he could not find it. When the party all met next morning, they found that they had taken a lot of horses, and they started north to go home. They reached the Pawnee village, and every one was glad of their success.

After this, whenever this young man saw anything that was nice or pretty, such as medals, ear-rings, finger rings for women, beadwork leggings, brace- lets, necklaces, wampum, beads—things that the Comanches did not have—he would give a pony for it. For one year he went on like this, gathering together these pretty things. When the year had gone by he had no horses left; he had given them all away to get these presents. He packed all these things up in a bundle, and then spoke one night to his friend, saying, "I intend to go off on the war-path again, and I would like to have you go with me; we two will go alone." His friend agreed to go.

II.

Before the time came to start, other young men heard of it, and several joined them. There were eight of them in all. *Kut-a'wi-kutz* was the leader. He told his young men that they were going to a certain place where he knew there were lots of spotted horses to steal. They started out on foot. After traveling many days, they came to the place where the camp had been at the time he saw the girl. There was now no camp there.

They went on further, and at length came to a camp and hid themselves. When night came the leader told his men to remain where they were hiding, and he would go into the camp and see if there were any horses to take. He went through all the camp looking for the lodge in which he had seen the girl, but he did not find it. Then he went back to where the young men were hiding, and told them that this was not the camp they were looking for;

that they did not have here the spotted horses that they wanted. In the camp of the year before there had been many spotted horses.

The young men did not understand this, and some of them did not like to leave this camp without taking any horses, but he was the leader and they did as he said. They left that camp and went on further.

After traveling some days they came to another camp, and hid themselves near it. When night came on *Kut-a'wi-kutz* said to his young men, "You stay here where you are hiding, and I will go into this camp and see if it is the one we are looking for." He went through the camp but did not find the lodge he sought. He returned to the hiding place, and told the party there that this was not the camp they were looking for, that the spotted horses were not there. They left the camp and went on.

When they had come close to the mountains they saw another camp. *Kut-a'wi-kutz* went into this camp alone, and when he had been through it, he went back to his party and told them that this was the camp they had been looking for. Then he sent the young men into the camp to steal horses, and he put on his fine leggings and moccasins that he had in his bundle, and painted himself and went with them. He took a horse and his friend took one. They met outside the village. He told his friend to get on his own horse and lead the other, and with the rest of the party to go off east from the camp to a certain place, and there to wait for him. "I have seen," he said, "another fine horse that I like, and I wish to go back and get it."

His friend looked sorrowfully at him and said, "Why are you all dressed up like this, and why is your face painted? What are you doing or what is in your mind? Perhaps you intend to do some great thing to-night that you do not want me, your friend, to know about. I have seen for a long time that you are hiding something from me."

Kut-a'wi-kutz caught his friend in his arms and hugged him and kissed him and said, "You are my friend; who is so near to me as you are? Go on as I have said, and if it turns out well I will tell you all. I will catch up with you before very long."

His friend said, "No, I will stay with you. I will not go on. I love you as a brother, and I will stay with you, and if you are going to do some great thing I will die with you."

When *Kut-a'wi-kutz* found that his friend was resolved to remain with him, he yielded and told him his secret. He said to him, "My brother, when we were on the warpath a year ago, and I took those two spotted horses, I heard a little noise in the lodge by which they were tied. I looked in and I saw there a girl sitting by the fire combing her hair. She was very pretty. When I took the spotted horses away, I could not put that girl out of my mind. I remembered her. Brother, when we went back home that girl was constantly in my mind. I could not forget her. I came this time on purpose to get her, even if it shall cost me my life. She is in this camp, and I have found the lodge where she lives."

His friend said, "My brother, whatever you say shall be done. I stay with you. You go into the camp. I will take the horses and go to that high rocky hill east of the camp, and will hide the horses there. When you are in the village I will be up in one of the trees on the top of the hill, looking down on the camp. If I hear shooting and see lots of people running to the lodge I will know that you are killed, and I will kill myself. I will not go home alone. If I do not see you by noon, I will kill myself."

Kut-a'wi-kutz said, "It is good. If I am successful I will go up there after you, and take you down into the camp."

They parted. The friend hid the horses and went up on the hill. *Kut-a'wi-kutz* went into the camp.

III.

It was now the middle of the night. When he came to the lodge, he saw there was a fire in it. He did not go in at once; he wanted the fire to go out. He stayed around the lodge, and gradually the fire died down. It was dark. He went into the lodge. He was painted and finely dressed, and had his bundle with him. He took his moccasins off and his leggings, and hung them up over the girl's bed; then strings of beads, then five or six medals, bracelets, ear-bobs, beaded leggings, everything he had—his shirt. He took his blanket, and spread it over the bed where the girl was lying, stepped over the bed, and crept under his own blanket, and lay down by her side.

When he lay down she woke up, and found that there was some one lying by her, and she spoke to him, but he did not answer. He could not understand her, for he did not know Comanche. She talked for a long time, but he did not speak. Then she began to feel of him, and when she put her hands on his head—*Pi-ta'-da*—Pawnee—an enemy! Then she raised herself up, took a handful of grass from under the bed, spread the fire and put the grass on it. The fire blazed up and she saw him. Then she sprang up and took the top blanket, which was his, off the bed, and put it about her, and sat by the fire. She called her father and said, "Father get up; there is a man here."

The old man got up, and got his pipe and began smoking. This old man was the Head Chief of the Comanches. He called the servant, and told him to make a fire. The girl got up and went over to where her mother was lying and called her. The mother got up; and they all sat by the fire.

The old man smoked for a long time. Every now and then he would look at the bed to see who it could be that was lying there, and then he would look at all the things hanging up over the bed—at the medals and other things. He did not know what they were for, and he wondered. At length the old man told the servant to go and call the chiefs of the tribe, and tell them to come to his lodge.

Presently the chiefs came in one by one and sat down. When they had come there was still one brave who ought to have come that was not there. His name was Skin Shirt; the father wanted him. He sent for him three times. He sent word back to the chief to go on with the council, and that he would agree to whatever they decided. The fourth time he was sent for he came, and took a seat by the chief, the girl's father. This brave spoke to *Kut-a'wi-kutz*, and told him to get up, and take a seat among them. He did so. The girl was sitting on the other side of the fire. When he got up, he had to take the blanket that was left, which was the girl's. He put it around him, and sat down among them.

When the chiefs came in, there was among them a Pawnee who had been captured long ago and adopted by the Comanches, and was now himself a chief; he talked with *Kut-a'wi-kutz* and interpreted for him, telling him everything that was said as each one spoke.

After the young man had seated himself, the chief filled his pipe, and gave the pipe to his brave to decide what should be done with this enemy. The brave took the pipe, but he did not wish to decide, so he did not light it, but passed it on to another chief to decide. He passed it on to another, and he to another, and so it went until the pipe came back

to the Head Chief.   When he got it again, he asked
Kut-a'wi-kutz, "Why have you come here this night
and lain down in my lodge, you who are an enemy to
my people?   And why have you hung up in the lodge
all these strange things which we see here?   I do not
understand it, and I wish to know your reasons."

The boy said to him, "A long time ago I came
south on the warpath to steal horses.   I traveled
until I came to your camp.   I saw three horses tied
outside a lodge, two spotted horses and a gray.
While I was cutting one of the ropes, I heard a little
noise inside the lodge, and pushing aside the door I
looked in, and saw that girl combing her hair.   I
stole the two spotted horses, and took them out of
the camp, and gave them to a friend of mine, and
came back to your lodge, and kept looking at the
girl.   I stayed there until she went to bed.   For a
long year I have been buying presents; beads and
many other things, for I had made up my mind that
I would go after this girl.   I came down here to find
her.   I have been to where you were camped last year,
and to two other camps that I discovered.   She was
not in these and I left them, and came on until I
found the right camp.   This is the fourth place.   Now
I am here.   I made up my mind to do this thing, and

if her relations do not like it they can do as they please. I would be happy to die on her account."

When he had spoken the old chief laughed. He said: "Those two spotted horses that you stole I did not care much about. The gray horse was the best one of the three, and you left him. I was glad that you did not take him. He was the best of all." Then for a little while there was silence in the lodge.

Then the chief, the girl's father, began to talk again; he said, "If I wanted to decide what should be done with this man, I would decide right now, but here is my brave, Skin Shirt, I want him to decide. If I were to decide, it would be against this man, but he has my daughter's blanket on, and she has his, and I do not want to decide. I pass the pipe to my brave, and want him to light it."

The brave said, "I want this chief next to me to decide," and he passed him the pipe, and so it went on around the circle until it came to the Head Chief again. He was just about to take it and decide the question, when they heard outside the lodge the noise made by some one coming, shouting and laughing; then the door was pushed aside and an old man came in, and as he passed the door he stumbled and fell on his knees. It was the girl's grandfather. He had been outside the lodge, listening.

The pipe was passed to the chief, and he gave it again to his brave to decide. While the brave was sitting there, holding the pipe, the old grandfather said, "Give me the pipe, if you men cannot decide, let me do it. In my time we did not do things this way. I never passed the pipe; I could always decide for myself."

Then Skin Shirt passed him the pipe, and he lit it and smoked. Then he said, "I do not wish to condemn to death a man who is wearing my granddaughter's blanket." The interpreter began to tell *Kut-a'wi-kutz* that the old man was going to decide in his favor, and that when he got through speaking he must get up and pass his hands over him, and thank him for taking pity on him, and so to all the others. The old man continued, "Now, chiefs, do not think hardly of what I am going to say, nor be dissatisfied with my decision. I am old. I have heard in my time that there is a tribe up north that is raising from the ground something that is long and white, and something that is round; and that these things are good to eat. Now, chiefs, before I die, I want to eat of these things, and I want my granddaughter to go and take her seat by this man, and for them to be man and wife. Since I was young we have been enemies, but now I want the two tribes to come together, join hands and be friends." And so it was decided.

The young man got up and passed his hands over the old man, and over the brave, and passed around the circle and blessed them all. The Pawnee, who was interpreter, now told him to get up, and get a medal and put it on the brave, and then another and put it on the chief, and so on until all the presents were gone. And he did so, and put on them the medals, and ear-rings, and strings of beads, and breast-plates of wampum, until each had something. And these things were new to them, and they felt proud to be wearing them, and thought how nice they looked.

IV.

By this time it was daylight, and it had got noised abroad through the camp that there was a Pawnee at the Head Chief's lodge, and all the people gathered there. They called out, "Bring him out; we want him out here." They crowded about the lodge, all the people, the old men and the women and the young men, so many that at last they pushed the lodge down. They shouted: "Let us have the Pawnee. Last night they stole many horses from us." The chiefs and braves got around the Pawnee, and kept the Comanches off from him, and protected him from the people. The Cheyennes were camped close by, near the hill southeast of the Comanches, and they, too, had heard that the Comanches had a Pawnee in the camp. They came over, and rode about in the crowd to try and get the Pawnee, and they rode over a Comanche or two, and knocked them down. So Skin Shirt got his bow and arrows, and jumped on his horse, and rode out and drove the Cheyennes away back to their camp again.

The Cheyennes saw that the Comanches did not want the Pawnee killed, so they sent a message inviting him over to a feast with them, intending to kill him, but Skin Shirt told them that he was married into the tribe. While the Cheyennes were parading round the Comanche camp, they were shooting off their guns in the air, just to make a noise. Now, the young Pawnee on the hill, who was watching the camp to see what would happen to his friend, saw the crowd and heard the shooting, and made up his mind that *Kut-a'wi-kutz* had been killed. So he took his knife, and put the handle against a tree and the

point against his breast, and put his arms around the
tree and hugged it, and the knife blade passed
through his heart and he fell down and died.

In the afternoon when all the excitement had
quieted down, the Cheyennes came over again to the
Comanche camp, and invited the Pawnee and his wife
to go to their village, and visit with them. Then Skin
Shirt said, "All right, we will go." Three chiefs of
the Comanches went ahead, the Pawnee followed
with his wife, and Skin Shirt went behind. They
went to the Cheyenne camp. The Cheyennes received them and made a great feast for them, and
gave the Pawnee many horses. Then they went back
to the Comanche camp. *Kut-a'wi-kutz* never went
up to the hill until the next morning. Then he went,
singing the song he had told his friend he would
sing. He called to him, but there was no reply. He
called again. It was all silent. He looked for his
friend, and at last he found him there dead at the
foot of the tree.

v.

Kut-a'wi-kutz then stayed with the Comanches.
The Cheyennes came north and east, and the Co-
manches went on west, nearer to the mountains.
While the Pawnee was with the Comanches, they had

several wars with the Utes, Lipans and Tonkaways. *Kut-a'wi-kutz* proved himself a brave man, and, as the son-in-law of the chief, he soon gained great influence, and was himself made a chief.

After some years the old man, his wife's grandfather, told the Pawnee that he thought it was time that he should eat some of those things that he had long wanted to eat that grew up north; that he was getting pretty old now. *Kut-a'wi-kutz* said, "It is time. We will go." So he had his horses packed, and with his immediate family and the old man, started north toward the Pawnee country. At this time he was called *Kut-a'wi-kutz-u si-ti'-da-rit*, which means "See! The Hawk." When going into battle he would ride straight out to strike his enemy, and the Comanches who were looking at him would say, "See! The Hawk." So that became his name.

They traveled a long time until they came to the Pawnee ground. As they were traveling along, they came to a field where were growing corn, beans and squashes. The Pawnee said to the old man, "Grandfather, look at that field. There are the things that you have desired to eat." He got off his horse and went into the field, and pulled some corn, some beans and some squashes, and took them to the old man,

and gave them to him. The old man supposed
they were to be eaten just as they were, and
he tried to bite the squashes. This made the
Pawnee laugh. When they came to the village,
the Pawnees were very glad to see him who had been
lost long ago. He told the people that he had
brought these Indians to eat of the corn and other
things; that they were his kinsfolk. He told them,
too, about the young man who had killed himself.
His relations went out into the fields, and gathered
corn and beans and squashes, and cooked them for
the Comanches.

They stayed there a long time at the Pawnee village. When they were getting ready to return, the
Pawnees dried their corn, and gave a great deal of it
to the Comanches, packing many horses with it for
the Indians at home. Then the Comanches started
south again, and some of the Pawnee young men,
relations of *Kut-a'wi-kutz*, joined him, and went back
with them. After they had returned to the Comanche camp, the old grandfather died, happy because
he had eaten the things he wanted to eat.

Soon after this, *Kut-a'wi-kutz* started back to the
Pawnee village, and some young men of the Comanches joined him. Some time after reaching the vil-

lage he went south again, accompanied by some young Pawnees, but leaving most of the Comanches behind. He had arranged with the chiefs of the Pawnees that they should journey south, meet the Comanches on the plains and make peace. When he reached the Comanches, the whole village started north to visit the Pawnees, and met them on their way south. When they met, the two tribes made friends, smoked together, ate together, became friends.

After they had camped together for some time, some Comanches stayed in the Pawnee camp, and some Pawnees in the Comanche camp. *Kut-a'wi-kutz* was called by the Pawnees Comanche Chief. He would have remained with the Comanches, but when he went back with them his wife fell sick. The Comanche doctors could not help her, and he wanted to take her north to see the Pawnee doctors, but the Comanches would not let him. They kept him there, and his wife died. Then he was angry, for he thought if he had taken her north her life might have been saved.

So he left the Comanches, and went and lived with the Pawnees, and was known among them always as Comanche Chief, the Peace-Maker, because he made peace between the Pawnees and Comanches. He was chief of the Ski'-di band, and a progressive man of modern times. He sent his children East to school at Carlisle, Pa.

Comanche Chief died September 9th, 1888.

PAWNEE PIPE.

LONE CHIEF.

Skur'-ar-a Le'-shar.

I.

LONE CHIEF was the son of the chief of the Kit-ke-hahk'-i band. His father died when the boy was very young, less than a year old. Until he was old enough to go to war, his mother had supported him by farming—raising corn, beans and pumpkins. She taught the boy many things, and advised him how to live and how to act so that he might be successful. She used to say to him, "You must trust always in *Ti-ra'-wa*. He made us, and through him we live. When you grow up, you must be a man. Be brave, and face whatever danger may meet you. Do not forget, when you look back to your young days, that I have raised you, and always supported you. You had no father to do it. Your father was a chief, but you must not think of that. Because he was a chief, it does not follow that you will be one. It is not the man who stays in the lodge that becomes great; it is the man who works, who sweats, who is always tired from going on the warpath."

Much good advice his mother gave him. She said, "When you get to be a man, remember that it is his ambition that makes the man. If you go on the warpath, do not turn around when you have gone part way, but go on as far as you were going, and then come back. If I should live to see you become a man, I want you to become a great man. I want you to think about the hard times we have been through. Take pity on people who are poor, because we have been poor, and people have taken pity on us. If I live to see you a man, and to go off on the warpath, I would not cry if I were to hear that you had been killed in battle. That is what makes a man: to fight and to be brave. I should be sorry to see you die from sickness. If you are killed, I would rather have you die in the open air, so that the birds of the air will eat your flesh, and the wind will breathe on you and blow over your bones. It is better to be killed in the open air than to be smothered in the earth. Love your friend and never desert him. If you see him surrounded by the enemy, do not run away. Go to him, and if you cannot save him, be killed together, and let your bones lie side by side. Be killed on a hill; high up. Your grandfather said it is not manly to be killed in a hollow. It is not a man who is talking to you, advising you. Heed my words, even if I am a woman."

The boy listened to these words, and he did not forget them.

II.

In the year 1867 he enlisted in the Pawnee Scouts under Major Frank North, and served in L. H. North's company. He was always a good soldier, ready, willing and brave. At a fight near the Cheyenne Pass in 1867, he counted *coup* on a woman and a man, Arapahoes who had stolen some horses at Fort Laramie.

At this time the boy's name was *Wi-ti-ti le-shar-uspi*, Running Chief. After he came back from this scout, he went on a war party of which Left Hand was the leader, and they went to the Osage country. He was no longer a servant, but a scout, a leading man in the party, one of those who went ahead as spies. He had good judgment and understood his duties. When they came to the Osage country, he was selected as one of the leaders of a small branch party to steal horses. His party took thirty head of horses. In the Osage country the young men were not allowed to take all the horses they could. On account of the few fords where they could cross the streams, they could not take a big herd, but only what they could ride and lead, and at the same time go fast. Across one river there was only one rocky ford, and over another stream with deep banks there was only one rocky ford where they could cross. Because they did not know this, in former times many Pawnees had been caught and killed in the Osage country. So now they took but few horses at a time, because these rivers were very deep and no one could cross them except at these rock fords. Out of the horses taken at this time Running Chief obtained one of the best and fastest ever known among the Pawnees—a cream-colored horse, long famous in the tribe. For his skillful leadership of this party he was given much credit.

After returning home—the same year—he led a party to go off on the warpath to the Cheyennes. He found a camp on the headwaters of the North Canadian, and his party took seven horses, but these horses looked thin and rough, and he was not satisfied with them; he was ashamed to go home with only these. He told his party to take them home, but that he was going off by himself to get some better ones. He had with him a friend, with whom he had grown up, and whom he loved. This young man was like a brother to Running Chief. These two went off together, and went to the Osage camp, and staid about it for three nights, and then took five horses, the best in the camp. They took them back to the village. It was customary for the leading man in a party to make a sacrifice to *Ti-ra'-wa*. Running-Chief did this, giving one horse to the chief priest. This sacrifice promoted him to be a warrior.

III.

The next year he led a party again to the Osage country. He took some horses and brought them home. This same year (1868) a party started south. He was not the leader, but he went with them. They went to the Wichita, Comanche and Kiowa villages—they were all camped together—stole some horses and started back with them. Before they had gone very far Running Chief stopped and said he was going back. His friend was with the party, and when he found that Running Chief had resolved to go back he said, "I will stop here with you."

The two went back toward the village that they had just left, and climbed a hill that stood near it, and hid themselves there. They waited, watching, for they had not decided what they would do. The next day in the afternoon they began to get hungry, and they began to talk together. Running Chief said to his friend, "My brother, are you poor in your mind?* Do you feel like doing some great thing—something that is very dangerous?"

His friend answered at once, "Yes, I am poor. I am ready. Why do you ask me?"

Running Chief thought a little while before he answered, and as he thought, all the pain and suffering of his life seemed to rise up before him, so that he could see it. He remembered how he had been a poor boy, supported by his mother, and all that they two had suffered together while he was yet a child. He remembered how his sister had been killed when he was a boy only ten years old, and how he had mourned for her, when her husband, who was jealous of her, had shot her through the body with an arrow and killed her. She was the only sister he

* Poor in mind; *i. e.*, despondent, unhappy, miserable.

had, and he had loved her. He felt that he was poor now, and that there was no hope of anything better for him, and he did not want to live any longer. After he had thought of all these things he said to his friend, "My life is not worth anything to me;" and then he told him of his bad feelings. Finally he said, "Now you go off and leave me here alone. I am tired of living, but you go home. You have relations who would mourn for you. I do not want you to lose your life on my account."

His friend answered him, "I will not go away from you. We have grown up together, and I will stick to you. Wherever you go I will go, and whatever you do I will do."

Then Running Chief meditated for a long time. He had not made up his mind what to do. He thought to himself, "This, my friend, will stay with me. I do not want to be the cause of his death." So he considered. Finally he said to his friend, "If I shall make up my mind to go to some place where there is great danger, I shall go."

His friend said, "I will go with you."

Running Chief thought again, and at last he said, "On account of my feelings I have decided to go into the camp of my enemies, and be eaten by their dogs."

The other man said, "Whatever you have determined on I also will do."

IV.

Then they jumped up out of the hole they were
hiding in, and tied up their waists, and prepared to
start. They were not very far from a trail which
connected two villages, along which persons kept
passing, and the Indians of these villages were all
about them. When they jumped up to go toward
the trail, they saw four or five persons passing at a
little distance. When they saw these people, Running Chief called out to them, "*High—eigh*," and
made motions for them to come to him. He wanted
to show his strong will, and that on account of his
bad feelings he wished to have his troubles ended
right there. He called to them twice, and each time
the Indians stopped and looked at the Pawnees, and
then went on. They did not know who it was that
was calling them; perhaps they thought the Pawnees
were two squaws.

The two young men went out to the trail and followed these persons toward the village. They went
over a little hill, and as soon as they had come to the
top and looked over it, they saw the village. On this

side of it, and nearest to them were three lodges. At the foot of the hill was a river, which they must cross to come to these three lodges. When they came to the river, the friend asked, "Shall we take off our moccasins and leggings to cross?" Running Chief replied, "Why should I take off my moccasins and leggings when I know that my life is just going over a precipice? Let us go in as we are." So they crossed with moccasins and leggings on. The river was only half-leg deep.

Just as they reached the further bank, all on a sudden, it came over Running Chief what they were doing—that they were going to certain death. All his courage seemed to leave him, and he felt as if he had no bones in his body. Then for a moment he faltered; but he could not give up now. He felt that if he was a man he must go forward; he could not turn back. He stopped for an instant; and his friend looked at him, and said, "Come, let us hurry on. We are near the lodges." He stepped forward then, but his feet seemed to be heavy and to drag on the ground. He walked as if he were asleep.

There was no one about near at hand, and as they went forward Running Chief prayed with all his mind to *Ti-ra'-wa* that no one might come until they had reached the lodge, and had got inside. When they had got to within about one hundred yards of the lodge, a little boy came out, and began to play around the door, and when they were about fifty yards from him he saw them. As soon as he looked at them, he knew that they did not belong to the camp, and he gave a kind of a scream and darted into the lodge, but no one came out. The people within paid no attention to the boy. As they walked toward the lodges Running Chief seemed not to know where he was, but to be walking in a dream. He thought of nothing except his longing to get to this lodge.

They went to the largest of the three lodges. Running Chief raised the door and put his head in, and as he did so, it seemed as if his breath stopped. He went in and sat down far back in the lodge, opposite the entrance, and though his breath was stopped, his heart was beating like a drum. His friend had followed him in, and sat down beside him. Both had their bows in their hands, strung, and a sheaf of arrows.

When they entered the lodge, the man who was lying down at the back of the lodge uttered a loud exclamation, " *Woof*," and then seemed struck dumb.

A plate of corn mush had just been handed him, but he did not take it, and it sat there on the ground by him. One woman was just raising a buffalo horn spoon of mush to her mouth, but her hand stopped before reaching it, and she stared at them, holding the mush before her face. Another woman was ladling some mush into a plate, and she held the plate in one hand and the ladle above it, and looked at them without moving. They all seemed turned into stone.

As the two Pawnees sat there, Running Chief's breath suddenly came back to him. Before it had all been dark about him, as if he had been asleep; but now the clouds had cleared away, and he could see the road ahead of him. Now he felt a man, and brave. As he looked around him, and saw the man lying motionless, and one woman just ready to take a mouthful, and the other woman with the ladle held over the dish, he perceived that they could not move, they were so astonished.

At length the Wichita had come to his senses. He drew a long breath, and sat up, and for a while looked at the two Pawnees. Then he made some sign to them which they did not understand, but they guessed that he was trying to ask who they

were. Running Chief struck his breast, and said,
"*Pi-ta'-da*" (Pawnee). As soon as the Wichita
heard that he caught his breath, and heaved a long
sigh. He did not know what to think of two Pawnees coming into his lodge. He could not think
what it meant. He drew a long breath. He did
not touch his plate of food, but motioned a woman
to take it away. Presently he called to some one in
the neighboring lodge. He was answered, and in a
moment a man came in. He called again, and another entered, and the three looked for a long time
at the two Pawnees. These were sitting motionless,
but watching like two wildcats to see what was going
to happen. Each had his bow and arrows by his
side, and his knife inside his robe. At length the
owner of the lodge spoke, and one of the men went
out, and after a little they heard the sound of horses'
hoofs coming, and they supposed some one was riding up. Every now and then Running Chief would
touch his friend's knee with his own, as if to say,
"Watch."

The owner of the lodge made a sign and pointed
to the east and said "*Capitan.*"* At the same time
he was dressing himself up, putting on a pair of

*A Spanish word meaning chief.

officer's trousers and a uniform coat. Meantime the Pawnees heard the rattle of one saddle, and then of another. The Wichita chief put on his blanket, and his pistol belt around it, and then made signs for them to go out. He led the way, and the Pawnees followed. As they went, Running Chief touched his friend, as if to say, "Watch. They may shoot us as we go out." But when they looked out of the lodge, the Wichita was walking toward the horses, so there was no danger. He mounted a horse, and signed to Running Chief to get up behind him. Another man mounted the other horse, and the friend got up behind him.

As they rode toward the main village, it came into the mind of Running Chief to kill the man he was riding behind, and to ride away. There was where he had to fight his hardest battle. He was tempted to kill this man in front of him, but he was not over-powered by this temptation. He overcame it. He thought that perhaps he might be mounted on a poor horse, and even if he did kill this man and his friend the other, they might be on slow horses and be caught at once. Every little while he would look at his friend and roll his eyes, as if to say, "Watch on your side and I will watch on mine."

As he came near to the village, the Wichita warrior called out, and began to sing a song, and all at once the village was in an uproar. The men, women and children seemed to start up out of the ground, and the lodges poured forth their inmates. Running Chief felt that he was in danger, but he knew that he was not in as much danger as the man before him. He could take the pistol out of the belt that he had hold of and kill him, or he could use his own knife. The Wichita knew that he was in danger. He knew that he was in the power of the enemy.

After the Wichita had called out to the people that they had enemies with them, he kept on talking, saying, "Keep quiet. Do not do anything. Wait. Keep away from me and be still. I am in danger." They would not have listened to him, if it had not been that he was a leading man, and a brave warrior. The riders came to the largest lodge, which stood in the middle of the village. Here they stopped. When Running Chief got off the horse, he held tightly the belt of the Wichita, who dismounted; and they went together into the lodge of the Head Chief, and the others followed and went in, and all sat down opposite the door. All this time there was a hubbub outside. People were flying from their lodges to that of the Head Chief, and lifting up the edge of the lodge, and peeping under it at the Pawnees. They chattered to each other, and called out to those who were coming; all was noise and confusion.

v.

The under chiefs came in one by one, until all were present. Then one of them made a speech, saying that it would be best to leave everything to the Head Chief, and that he should decide what ought to be done with these enemies. Then it was silent for a time, while the Chief was making up his mind what should be done; and during this silence Running Chief felt a touch on his shoulder, and looked behind him, and there was handed to him under the edge of the lodge a dish of meat. He took it and began to eat, and his companion also ate with him. After he had eaten a few mouthfuls, he took his arrows, which he had held in his hand, and put them in his quiver, and unstrung his bow and laid it aside, and his friend did the same.

Then the Chief stood up and spoke to those sitting there and said, "What can I do? They have eaten of my food. I cannot make war on people who have been eating with me." While he was saying this, Running Chief was again touched on the shoulder, and some one handed him a cup of water, and he drank; and the Chief, as he saw this, added, "and have also drunk of my water." He then turned and called to a certain man, who could speak Pawnee, and told him to ask these men if they were on the warpath. He asked them, "Are you on the warpath?" and they replied, "Yes, we are on the warpath."

Then said he, "What are you here for?"

Running Chief answered, "You have plenty of dogs. I am here that my body may be eaten by them."

When the Wichitas heard this they all made a sound, *Ah-h-h-h!* for they were surprised at his bravery. The Chief asked him, "Do you know anything about the horses that were missed last night?"

He said, "Yes."

"Where are they?" said the Head Chief.

Running Chief replied, "The party have gone off with them—Pawnees."

"Were you with them?"

"Yes, I was with them, and I stopped behind on purpose to come into your village."

The Head Chief then turned to the others and talked for a little while. He said, "See what a brave man this is. He had resolved to die. But he shall not die, because he has eaten our food and drunk of our water. Although we are enemies of this man's tribe, yet we are the same people with them, who have been apart for a long time. I cannot help it; my heart is touched by his talk and by their bravery. By their bravery they are safe." And all the Wichitas said "*Waugh.*"

Then the Head Chief through the interpreter talked to Running Chief. He said, "Are you a chief?"

Running Chief replied, "No, I am not a chief; I am like a dog; I am poor."

The Head Chief said to him, "By your bravery you have saved yourselves. You shall have the road to your home made white before you. Let there not be one blood spot on it." Then he turned to those who were sitting about the lodge and said, "Now, my young men, do something for them."

A young man named Crazy Wolf stood up and spoke; and when he had finished, the interpreter said, "That man has given you a black horse, the best that he has."

Another young man on the other side of the lodge spoke, and the interpreter said, "He has given you a roan horse, the best that he has." Then all the Wichitas began to speak at once, and before they knew it, the Pawnees had ten head of horses, and robes and blankets, saddles, bridles, shields, spears and moccasins—many beautiful presents. So they were well provided.

The Head Chief again stood up and talked to the assembly, praising these Pawnees; and he stepped over to Running Chief and shook hands with him, and when he did so, Running Chief stood up and put his arms around the Chief and pressed him to his breast, and the Chief did the same to him, and when Running Chief had his arms around the Chief, the Chief trembled, and came near to crying. The Chief embraced the other Pawnee, and looked him in the face and said, "What brave men you are!"

The friend said, "What my friend stepped, that I stepped; I trod in his footprints; I had one mind with him."

As the Chief stepped back to his place he spoke through the interpreter, "Now you have eaten of my food and drunk of my water. Everything that I have is yours. My women and my children are

yours. You are not a chief, but you are a chief."*
Then he spoke to the crowd and they all went away,
leaving only the principal men in the lodge.

That afternoon the Pawnees were feasted everywhere, and had to eat till they were almost dead;
and as they went about, all of their former sadness
seemed to be swept away, and Running Chief felt
like crying for joy.

While they were feasting, the man who had given
the black horse went out, and caught it up, and
painted it handsomely, and rode into the village, and
put on it a silver bridle, and eagle feathers in its
mane and tail, and when Running Chief was going
from one lodge to another he met him, and jumped
off the horse and said, "Brother, ride this." He gave
him also a shield and a spear.

These Pawnees staid two months with the Wichitas,
and all their troubles seemed at an end. At length
Running Chief called a council of the chiefs, and
told them that now he wished to make ready to go
home to his village. He thanked them for all that
they had done for him, and said that now he would
go. The chiefs said, "It is well. We are glad that

* You are not a chief, but you have made yourself a chief by
your great qualities.

you have been with us and visited us. Take the good news back to your tribe. Tell them that we are one people, though long separated. Let the road between our villages be made white. Let it no more show any spots of blood."

Running-Chief thanked them and said, "I will go and take the good news to my people. I shall show them the presents you have made us, and tell them how well we have been treated. It may be that some of the chiefs of my tribe will wish to come down to visit you, as I have done." The Head Chief said, "Can I rely on your words, that I shall be visited?" Running Chief replied, "You can rely on them if I have to come alone to visit you again." The Chief got up and put his arms about him, and said, "I want to be visited. Let there be no more war between us. We are brothers; let us always be brothers." Then they gave him many more presents, and packed his horses, and six braves offered to go with him through the Cheyenne country. They went through in the night. Running Chief said afterward, "I could have stolen a lot of horses from the Cheyennes, but I thought, I will be coming back through this country and it is better not."

At the Pawnee village these two young men had

been mourned by their relations as lost or dead. It was in the spring (March, 1869) when they reached home, and there was joy in the tribe when they came in with the presents. Running Chief was praised, and so was his friend. Both had been brave and had done great things.

Now Running Chief's name was changed from *Wi-ti-ti le-shar'-uspi* to *Skŭ'r-ar-a le-shar* (Lone Chief).

VI.

The following summer in August, at the close of the summer hunt, three hundred Pawnees, old men and young, under the leadership of Lone Chief, visited the Wichitas, who received them well, and gave them many horses. Lone Chief was not satisfied with the peace that he had made with the Wichitas. He also visited the Kiowas, and made peace, and was given by them eight fine horses. He also led his party to the Comanches, and visited them, and got many presents. In the fall the Pawnees returned to their village. Many of them fell sick on the way, and some died.

In the winter of 1869–70 Lone Chief and his friend led a war party against the Cheyennes. They took six hundred head of horses. The Cheyennes now

tell us that in the seventy-five lodges of that camp
there was not left a hoof.   All night and all next day
they ran the herd.   Then Lone Chief said, "Let us
not run the horses any longer, they will not come
after us; they are afoot."   When the party got on
the north side of the Republican, on the table lands,
a terrible storm of snow and wind came upon them,
and they were nearly lost.   For three days and three
nights they lay in the storm.   All were frozen, some
losing toes and fingers.   They survived, however,
and brought in all their horses.   Again Lone Chief
sacrificed to *Ti-ra'-wa*.   A second sacrifice is very
unusual and a notable event.

OLD-FASHIONED "T. GRAY" AX.

THE PRISONERS OF COURT
HOUSE ROCK.

COURT HOUSE ROCK is a high, square-shaped bluff, or butte, on the North Platte River. It is composed of a hard, yellowish clay, which is but slowly eroded by the weather, though soft enough to be cut readily with a knife. On all sides except one, this rock or butte is nearly or quite vertical, and its sides, smoothed and polished by the wind and the rain, offer no projecting points, to serve as foot or hand holds for one who might wish to climb up or down. On one side there is a way by which an active man may reach the summit, where he finds a flat tableland of moderate extent.

A number of years ago a war party of Skidi, who were camped near Court House Rock, were surprised by a party of Sioux. There were many of them, and they drove the Skidi back, and at length these were

obliged to climb the steep side of Court House Rock.
The Sioux dared not follow them up on to the rock,
but guarded the only place where it was possible to
come down, and camped all around the rock below
to starve the Skidi out. The Skidi had nothing to
eat nor to drink, and suffered terribly from hunger
and still more from thirst. The leader of the party
suffered most of any, for he thought that he would
surely lose all his men. He felt that this was the
worst of all. He must not only die, but must also be
disgraced, because under his leadership the young
men of his party had been lost. He used to go off
at night, apart from the others, and pray to *Ti-ra'-wa*
for help; for some way to save his party.

One night while he was praying, something spoke
to him, and said, "Look hard for a place where you
may get down from this rock, and so save both your
men and yourself." He kept on praying that night,
and when day came, he looked all along the edge of
the rock for a place where it might be possible to get
down. At last he found near the edge of the cliff a
point of the soft clay rock sticking up above the level
of the rest. The side of the rock below it was straight
up and down, and smooth. At night he took his
knife, and began to cut about the base of this point

of rock, and night after night he kept at this until he had cut away the base of the point, so that it was no larger around than a man's body. Then he secretly took all the lariats that the party had, and tied them together, and let them down, and found that his rope was long enough to reach the ground. He put the rope around the point, and made a loop in it for his feet, and slowly let himself down to the ground. He got there safely, and then climbed back again. The next night he called his men about him, and told them how it was, and that they might all be saved. Then he ordered the youngest and least important man of the party to let himself down, and after him the next youngest, and so on, up to the more important men, and last of all the leader's turn came. He let himself down, and they all crept through the Sioux camp and escaped.

They never knew how long the Sioux stayed there watching the rock. Probably until they thought that the Skidi had all starved to death.

WOLVES IN THE NIGHT.

IN the year 1879 Little Warrior, with a Chaui boy and a soldier, was off scouting on the plains east of the mountains. They saw a long way off—perhaps twenty miles—some objects that seemed to be moving. It was one of those hot dry days in summer, when all the air is quivering and all things are distorted by the mirage. They watched these objects through their glasses for a long time. They seemed to move and quiver, and they could not tell what they were, but Little Warrior thought they were mounted men. They seemed to be traveling in the same direction with this scouting party. At length they could see that they were mounted men, and were driving some loose animals.

When night came, the two Pawnees left their horses with the soldier and started on foot to look for the camp of the strangers, and to find out who they were. They formed the plan to make themselves look like coyotes, so that they could go close to the camp. Each took from under his saddle a white sheet, which, when the time came, they would tie around their bodies, having their guns inside, held under their arms, and their pistols in their belts about their waists. It was a bright moonlight night, the moon being so bright that it made it hard to see far on the prairie.

The camp was found in a little hollow, and was occupied by seven Ute Indians. They had a dog with them. The Pawnees could hear them talking and laughing, as they sat about the big fire they had built. They could see the horses too.

The men put on their white sheets, and getting down on all fours, prowled about *l*ike wolves, gradually drawing nearer and nearer to the camp. Two or three times the dog smelt them and barked, but they paid no attention to it, but trotted hither and thither, smelling the ground and sometimes sitting up on their haunches like wolves, and then going on again. After a little while they came so close to the camp that they could see that the horses were staked out, and that there were some mules feeding about, hobbled. One of the Utes, who noticed the wolves prowling near the camp, got his gun and shot at the Chaui boy, but he did not hit him. The boy loped off and joined Little Warrior behind a hill, and there the two waited.

Little Warrior said to his companion, "These men have come far to-day. They are pretty tired. Wait and they will lie down and go to sleep." Presently the camp quieted down and the Utes slept.

The Pawnees then made themselves wolves again, and went close to the Ute camp. The horses were staked close to where the men were sleeping, but the mules had wandered off a little to one side. Six mules were together, and one was by itself on the other side of the camp. Little Warrior went around the camp to this one, and cut its hobbles, and then drove it slowly toward the others. Then they drove the whole seven quietly away from the camp. If it had not been for the dog, they could very likely have stolen the horses too, and left the Utes afoot, and perhaps they might have been able to kill the Utes.

They drove the mules about two miles, and then went on to where they had left their horses. They found the soldier nearly frightened to death. He said he did not like to be left by himself in such a lonely place; he wanted to go to camp. They told him they were going to return and get those mules. They did so, and secured them, and drove them in to their own camp, which they reached about six o'clock the next morning.

It was learned afterward that fourteen mules had been stolen from a Government train, and a reward of $200 had been offered for their recovery. These taken by the two Pawnees were seven of the stolen animals, and each of the men received $50 as his proportion of the reward.

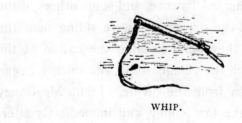

WHIP.

A LEADER OF SOLDIERS.

IN 1876, when the attack was made by General
Mackenzie on the village of the Cheyenne chief,
Dull Knife, the Pawnee Scouts charged down on the
village on the south side of the creek, while on the
north side of the stream, a company of United States
cavalry, under Lieut. McKinney, were making a
charge. Before the village was reached, Ralph J.
Weeks, an educated Pawnee, and some others of the
scouts crossed the stream and were riding near the
soldiers. As they were crossing the cañon at the
mouth of which the village stood, the enemy began
to fire at them from the ravine. Lieut. McKinney
was killed at the first volley, and immediately afterward his first sergeant fell, leaving the troop without
a commander. The soldiers hesitated, stopped, and
then turned round, and began to retreat.

Ralph rode up behind them, and got off his horse, and called out, "Hold on boys, don't run. There are only seven Indians there. Come on, and we will kill them all. Get off your horses and come ahead on foot. There are only seven of them. We will kill them all."

The men stopped in their retreat, dismounted, and under Ralph's direction and leadership, went forward, and did kill all the Indians in the ravine.

KNIFE SCABBARD.

A CHEYENNE BLANKET.

THE Cheyennes, like other Indians, do not speak to each other when they are away from the camp. If a man goes away from the village, and sits or stands by himself on the top of a hill, it is a sign that he wants to be alone; perhaps to meditate; perhaps to pray. No one speaks to him or goes near him.

Now, there was once a Pawnee boy, who went off on the warpath to the Cheyenne camp. In some way he had obtained a Cheyenne blanket. This Pawnee came close to the Cheyenne camp, and hid himself there to wait. About the middle of the afternoon, he left his hiding place, and walked to the top of the hill overlooking the village. He had his Cheyenne blanket wrapped about him and over his head, with only a little hole for his eyes.

He stood there for an hour or two, looking over the Cheyenne camp.

They were coming in from buffalo hunting, and some were leading in the pack horses loaded down with meat. A man came along, riding a horse packed with meat, and leading another pack horse, and a black spotted horse that was his running horse. These running horses are ridden only on the chase or on war parties, and are well cared for. After being used they are taken down to the river and are washed and cleaned with care. When the boy saw this spotted horse, he thought to himself that this was the horse that he would take. When the man who was leading it reached his lodge, he dismounted and handed the ropes to his women, and went inside.

Then the Pawnee made up his mind what he would do. He started down the hill into the village, and walked straight to this lodge where the women were unloading the meat. He walked up to them, reached out his hand, and took the ropes of the spotted horse and one of the others. As he did so the women fell back. Probably they thought that this was some one of the relations of the owner, who was going to take the running horse down to the river to wash it. The Pawnee could not talk Cheyenne, but as he turned away he mumbled something —*m-m-m-m*—as if speaking in a low voice, and then walked down toward the river. As soon as he had gone down over the bank and was out of sight, he jumped on the spotted horse and rode into the brush, and pretty soon was away with two horses, stolen out of the Cheyenne camp in broad daylight.

A WAR SHIELD.

LITTLE WARRIOR'S COUNSEL.

MOST of the Pawnee heroes are so regarded because of victories, daring deeds, the *coups* they have counted and the horses they have stolen. The glory of Comanche Chief and of Lone Chief depends mainly on their bravery, rather than on the fact that they were peace-makers. Yet there should be room among these stories for the account of an educated Pawnee—a brave—who by his wise counsel to an Indian of a hostile tribe saved many lives, both of Indians and of white men. Little Warrior was educated at a Western college, but has shown his bravery on the field of battle, and has sacrificed a scalp to *Ti-ra'-wa*.

In the year 1879, at the time of the Ute outbreak, after Major Thornburgh's command had been annihilated, Little Warrior was employed as a scout for the troops. On the headwaters of the Arkansas River he was one day scouting in advance of the command, in company with four white soldiers and four Indian scouts. One day, the party saw far off on the prairie an Indian, who showed a white flag, and came toward them. When he had come near to them, the soldiers proposed to kill him, and report that he was a Ute, one of the Indians that they were looking for. But Little Warrior said, "No. He has a white flag up, and it may be that he is carrying a dispatch, or, perhaps, he is a white man disguised as an Indian."

When the man had come close to them, they saw that he was dressed like a Comanche; he did not have the bristling fringe of hair over the forehead that the Utes wear, and his side locks were un-braided. Little Warrior asked him, by signs, if he was alone, to which he replied in the same language that he was alone. Then Little Warrior inquired who he was. The stranger made the sign for Comanche—a friendly tribe.

They took him into the camp, and after a while Little Warrior began to talk to him in Comanche. He could not understand a word of it.

Then the Pawnee said to him, "My friend, you

are a Ute." The stranger acknowledged that he
was.

Then Little Warrior talked to him, and gave him
much good advice. He said, "My friend, you and I
have the same skin, and what I tell you now is for
your good. I speak to you as a friend, and what I
say to you now is so that you may save your women
and your children. It is of no use for you to try to
fight the white people. I have been among them,
and I know how many they are. They are like the
grass. Even if you were to kill a hundred it would
be nothing. It would be like burning up a few
handfuls of prairie grass. There would be just as
many left. If you try to fight them they will hunt
you like a ghost. Wherever you go they will follow after you, and you will get no rest. The soldiers will be continually on your tracks. Even if
you were to go up on top of a high mountain, where
there was nothing but rocks, and where no one else
could come, the soldiers would follow you, and get
around you, and wait, and wait, even for fifty years.
They would have plenty to eat, and they could wait
until after you were dead. There is one white man
who is the chief of all this country, and what he says
must be done. It is no use to fight him.

"Now if you are wise you will go out and get all your people, and bring them in, on to the reservation, and give yourself up. It will be better for you in the end. I speak to you as a friend, because we are both the same color, and I hope that you will listen to my words."

The Ute said, "My friend, your words are good, and I thank you for the friendly advice you have given me. I will follow it and will agree to go away and bring in my people."

Little Warrior said, "How do you make a promise?"

The Ute said, "By raising the right hand to one above."

Little Warrior said, "That is the custom also among my people."

The Ute raised his hand and made the promise.

After he had been detained two or three weeks, he was allowed to go, and about a month afterward, he brought in the band of which he was chief, and surrendered. Through his influence afterward, the whole tribe came in and gave themselves up. He was grateful to Little Warrior for what he had done for him, and told him that if he ever came back into his country he would give him many ponies.

A COMANCHE BUNDLE.

A PAWNEE boy went to the Comanche village after horses. At night he went into the camp, crept to the door of a lodge, and took a horse that was tied there. It was bright moonlight, and as he was cutting the rope he saw, hanging before the lodge, a handsome shield and a spear, which he took. There was also a bundle hanging there. He took this down, opened it, and found in it a war bonnet, beaded moccasins and leggings, and a breast-plate of long beads. He dressed himself in all these fine things, mounted the horse and rode away.

FOLK-TALES.

THE DUN HORSE.

I.

MANY years ago, there lived in the Pawnee tribe an old woman and her grandson, a boy about sixteen years old. These people had no relations and were very poor. They were so poor that they were despised by the rest of the tribe. They had nothing of their own; and always, after the village started to move the camp from one place to another, these two would stay behind the rest, to look over the old camp, and pick up anything that the other Indians had thrown away, as worn out or useless. In this way they would sometimes get pieces of robes, worn out moccasins with holes in them, and bits of meat.

Now, it happened one day, after the tribe had moved away from the camp, that this old woman and her boy were following along the trail behind the rest, when they came to a miserable old worn out dun horse, which they supposed had been abandoned by some Indians. He was thin and exhausted, was blind of one eye, had a bad sore back, and one of his forelegs was very much swollen. In fact, he was so worthless that none of the Pawnees had been willing to take the trouble to try to drive him along with them. But when the old woman and her boy came along, the boy said, "Come now, we will take this old horse, for we can make him carry our pack." So the old woman put her pack on the horse, and drove him along, but he limped and could only go very slowly.

II.

The tribe moved up on the North Platte, until they came to Court House Rock. The two poor Indians followed them, and camped with the others. One day while they were here, the young men who had been sent out to look for buffalo, came hurrying into camp and told the chiefs that a large herd of buffalo were near, and that among them was a spotted calf.

The Head Chief of the Pawnees had a very beautiful daughter, and when he heard about the spotted calf, he ordered his old crier to go about through the village, and call out that the man who killed the spotted calf should have his daughter for his wife. For a spotted robe is *ti-war'-uks-ti*—big medicine.

The buffalo were feeding about four miles from the village, and the chiefs decided that the charge should be made from there. In this way, the man who had the fastest horse would be the most likely to kill the calf. Then all the warriors and the young men picked out their best and fastest horses, and made ready to start. Among those who prepared for the charge was the poor boy on the old dun horse. But when they saw him, all the rich young braves on their fast horses pointed at him, and said, "Oh, see; there is the horse that is going to catch the spotted calf;" and they laughed at him, so that the poor boy was ashamed, and rode off to one side of the crowd, where he could not hear their jokes and laughter.

When he had ridden off some little way, the horse stopped, and turned his head round, and spoke to the boy. He said, "Take me down to the creek, and plaster me all over with mud. Cover my head and neck and body and legs." When the boy heard the horse speak, he was afraid; but he did as he was told. Then the horse said, "Now mount, but do not ride back to the warriors, who laugh at you because you have such a poor horse. Stay right here, until the word is given to charge." So the boy stayed there.

And presently all the fine horses were drawn up in line and pranced about, and were so eager to go that their riders could hardly hold them in; and at last the old crier gave the word, *"Loo-ah"*—Go! Then the Pawnees all leaned forward on their horses and yelled, and away they went. Suddenly, away off to the right, was seen the old dun horse. He did not seem to run. He seemed to sail along like a bird. He passed all the fastest horses, and in a moment he was among the buffalo. First he picked out the spotted calf, and charging up alongside of it, *U-ra-rish!* straight flew the arrow. The calf fell. The boy drew another arrow, and killed a fat cow that was running by. Then he dismounted and began to skin the calf, before any of the other warriors had come up. But when the rider got off the old dun horse, how changed he was! He pranced about and would hardly stand still near the dead buffalo. His back was all right again; his legs were well and fine; and both his eyes were clear and bright.

The boy skinned the calf and the cow that he had killed, and then he packed all the meat on the horse, and put the spotted robe on top of the load, and started back to the camp on foot, leading the dun horse. But even with this heavy load the horse pranced all the time, and was scared at everything he saw. On the way to camp, one of the rich young chiefs of the tribe rode up by the boy, and offered him twelve good horses for the spotted robe, so that he could marry the Head Chief's beautiful daughter; but the boy laughed at him and would not sell the robe.

Now, while the boy walked to the camp leading the dun horse, most of the warriors rode back, and one of those that came first to the village, went to the old woman, and said to her, "Your grandson has killed the spotted calf." And the old woman said, "Why do you come to tell me this? You ought to be ashamed to make fun of my boy, because he is poor." The warrior said, "What I have told you is true," and then he rode away. After a little while another brave rode up to the old woman, and said to her, "Your grandson has killed the spotted calf." Then the old woman began to cry, she felt so badly because every one made fun of her boy, because he was poor.

Pretty soon the boy came along, leading the horse up to the lodge where he and his grandmother lived. It was a little lodge, just big enough for two, and was made of old pieces of skin that the old woman had picked up, and was tied together with strings of rawhide and sinew. It was the meanest and worst lodge in the village. When the old woman saw her boy leading the dun horse with the load of meat and the robes on it, she was very much surprised. The boy said to her, "Here, I have brought you plenty of meat to eat, and here is a robe, that you may have for yourself. Take the meat off the horse." Then the old woman laughed, for her heart was glad. But when she went to take the meat from the horse's back, he snorted and jumped about, and acted like a wild horse. The old woman looked at him in wonder, and could hardly believe that it was the same horse. So the boy had to take off the meat, for the horse would not let the old woman come near him.

III.

That night the horse spoke again to the boy and said, "*Wa-ti-hes Chah'-ra-rat wa-ta*. To-morrow the Sioux are coming—a large war party. They will attack the village, and you will have a great battle.

Now, when the Sioux are drawn up in line of battle, and are all ready to fight, you jump on to me, and ride as hard as you can, right into the middle of the Sioux, and up to their Head Chief, their greatest warrior, and count *coup* on him, and kill him, and then ride back. Do this four times, and count *coup* on four of the bravest Sioux, and kill them, but don't go again. If you go the fifth time, may be you will be killed, or else you will lose me. *La-ku'-ta-chix*—remember." So the boy promised.

The next day it happened as the horse had said, and the Sioux came down and formed a line of battle. Then the boy took his bow and arrows, and jumped on the dun horse, and charged into the midst of them. And when the Sioux saw that he was going to strike their Head Chief, they all shot their arrows at him, and the arrows flew so thickly across each other that the sky became dark, but none of them hit the boy. And he counted *coup* on the Chief, and killed him, and then rode back. After that he charged again among the Sioux, where they were gathered thickest, and counted *coup* on their bravest warrior, and killed him. And then twice more, until he had gone four times as the horse had told him.

But the Sioux and the Pawnees kept on fighting, and the boy stood around and watched the battle. And at last he said to himself, "I have been four times and have killed four Sioux, and I am all right, I am not hurt anywhere; why may I not go again?" So he jumped on the dun horse, and charged again. But when he got among the Sioux, one Sioux warrior drew an arrow and shot. The arrow struck the dun horse behind the forelegs and pierced him through. And the horse fell down dead. But the boy jumped off, and fought his way through the Sioux, and ran away as fast as he could to the Pawnees. Now, as soon as the horse was killed, the Sioux said to each other, "This horse was like a man. He was brave. He was not like a horse." And they took their knives and hatchets, and hacked the dun horse and gashed his flesh, and cut him into small pieces.

The Pawnees and Sioux fought all day long, but toward night the Sioux broke and fled.

IV.

The boy felt very badly that he had lost his horse; and, after the fight was over, he went out from the village to where it had taken place, to mourn for his horse. He went to the spot where the horse lay, and gathered up all the pieces of flesh, which the Sioux had cut off, and the legs and the hoofs, and put them all together in a pile. Then he went off to the top of a hill near by, and sat down and drew his robe over his head, and began to mourn for his horse.

As he sat there, he heard a great wind storm coming up, and it passed over him with a loud rushing sound, and after the wind came a rain. The boy looked down from where he sat to the pile of flesh and bones, which was all that was left of his horse, and he could just see it through the rain. And the rain passed by, and his heart was very heavy, and he kept on mourning.

And pretty soon, came another rushing wind, and after it a rain; and as he looked through the driving rain toward the spot where the pieces lay, he thought that they seemed to come together and take shape, and that the pile looked like a horse lying down, but he could not see well for the thick rain.

After this, came a third storm like the others; and now when he looked toward the horse he thought he saw its tail move from side to side two or three times, and that it lifted its head from the ground. The boy was afraid, and wanted to run away, but he stayed.

And as he waited, there came another storm. And while the rain fell, looking through the rain, the boy saw the horse raise himself up on his forelegs and look about. Then the dun horse stood up.

v.

The boy left the place where he had been sitting on the hilltop, and went down to him. When the boy had come near to him, the horse spoke and said, "You have seen how it has been this day; and from this you may know how it will be after this. But *Ti-ra'-wa* has been good, and has let me come back to you. After this, do what I tell you; not any more, not any less." Then the horse said, "Now lead me off, far away from the camp, behind that big hill, and leave me there to-night, and in the morning come for me;" and the boy did as he was told.

And when he went for the horse in the morning, he found with him a beautiful white gelding, much more handsome than any horse in the tribe. That night the dun horse told the boy to take him again to the place behind the big hill, and to come for him the next morning; and when the boy went for him again, he found with him a beautiful black gelding.

And so for ten nights, he left the horse among the hills, and each morning he found a different colored horse, a bay, a roan, a gray, a blue, a spotted horse, and all of them finer than any horses that the Pawnees had ever had in their tribe before.

Now the boy was rich, and he married the beautiful daughter of the Head Chief, and when he became older, he was made Head Chief himself. He had many children by his beautiful wife, and one day when his oldest boy died, he wrapped him in the spotted calf robe and buried him in it. He always took good care of his old grandmother, and kept her in his own lodge until she died. The dun horse was never ridden except at feasts, and when they were going to have a doctors' dance, but he was always led about with the Chief, wherever he went. The horse lived in the village for many years, until he became very old. And at last he died.

A STORY OF FAITH.

LONG ago, before they ever had any of these doctors' dances, there was, in the Kit-ke-hahk'-i tribe, a young boy, small, growing up. He seemed not to go with the other boys nor to play with them, but would keep away from them. He would go off by himself, and lie down, and sometimes they would find him crying, or half crying. He seemed to have peculiar ways. His father and mother did not try to interfere with him, but let him alone. Sometimes they would find him with mud or clay smeared over his face and head. That is the sign of a doctor. When you see a person putting mud on his face or head, it shows that he has faith in the earth. From the earth are taken the roots that they use in medicine.

When the parents saw this, they did not understand it. How should he know anything about mud being the sign of a doctor? They did not understand, but they just let him do it.

The boy grew up till he came to have the ways of a young man, but he never went with any of the other boys. After he had grown up, they saw that he had something in his mind. Sometimes he would fast for two days, and sit by himself, smoking and praying to *Ti-ra'-wa*, and not saying anything to any one. His father was a brave but not a chief, and had plenty of horses. The son was well dressed and comfortably off.

When any one in the camp was sick, this young man would take pity on him, and of his own accord would go and doctor him, and pretty soon the person would be well again. Through his doing this, the people began to hear about him, and his name became great. He was humble, and did not want to be thought well of. He was not proud, but he was always doing good. At that time, there were many doctors in the tribe, and they wondered how it was that he could cure so many people, when he had never been taught by any of them. They could not understand it, and they began to be jealous of him.

He never wanted to be with the doctors, but liked to stay by himself. He wanted to be alone rather than with any one.

In that time there were bad doctors, and they began to hear about this humble man and to be jealous of him. These bad doctors could curse a man, and he would be cursed, and could poison one. They had great power and influence, for everybody feared them.

The bands of the Pawnees were not then together, as they are now. As the people talked about this young man, one of the other bands heard about him. In this band was a great doctor, and this doctor thought to himself, "This young man's influence is growing. If I do not do something, he will soon be ahead of me."

This great doctor went to the village to visit this young man, to see how he looked, and to find out how he got his knowledge and his power, for he knew he had never been taught. He wanted to eat with him, and talk with him, and find out whence his learning came. He reached the Kit-ke-hahk'-i village. He was welcomed, and the young man treated him with respect, and asked him to come into the lodge, and sit down with him. At night they talked together. The great doctor said, "I am glad to see you. You can come to me for advice sometimes." The young man thanked him. They smoked together. It is the custom always when an Indian is visiting another, for the one that is being visited to present all the smokes; but at this time the great doctor said, "We will smoke my tobacco." So all night they smoked his tobacco. The next morning he went away. He did not again eat with the young man. He said, "I am glad, and I am going." And he went away to his village. This happened in the winter.

This young man was not married. His father had asked him to marry, but he would not. He said he had reasons.

About summer time, he felt different from what he had. He was drowsy and felt badly. He felt heavy. He seemed to be swelling up with some strange new disease. The great doctor had poisoned him with this result. How it was no one can tell, but it was so. This was a disgrace, and he did not know how to get out of it. There was no way. He would go off and cry, and pray to *Ti ra'-wa*, and sometimes would stay for three or four days without anything to eat. He was so miserable that one time he was going to kill himself. He did not tell his father or any one about this, but kept it to himself. The tribe went off on a hunt and left the old village. Before they started, the man went off on a hill somewhere to meditate and pray, and his father told him that when he was ready to start he should ride such a horse, and he left it in the village for him when he should come in.

When he came into the empty village he found the horse tied there, and he saddled it and started; but instead of going in the direction the tribe had taken, he went east. His horse was a fine one. He went away off by himself for some days, and at last he stopped, and got off his horse, and tied it to a tree. Then he called aloud and said, "*A-ti-us ta'-kaw-a* (My Father, in all places), it is through you that I am living. Perhaps it was through you that this man put me in this condition. You are the ruler. Nothing is impossible to you. If you see fit, take this away from me." Then he turned round and said, "Now, you, all fish of the rivers, and you, all birds of the air, and all animals that move upon the earth, and you, oh Sun! I present to you this animal." He said again, "You birds in the air, and you animals upon the earth, we are related, we are alike in this respect, that one ruler made us all. You see me, how unhappy I am. If you have any power, intercede for me."

When he had finished his prayer, he went up to the horse, and stabbed it with his knife and killed it, and it fell down dead. He turned it so that its head was toward the east, and raised it on its belly, doubling its knees under it, and cut the hide down the back, and skinned it down on both sides, so that the birds of the air and the animals of the earth might feed on it.

The tribe at this time was camped on the head of the Republican River. He went on toward the east until he came to the place on the Platte River called *Pa-huk'* (hill island). He saw that there were many wild animals on this point, and he liked it, and thought he would stay there, and perhaps dream. He stopped there a while, feeling very badly, and mourning all the time on this point. He was there several days, and one night it happened that he went to sleep [fainted], for he was exhausted with much weeping and praying. Something spoke to him, and said, "What are you doing here?" He woke up, and looked around, but saw no one. It was only a voice. Another night when he was asleep a voice asked him, "What are you doing here?" He awoke and looked about, but saw no one. A third night the same thing happened, and he was wondering what it meant. Then he answered and said, "Who ever you are who speaks to me, look at me and you will see that I am poor in mind.* I am a man, and yet I am in a condition that no man was ever in before. I am here only to suffer and to die. Whoever you are who speaks to me, take pity on me and help me." He received no answer.

The fourth night something touched him. He was half awake when he felt it. Something said, "What are you doing here?" He was lying on his side, his head toward the east and his feet toward the west. Something tapped him on the shoulder, and he looked up and saw a great big animal, big black eyes and a whitish body, *Pah'*, big elk. When he looked at it, the animal said, "Get up and sit down;" and the elk too sat down. The elk said, "I have heard of you and of your condition, and I am here to tell you that we all know your trouble. Right here where you are, under you, is the home of the *Nahu'rac* (animals). I know that it is impossible to help you, but I shall let them know—they already know—that

---

* Poor in mind, *i. e.*, despondent, miserable, unhappy.

you are here. I can only help you so far as to take you to the places where these animals are. If this animal home cannot help you, I will take you to another place; if that fails, I will take you to another place; if that fails, to another. Then you will see that I have done my part. If it is impossible for the animals to do it, we have still one above that we look to." As soon as he had said, this he vanished like a wind; disappeared all at once.

While the boy sat there, thinking about what the animal had said to him, he fell asleep with his mind full of these things. In his sleep something talked to him. It said, "I know that you feel badly, and that your mind is poor. I have passed you many times, and I have heard you crying. I belong here, but I am one of the servants. I have informed my leaders, those who command me, about you, and that you are so poor in your mind, and they have said to me, 'If you take pity on him, do as you please because you are our servant.'"

At this time he woke up, and saw sitting by him a little bird.* He talked to it. He said, "Oh, my

---

* This is a small bird, blue above, white below, with red legs. It is swift-flying, and sometimes dives down into the water. It is the messenger bird of the *Nahu'rac*. See also story of the Boy who was Sacrificed.

brother, I feel pleased that you understand my poor mind. Now take pity on me and help me." The bird said to him, "You must not talk in this way to me. I am only a servant. To-morrow night I will come this way, and will show you what to do. To-morrow night I will come this way, and whatever you see me do, you do the same thing." Then he disappeared. The man then felt a little easier in his mind, and more as if there were some hope for him.

The next night the bird came, and was flying about near him after dark, waiting for the time. When the time came, the bird flew close to him, and said, "Come. Let us go to the edge of the cut bank." When they had come to the edge of the bank above the water in the river, the bird said, "Now, my friend, you are poor. What I do, you do. When I dive down off this bank, you follow me." The man replied to him, "Yes, I am poor. Whatever you tell me to do, I will do." So when the bird dived down off the cut bank, the man threw off everything, and cared nothing for what he did except to follow the bird. He leaped down after it, and as he sprang, it seemed to him that he felt like a bird, and could sail this way and that. He did not feel as if he were falling, and were going to be hurt, but as if he were flying, and could control his movements. Just as he reached the water in his fall, it seemed to him that he was standing in the entrance way of a lodge, and could look through into it and see the fire burning in the middle.

While he was standing there, the bird flew in ahead of him, and he heard it say, "Here he is." He stepped toward the entrance, and just as he came to it the *Nahu'rac* all made their different noises, for they are not used to the smell of human beings. The bears growled, and the panthers and wild cats and wolves and rattlesnakes and other animals all made their sounds. As he went in, there was a bear standing on one side, and a great snake on the other, and it was very difficult for the man to go in. He hesitated a little to enter that narrow passage, but something behind him seemed to push him ahead, although the bear stood ready to seize him, and the snake was rattling and standing up as if about to strike. If he had not had the courage to pass them he would have been lost, but he looked neither to the right nor to the left, but walked straight ahead past them. As soon as he had passed them, they both sank back and were quiet. Then all the *Nahu'rac* made another kind of a noise, as if welcoming him. The bear began to lie down; and the snake stretched itself out again. As he went in he just stood there and looked around. He saw there all kinds of animals. The head doctor was a white beaver, very large, there was another a garfish, another an otter, and the fourth was a sandhill crane.

The man sat down, and he looked very pitiful. Then for a while everything was silent. Then the servant said to the four head doctors, "I have brought this man here. I have taken pity on him, and I want you to take pity on him." Then it was more silent than ever. The man looked about him, and saw all the animals, and saw them roll their eyes around at him.

Presently the servant got up, and stood right in the midst. The head doctors sat at the back of the lodge opposite the door on the other side of the fire. The bird said, "My rulers, you know me. I am your servant, and I am always obedient to your commands. No matter what you tell me to do, I do it. No matter how long the journeys you send me on, I go. Many nights I have lost sleep because of carrying out your commands. I have seen this man many times, and I am weary of his crying as I fly back and forth. Now, I want you to take pity on this man, because I pity him. Look on this poor-minded man and pity him."

Then the bird went to the young man, and took from him his pipe, which was filled, and carried it round and stood before the beaver, the head doctor, and held out the pipe to him to take. The white beaver did not stretch out his hand for it, and the bird stood there for a long time. At last the bird began to cry, and the tears began to run down its face, and it cried hard; and at last the white beaver stretched out his hand, and then drew it back again, and hesitated; and the bird kept on crying, and at length the head doctor reached out his hand and took the pipe. Just as soon as he took the pipe, all the animals made a kind of a hissing sound, as much as to say, *Loo'ah*—Good. They were pleased. Then the white beaver, holding the pipe, said, "I cannot help but reach out for this pipe, for I take pity on my servant. But it is impossible for me to promise that I will do this thing, but I will do what I can. I will leave it to this other *Nahu'rac* to say what shall be done;" and he passed the pipe to the other *Nahu'rac* who sat next to him. This animal reached for the pipe, and took it. He made a speech, and said, "My friends, I am poor, I am poor. I have not such power as that;" and he passed the pipe to another; and he said, "I have not the power;" and he passed it to another; and so it went around the circle. The pipe had passed around, and none of the *Nahu'rac* had the power. None of them seemed to understand how to help the man. Then the white beaver said, "My friend, you see that no one of us have the power to help you. There is another lodge of *Nahu'rac* at *Pa'howa*. You must go there and ask them." Then the *Nahu'rac* made medicine, and the young man went to sleep, and when he awoke at daylight, he found himself on the point where he had lain down to sleep the night before.

He was discouraged and wept all day long. At night the elk came to him and said, "Go to sleep; I will take you over to *Pa'howa*." The man slept and the elk took him on its back and carried him while asleep, and the next morning he found himself on that point of *Pa'howa*.

That night the messenger bird came to him and said, "Now, my friend, follow me, and what you see me do, that do yourself. When I dive down into *Pa'howa*, you follow me." The bird dived down into the spring, and the young man jumped after him, and again found himself standing at the door of a lodge, and the same things took place as before. Here the same animals were the head doctors. The chief head doctor talked to the boy and said, "My friend, I am sorry you have come to me in the condition you are in. My friend, this is something impossible. If it were anything else it might be possible for us to cure your trouble. Nothing like it was ever known before."

When he had said this he turned to the *Nahu'rac* and said, "Now you shall be the leaders. If there are any of you who understand things like this; if any of you can take the lead in things like this, why do it. It is beyond my power. Say what shall be done, any of you. My mind would be big if any of you could take pity on this poor man."

Another one of the *Nahu'rac* stood up and spoke, "My brother [to the white beaver], and my brother [to the young man], do not feel hard at me. This is beyond my power. I cannot do anything to help him." So it went around the circle, every one saying that it was impossible. After it had gone round, the head doctor again stood up and said, "Now, my friend, you can see that it is impossible to cure you of this trouble, but there is another lodge of the *Nahu'rac* on the west side of the Loup River. You go there." Then they put him to sleep, and when he awoke next morning, he was on top of the ground near *Pa'howa.*

That night the elk took him while he was asleep to the place on the Loup. The next night he was sitting on the ground there, and the bird came to him, and he followed the bird down over the bank and into the *Nahu'rac* lodge. Here the head doctors were the same animals, and they made speeches as had been done at the other places, and, as before, it was left to the assembly, and all agreed that it was beyond their power. Then the white beaver directed him to go to an island in the Platte, near the Lone Tree, where there was another lodge of the *Nahu'rac.* The elk took him to this island. Under the center of this island was the lodge. The messenger bird was with him and went into the lodge and asked the *Nahu'rac* to help him. The white beaver made a speech, and said, "My friend, I have heard the condition that you are in. Of all these lodges that you have visited, that lodge at *Pa-huk'* is the head. I want you to go back there, and tell the leaders there that they are the rulers, and that whatever they shall do will be right, and will be agreed to by the other lodges. They must help you if they can. If they cannot do it, no one can."

When the elk took him back to *Pa-huk'*, the bird again conducted him into the lodge. He had left his pipe here. When he entered the lodge all the animals made a hissing sound—*No'a*—they were glad to see him again. The man stood in the middle of the lodge and spoke. He said, "Now you animals all, you are the leaders. You see how poor my mind is. I am tired of the long journeys you have sent me on. I want you to take pity on me."

The white beaver stood up and took the pipe and said, "Oh, my brother, I have done this to try these other lodges of *Nahu'rac*, to see if any of them were equal to me. That was the reason that I sent you around to all these other lodges, to see if any of them would be willing to undertake to rid you of your burden. But I see that they all still acknowledge that I am the leader. Now I have here an animal that I think will undertake to help you and to rid you of your trouble." Saying this he stepped out to the right, and walked past some of the *Nahu'-rac* until he came to a certain animal—a ground dog—and held out the pipe to it. There were twelve of these animals, all alike—small, with round faces and

black whiskers—sitting on their haunches. He held
out the pipe to the head one of these twelve. When
the white beaver reached out the pipe to this animal
he did not take it. He hesitated a long time, and
held his head down. He did not want to take the
pipe. He looked around the lodge, and at the man,
and drew in his breath. At last he reached out his
paws and took the pipe, and as he did so, all the
Nahu'rac made a noise, the biggest kind of a noise.
They were glad.

Then the head ground dog got up and said, "Now,
doctors, I have accepted this pipe on account of our
servant, who is so faithful, and who many a night has
lost sleep on account of our commands. I have accepted it for his sake. It is impossible to do this
thing. If it had been earlier, I could perhaps have
done it. Even now I will try, and if I fail now, we
can do nothing for him."

After they had smoked, they told the man to go
and sit down opposite the entrance to the lodge, between the head doctors and the fire. These twelve
animals stood up and walked back and forth on the
opposite side of the fire from him, facing him. After
a while they told him to stand up. The head ground
dog now asked the other *Nahu'rac* to help him, by

singing, and they all sang; and the ground dogs danced, keeping time to the singing, and moved their hands up and down, and made their jaws go as if eating, but did not open their mouths.

After a while they told him to lie down with his head toward the doctors and his feet toward the entrance. After he had lain down, they began to move and went round the lodge toward him, and the head ground dog jumped over the man's belly, and as he jumped over him he was seen to have a big piece of flesh in his mouth, and was eating it. Another ground dog followed him, and another, and each one ran until he came to the man, and as each one jumped over him, it had a piece of flesh in its mouth, eating it. So they kept going until they had eaten all the swelling. The young man was unconscious all this time, for he afterward said he knew nothing of what had happened.

The head ground dog spoke to the animals, and said, "Now, *Nahu'rac*, you have seen what I can do. This is the power that I have. That is the reason I am afraid to be out on the prairie, because when I get hungry I would kill men and would eat them. My appetite would overpower me, and I do not want to do these things, I want to be friendly. This is the reason that I do not travel around on top of the ground. I stay hid all the time."

The man was still unconscious, and the head ground dog said, "Now, *Nahu'rac*, I do not understand how to restore this man. I leave that to you." Then the ground dogs went back to their places and sat down. Then the head doctor, the beaver, spoke to the bears. He said, "Now this man belongs to you. Let r e see what you can do." The head bear got up and said, "Very well, I will come. I will let you see what I can do." Then the bears stood up and began to sing. The head bear would jump on top of the man, and act as if he were going to tear him to pieces, and the others would take hold of him, and shake him around, and at last his blood began to flow and the man began to breathe, but he was still unconscious. After a while he moved and came to life, and felt himself just as he had been many months before. He found that his trouble was gone and that he was cured.

The head bear still stood by him and spoke to the *Nahu'rac*. He said, "Now, *Nahu'rac*, this is what I can do. I do not care how dangerously wounded I may be, I know how to cure myself. If they leave any breath at all in me, I know how to cure myself." Then the bears went to their place and sat down.

The man got up and spoke to the *Nahu'rac*, thanking them for what they had done for him. He stayed there several nights, watching the doings of the *Nahu'rac*. They taught him all their ways, all the animal secrets. The head doctor said to him, "Now, I am going to send you back to your home, but I will ask a favor of you, in return for what I have done for you."

The man answered him, "It will be so, whatever you say."

The doctor said, "Through you let my animals that move in the river be fed. Now you can see who we are. I move in the water. I have no breath, but I exist. We every one of us shall die except *Ti-ra'-wa*. He made us, just as he made you. He made you to live in the air. We live where there is no air. You see the difference. I know where is that great water that surrounds us [the ocean]. I know that the heaven [sky] is the house of *Ti-ra'-wa*, and we live inside of it. You must imitate us. Do as we do. You must place your dependence on us, but still, if anything comes up that is very difficult, you must put your dependence on *Ti-ra'-wa*.

Ask help from the ruler. He made us. He made
every thing. There are different ways to different
creatures. What you do I do not do, and what I do
you do not do. We are different. When you
imitate us you must always blow a smoke to each one
of these four chief doctors, once to each; but to
Ti-ra'-wa you must blow four smokes. And always
blow four to the night, to the east, because something may tell you in your sleep a thing which will
happen. This smoke represents the air filled with
the smoke of hazy days. That smoke is pleasant to
Ti-ra'-wa. He made it himself. Now go home, and
after you have been there for a time, go and pay a
visit to the doctor who put you in this condition."

The young man went home to his village, and got
there in the night. He had long been mourned as
dead, and his father was now poor in mind on
account of him. He went into his father's lodge,
and touched him, and said, "Wake up, I am here."

His father could not believe it. He had thought
him dead a long time. He said, "Is it you, or is it
a ghost?"

The young man answered, "It is I, just the same
as ever. Get up, and go and tell my uncles and all
my relations that I am here. I want you to give me

something; a blue bead, and some Indian tobacco, and some buffalo meat, and a pipe."

The father went about and told his relations that his son had come back, and they were very glad, and came into the lodge, bringing the presents, and gave them to the boy. He took them, and went down to the river, and threw them in, and they were carried down to the *Nahu'rac* lodge at *Pa-huk'*.

A few days after this the boy got on his horse, and rode away to visit the doctor who had brought his trouble on him. When he reached the village, the people said to the doctor, "A man is coming to visit you," and the doctor was troubled, for he knew what he had done to the boy. But he thought that he knew so much that no one could get the better of him. When the boy came to the lodge, he got off his horse, went in and was welcomed. After they had eaten, the boy said to him, "When you visited me we smoked your tobacco; to-day we will smoke mine."

They did so, for the doctor thought that no one could overcome him. They smoked until daylight, and while they were smoking, the boy kept moving his jaws as if eating, but did not open his mouth. At daylight the boy said he must be going. He went, and when he got down to the river, he blew strongly upon the ice, and immediately the water in the river was full of blood. It was the blood of the doctor. It seems that the ground dogs had taught the young man how to do their things.

When the people found the doctor he was dead in his lodge, and he was all hollow. All his blood and the inside of him had gone into the river, and had gone down to feed the animals. So the boy kept his promise to the *Nahu'rac* and had revenge on the doctor.

The boy was the greatest doctor in the Kit-ke-hahk'-i band, and was the first who taught them all the doctors' ceremonies that they have. He taught them all the wonderful things that the doctors can do, and many other things.

OLD-FASHIONED KNIFE.

THE BEAR MAN.

THERE was once a young boy, who, when he was playing with his fellows, used often to imitate the ways of a bear, and to pretend that he was one. The boys did not know much about bears. They only knew that there were such animals.

Now, it had happened that before this boy was born his mother had been left alone at home, for his father had gone on the warpath toward the enemy, and this was about five or six months before the babe would be born. As the man was going on the warpath, he came upon a little bear cub, very small, whose mother had gone away; and he caught it. He did not want to kill it because it was so young and helpless. It seemed to him like a little child. It looked up to him, and cried after him, because it knew no better; and he hated to kill it or to leave it there. After he had thought about this for a while, he put a string around its neck and tied some medicine smoking stuff, Indian tobacco, to it, and said, "*Pi-rau'*—child, you are a *Nahu'rac; Ti-ra'-wa* made you, and takes care of you. He will look after you, but I put these things about your neck to show that I have good feelings toward you. I hope that when my child is born, the *Nahu'rac* will take care of him, and see that he grows up a good man, and I hope that *Ti-ra'-wa* will take care of you and of mine." He looked at the little bear for quite a long time, and talked to it, and then he went on his way.

When he returned to the village from his warpath, he told his wife about the little bear, and how he had looked at it and talked to it.

When his child was born it had all the ways of a bear. So it is among the Pawnees. A woman, before her child is born, must not look hard at any animal, for the child may be like it. There was a woman in the Kit-ke-hahk'-i band, who caught a rabbit, and, because it was gentle and soft, she took it up in her hands and held it before her face and petted it, and when her child was born it had a split nose, like a rabbit. This man is still alive.

This boy, who was like a bear, as he grew up, had still more the ways of a bear. Often he would go off by himself, and try to pray to the bear, because he felt like a bear. He used to say, in a joking way, to the other young men, that he could make himself a bear.

After he had come to be a man, he started out once on the warpath with a party of about thirty-five others. He was the leader of the party. They went away up on the Running Water, and before they had come to any village, they were discovered by Sioux. The enemy pursued them, and surrounded them, and fought with them. The Pawnees were overpowered, their enemies were so many, and all were killed.

The country where this took place is rocky, and much cedar grows there. Many bears lived there. The battle was fought in the morning; and the Paw-nees were all killed in a hollow. Right after the fight, in the afternoon, two bears came traveling along by this place. When they came to the spot where the Pawnees had been killed, they found one of the bodies, and the she bear recognized it as that of the boy who was like a bear. She called to the he bear, and said, "Here is the man that was very good to us. He often sacrificed smokes to us, and every

time he ate he used always to take a piece of food
and give it to us, saying, 'Here is something for you
to eat. Eat this.' Here is the one that always
imitated us, and sung about us, and talked about us.
Can you do anything for him?" The he bear said,
"I fear I cannot do it. I have not the power, but I
will try. I can do anything if the sun is shining. I
seem to have more power when the sun is shining on
me." That day it was cloudy and cold and snowing.
Every now and then the clouds would pass, and the
sun come out for a little while, and then the clouds
would cover it up again.

The man was all cut up, pretty nearly hacked in
small pieces, for he was the bravest of all. The two
bears gathered up the pieces of the man, and put
them together, and then the he bear lay down and
took the man on his breast, and the she bear lay on
top of it to warm the body. They worked over it
with their medicine, and every now and then the he
bear would cry out, and say, "*A-ti'-us*—Father, help
me. I wish the sun was shining." After a while the
dead body grew warm, and then began to breathe a
little. It was still all cut up, but it began to have life.
Pretty soon the man began to move, and to come to
life, and then he became conscious and had life.

When he came to himself and opened his eyes he was in the presence of two bears. The he bear spoke to him, and said, "It is not through me that you are living. It was the she bear who asked for help for you, and had you brought back to life. Now, you are not yet whole and well. You must come away with us, and live with us for a time, until all your wounds are healed." The bears took him away with them. But the man was very weak, and every now and then, as they were going along, he would faint and fall down; but still they would help him up and support him; and they took him along with them, until they came to a cave in the rocks among the cedars, which was their home. When he entered the cave, he found there their young ones that they had left behind when they started out.

The man was all cut up and gashed. He had also been scalped, and had no hair on his head. He lived with the bears until he was quite healed of his wounds, and also had come to understand all their ways. The two old bears taught him everything that they knew. The he bear said to him, "None of all the beings and animals that roam over the country are as great and as wise as the bears. No animal is equal to us. When we get hungry, we go out and kill something and eat it. I did not make the wisdom that I have. I am an animal, and I look to one above. He made me, and he made me to be great. I am made to live here and to be great, but still there will be an end to my days, just as with all of us that *Ti-ra'-wa* has created upon this earth. I am going to make you a great man; but you must not deceive yourself. You must not think that I am great, or can do great things of myself. You must always look up above for the giver of all power. You shall be great in war and great in wealth.

"Now you are well, and I shall take you back to your home, and after this I want you to imitate us. This shall be a part of your greatness. I shall look after you. I shall give to you a part of myself. If I am killed, you shall be killed. If I grow old, you shall be old.

"I want you to look at one of the trees that *Ti-ra'-wa* made in this earth, and place your dependence on it. *Ti ra'-wa* made this tree (pointing to a cedar). It never gets old. It is always green and young. Take notice of this tree, and always have it with you; and when you are in the lodge and it thunders and lightens,* throw some of it on the fire and let the smoke rise. Hold that fast."

* A cedar is never struck by lightning.

The he bear took the skin of a bear, and made a cap for him, to hide his naked skull. His wounds were now all healed, and he was well and strong. The man's people had nearly forgotten him, it had been so long ago, and they had supposed that the whole party had been killed.

Soon after this the he bear said, "Now we will take that journey." They started, and went to the village, and waited near it till it was night. Then the bear said to him, "Go into the village, and tell your father that you are here. Then get for me a piece of buffalo meat, and a blue bead, and some Indian tobacco, and some sweet smelling clay." *

The man went into the village, and his father was very much surprised, and very glad to see him again. He got the presents, and brought them to the bear, and gave them to him, and the bear talked to him.

When they were about to part, the bear came up to him, and put his arms about him, and hugged him, and put his mouth against the man's mouth, and said, "As the fur that I am in has touched you it will make you great, and this will be a blessing to you." His paws were around the man's shoulders, and he drew them down his arms, until they came to

* A green clay, which they roast, and which then turns dark red, and has a sweet smell.

his hands, and he held them, and said, "As my hands have touched your hands, they are made great, not to fear anything. I have rubbed my hands down over you, so that you shall be as tough as I am. Because my mouth has touched your mouth you shall be made wise." Then he left him, and went away.

So this man was the greatest of all warriors, and was brave. He was like a bear. He originated the bear dance which still exists among the tribe of Pawnees. He came to be an old man, and at last died of old age. I suspect the old bear died at the same time.

A RATTLE.

THE GHOST WIFE.

ONE time there were living together a man and his wife. They had a young child. The woman died. The man was very sad, and mourned for his wife.

One night he took the child in his arms, and went out from the village to the place where his wife was buried, and stood over the grave, and mourned for his wife. The little child was very helpless, and cried all the time. The man's heart was sick with grief and loneliness. Late in the night he fell asleep, fainting and worn out with sorrow. After a while he awoke, and when he looked up, there was a form standing by him. The form standing there was the one who had died. She spoke to her husband, and said, "You are very unhappy here. There is a place to go where we would not be unhappy. Where I have been nothing bad happens to one. Here, you never know what evil will come to you. You and the child had better come to me."

The man did not want to die. He said to her, "No; it will be better if you can come back to us. We love you. If you were with us we would be unhappy no longer."

For a long time they discussed this, to decide which one should go to the other. At length the man by his persuasions overcame her, and the woman agreed to come back. She said to the man, "If I am to come back you must do exactly as I tell you for four nights. For four days the curtain must remain let down before my sleeping place; it must not be raised; no one must look behind it."

The man did as he had been told, and after four days had passed, the curtain was lifted, and the woman came out from behind it. Then they all saw her, first her relations, and afterward the whole tribe. Her husband and her child were very glad, and they lived happily together.

A long time after this, the man took another wife. The first wife was always pleasant and good-natured, but the new one was bad-tempered, and after some time she grew jealous of the first woman, and quarreled with her. At length, one day the last married became angry with the other, and called her bad names, and finally said to her, "You ought not to be here. You are nothing but a ghost, anyway."

That night when the man went to bed, he lay down, as was his custom, by the side of his first wife. During the night he awoke, and found that his wife had disappeared. She was seen no more. The next night after this happened, the man and the child both died in sleep. The wife had called them to her. They had gone to that place where there is a living.

This convinced everybody that there is a hereafter.

TI-KE-WA-KUSH.

THE MAN WHO CALLED THE BUFFALO.

THIS happened in the olden time before we had met the white people. Then the different bands lived in separate villages. The lodges were made of dirt. The Kit-ke-hahk'-i band went off on a winter hunt, roaming over the country, as they used to do, after buffalo. At this time they did not find the buffalo near. They scouted in all directions, but could discover no signs of them. It was a hard time of starvation. The children cried and the women cried; they had nothing at all to eat.

There was a person who looked at the children crying for something to eat, and it touched his heart. They were very poor, and he felt sorry for them. He said to the Head Chief, "Tell the chiefs and other head men to do what I tell them. My heart is sick on account of the suffering of the people. It may be that I can help them. Let a new lodge be set up outside the village for us to meet in. I will see if I can do anything to relieve the tribe." The Chief said that it was well to do this, and he gave orders for it.

While they were preparing to build this lodge they would miss this man in the night. He would disappear like a wind, and go off a long way, and just as daylight came, he would be there again. Sometimes, while sitting in his own lodge during the day, he would reach behind him, and bring out a small piece of buffalo meat, fat and lean, and would give it to some one, saying, "When you have had enough, save what is left, and give it to some one else." When he would give this small piece of meat to any one, the person would think, "This is not enough to satisfy my hunger;" but after eating until he was full, there was always enough left to give to some other person.

In those days it was the custom for the Head Chief of the tribe, once in a while, to mount his horse, and ride about through the village, talking to the people, and giving them good advice, and telling them that they ought to do what was right by each other. At this time the Chief spoke to the people, and explained that this man was going to try to benefit the tribe. So the people made him many fine presents, otter skins and eagle feathers, and when they gave him these things each one said, "I give you this. It is for yourself. Try to help us." He thanked them for these presents, and when they were all gathered together he said, "Now you chiefs and head men of the tribe, and you people, you have done well to give me these things. I shall give them to that person who gives me that power, and who has taken pity on me. I shall let you starve yet four days. Then help will come."

During these four days, every day and night he disappeared, but would come back the same night. He would say to the people that he had been far off, where it would take a person three or four days to go, but he was always back the same night. When he got back on the fourth night, he told the people that the buffalo were near, that the next morning they would be but a little way off. He went up on the hill near the camp, and sacrificed some eagle feathers, and some blue beads, and some Indian tobacco, and then returned to the camp. Then he said to the people, "When that object comes to that place of sacrifice, do not interfere with it; do not turn it back. Let it go by. Just watch and see."

The next morning at daylight, all the people came out of their lodges to watch this hill, and the place where he had sacrificed. While they were looking they saw a great buffalo bull come up over the hill to the place. He stood there for a short time and looked about, and then he walked on down the hill, and went galloping off past the village. Then this man spoke to the people, and said, "There. That is what I meant. That is the leader of the buffalo; where he went the whole herd will follow."

He sent his servant to the chiefs to tell them to choose four boys, and let them go to the top of the hill where the bull had come over, and to look beyond it. The boys were sent, and ran to the top of the hill, and when they looked over beyond it they stopped, and then turned, and came back, running. They went to the chiefs' lodge, and said to the chiefs sitting there, "Beyond that place of sacrifice there is coming a whole herd of buffalo; many, many, crowding and pushing each other."

Then, as it used to be in the old times, as soon as the young men had told the Chief that the buffalo were coming, the Chief rode about the village, and told every one to get ready to chase them. He said to them besides, " Do not leave anything on the killing ground. Bring into the camp not only the meat and hides, but the heads and legs and all parts. Bring the best portions in first, and take them over to the new lodge, so that we may have a feast there." For so the man had directed.

Presently the buffalo came over the hill, and the people were ready, and they made a surround, and killed all that they could, and brought them home. Each man brought in his ribs and his young buffalo, and left them there at that lodge. The other parts they brought into the village, as he had directed. After they had brought in this meat, they went to the lodge, and staid there four days and four nights, and had a great feast, roasting these ribs. The man told them that they would make four surrounds like this, and to get all the meat that they could, "But," he said, "in surrounding these buffalo you must see that all the meat is saved. *Ti-ra'-wa* does not like the people to waste the buffalo, and for that reason I advise you to make good use of all you kill." During the four nights they feasted this man used to disappear each night.

On the night of the fourth day he said to the peo-

ple, "To-morrow the buffalo will come again, and
you will make another surround. Be careful not to
kill a yellow calf—a little one—that you will see with
the herd, nor its mother." This was in winter, and
yet the calf was the same color as a young calf born
in the spring. They made the surround, and let the
yellow calf and its mother go.

A good many men in the tribe saw that this man
was great, and that he had done great things for the
tribe, and they made him many presents, the best
horses that they had. He thanked them, but he did
not want to accept the presents. The tribe believed
that he had done this wonderful thing—had brought
them buffalo—and all the people wanted to do just
what he told them to.

In the first two surrounds they killed many buffalo,
and made much dried meat. All their sacks were
full, and the dried meat was piled up out of doors.
After the second surround, they feasted as before.

After four days, as they were going out to surround the buffalo the third time, the wind changed,
and before the people got near them, the buffalo
smelt them, and stampeded. While they were galloping away, the man ran up on to the top of the
hill, to the place of sacrifice, carrying a pole, on

which was tied the skin of a kit fox; and when he saw the buffalo running, and that the people could not catch them, he waved his pole, and called out *Ska-a-a-a!* and the buffalo turned right about, and charged back right through the people, and they killed many of them. He wished to show the people that he had the power over the buffalo.

After the third surround they had a great deal of meat, and he called the chiefs together and said, "Now, my chiefs, are you satisfied?" They said, "Yes, we are satisfied, and we are thankful to you for taking pity on us and helping us. It is through your power that the tribe has been saved from starving to death." He said, "You are to make one more surround, and that will be the end. I want you to get all you can. Kill as many as possible, for this will be the last of the buffalo this winter. Those presents that you have made to me, and that I did not wish to take, I give them back to you." Some of the people would not take back the presents, but insisted that he should keep them, and at last he said he would do so.

The fourth surround was made, and the people killed many buffalo, and saved the meat. The night after this last surround, he disappeared and drove the buffalo back. The next morning he told the people to look about, and tell him if they saw anything. They did so, but they could not see any buffalo.

The next day they moved camp, and went east toward their home. They had so much dried meat that they could not take it all at once, but had to come back and make two trips for it. When they moved below, going east, they had no fresh meat, only dried meat; but sometimes when this man would come in from his journeys, he would bring a piece of meat—a little piece—and he would divide it up among the people, and they would put it into the kettles and boil it, and everybody would eat, but they could not eat it all up. There would always be some left over. This man was so wonderful that he could change even the buffalo chips that you see on the prairie into meat. He would cover them up with his robe, and when he would take it off again, you would see there pounded buffalo meat and tallow (pemmican), *tup-o-har'-ash.*

The man was not married; he was a young man, and by this time the people thought that he was one of the greatest men in the tribe, and they wanted him to marry. They went to one of the chiefs and told him that they wanted him to be this man's father-in-law, for they wanted him to raise children, thinking that they might do something to benefit the tribe. They did not want that race to die out. The old people say that it would have been good if he had had children, but he had none. If he had, perhaps they would have had the same power as their father.

That person called the buffalo twice, and twice saved the tribe from a famine. The second time the suffering was great, and they held a council to ask him to help the tribe. They filled up the pipe and held it out to him, asking him to take pity on the tribe. He took the pipe, and lighted it, and smoked. He did it in the same way as the first time, and they made four surrounds, and got much meat.

When this man died, all the people mourned for him a long time. The Chief would ride around the village and call out, "Now I am poor in mind on account of the death of this man, because he took pity on us and saved the tribe. Now he is gone and there is no one left like him."

This is a true and sacred story that belongs to the Kit-ke-hahk'-i band. It happened once long ago, and has been handed down from father to son in this band. The Skidi had a man who once called the buffalo, causing them to return when stampeded, as was done in this story.

Note.—Big Knife, a Skidi, who died only recently, said that the man was alive in his time. *Kuru'ks-u le-shar* (Bear Chief), a Skidi, says that he knew the man. His name was Carrying Mother.

BABY ON BOARD.

PA-HU-KA'-TAWA.

ABOUT the end of the winter, before the grass began to grow in the spring, a company of three brothers and two other men went out from the village to trap beaver. When they had been gone about ten days, and had got up above the Forks of the Loup River, they camped on the South Fork, and in the morning sent one man ahead to see if he could find any beaver sign, and could look out a good trapping ground.

When he had gone a little distance from the camp, he saw some Sioux, and at the same moment they saw him. He did not run back to the camp; he was too anxious to save himself; but ran across to a little creek, and hid in the brush, not trying to let his brothers know that the enemy were near. The Sioux followed him and found him, and chased him about, and shot at him all day, until near sundown, when they killed him.

The four other men had stopped in camp, but were not so far off but that they could hear the shouts and yells, and they ran off from the camp, and hid themselves and waited. When the other man did not come back, they knew that he had been killed.

The next morning, the four men talked together. One said, "We had better go up and see if he is killed." Another said, "Yes, let us go there. It may be that we can bury him." So they went up where he had been, going very carefully, and looking over all the hills as they went, so as to see any enemies if they were about. They found him. He was dead, shot full of arrows, scalped, his whole head skinned, his arms and legs unjointed, his head cut off; he was all cut to pieces. So they thought that there was not enough of him left to bury, and besides, those killed in battle are often left unburied. When they found how it was, they started back to the village, and when they came close to it, one of the men called out, "*Pa-hu-ka'-tawa* is killed!" He called that out so that the people might know, and might begin to mourn.

When they came into the village, the relations of

this man felt very badly because he was killed. It was coming on toward the time when they begin to clear up their patches, to plant the corn, and to hoe, and his father and mother mourned, and said, "Now we have no one to help us hoe. We are old, and he helped us; but now he is gone." So they mourned for him.

They did not visit the place where he had been killed for some time. It was now spring, and they were planting, and hoeing the corn, and when they got through their work, the whole tribe started out on the summer hunt to get buffalo, as they used to do. They started up the Loup, and when they had traveled along a number of days, they came near the place where the man had been killed. When they got there, the men who had been with him said, "This is the place where *Pa-hu-ka'-tawa* was killed," and his father and mother and all his relations went over to the place where he had lain, to gather his bones together and then to bury them. When they got to the place, they could find no bones at all, but the arrows were there, sticking straight up in the ground; all the arrows that had been shot into the body. They wondered that they had not fallen down, for they thought that the wolves might have dragged the body, but when they looked everywhere about for the bones, they could find no sign of them anywhere. It seemed strange to them that the arrows should be there standing up in the ground, and they wondered what had become of the bones. At length they gave up looking for them, and went back to the camp. When they could not find the bones, they went on and hunted buffalo, and killed plenty, and made dried meat. After two months they started back to the village, going down the Platte River. His mother had cried so much for *Pa-hu-ka'-tawa*, that she had become blind.

One pleasant afternoon they were camped on the Platte. The evening was warm and soft and still. As the sun went down toward the earth, long shining rays seemed to come down from it to the ground. All through the air was a light smoke, and in the west the sky was red. Just as the sun was setting, the people all heard a voice calling from the other side of the river. They listened; and the voice said, "*Pa-hu-ka'-tawa* is coming back to you." Then all the Indians jumped up, and ran across the river to meet him, for they thought perhaps he was coming back. When they had got to the other side, they looked about, but could see no one. Then they heard a voice from behind them, on the other side of the camp, which said, "He is coming from here." They all turned round and ran back to the other side of the camp; but no one was there; and in a little while they heard the voice again, on the other side of the river, saying, "He is coming." Then they knew it was only a voice and not a person. They stopped running about, and that night they talked about the voice. The next day they went on down the river, and at length got back to the main village. There they stayed six months, and by this time their dried meat was all eaten, and it was toward spring.

The mother of *Pa-hu-ka'-tawa* had her bed near the door of the lodge on the left hand side, the last bed next to the door. One night, at midnight, he came into the lodge, and touched his mother and said, "Mother! mother!" His mother used to dream of him almost every night, and she thought she was dreaming now. She said, "Oh, my son, do not do this. You are deceiving me again." He stopped; but presently he touched her again, and pushed her shoulder, and she awoke.

He said to her, "Mother, I am here," and she reached out and felt him.

She said, "Are you really my son?"

He answered, "Yes, I am your son."

Then she put her arms around him, and hugged him, and said to him, "Oh, my son, my son, you have come back to me." She cried, she was so glad.

Then they talked together. He gave her a piece of meat—a piece of fresh buffalo meat—though they had had no fresh meat in the village for six months. He said to his mother, "I am really alive, though I was killed. The *Nahu'rac* (animals) took pity on me, and have made me alive again. And now I am going off; but do not cry about me any more." Then he went away.

The next morning, when his mother awoke, she found by her side the piece of fresh meat, and she began to cook it on the coals. The people wondered where she got the fresh meat, and asked her about it, but she would not tell them where she got it, for her son had told her to say nothing. They asked her again where she got it, and she told them she found it in her bed.

After a long time her son came again in the night, and went into the lodge, and spoke to his mother, saying, "Mother, I am here again." She awoke, and rejoiced that he had come back. He said to her, "My mother, I know that you are poor. You are blind on account of me, because you have cried so much. Now, my mother, there is standing by the side of your daughter's bed, water in a wooden bowl. After I have left you to-night, go over there, and put your face down deep into the water, and open your eyes in the water, and then you will see." Before he left her he gave her some *ka'wis.* *

After he had gone, she did as he had told her. She got up, and feeling her way along with her hands, crept into the place where her daughter slept. There she felt the wooden bowl with water in it, and she put her face deep down into the water, and opened her eyes in it, and when she took her face out of the water, and opened her eyes again, she could see. Then she was glad. Everybody wondered how the mother's eyes had been cured, but she told no one, except only her oldest son.

After a long time *Pa-hu-ka'-tawa* came down again to see his mother. He said to her, "Mother, I am going up to see my oldest brother." He went to see his brother in the night. His brother was expecting him, for his mother had warned him. *Pa-hu-ka'-tawa* said, "Now, my brother, I think you

---

* Chopped buffalo meat tied up in the small intestine.

have heard that I come all the time to see our mother. I wish that you would put up your lodge outside the camp, so that I can come and see you often. I want to talk to you, and tell you my thoughts and all my troubles. I am a spirit." His brother answered him that he would do as he had asked, and the first night after the lodge had been set up outside the camp, *Pa-hu-ka'-tawa* came down, and said to his brother, "To-morrow night I want you to select the two bravest men in the tribe, and let them go about through the camp, and call all the chiefs and all the bravest warriors in the tribe, and let them gather at your home. Do not build any fire in the lodge. Let it all be dark, for I am coming down in the night to see them."

When the next night came, the chiefs and the braves gathered at the lodge just about dark. They made no fire, but sat there waiting for *Pa-hu-ka'-tawa* to come down. After a while he came down to the lodge, and came in where they were sitting. When they were all silent, he came in, and every step he made it seemed that sparks of fire were flying out from him. He went and stood before his brother, and said to him, "I am in everything; in the grass, the water, the trees. I am a part of all these things.

I know every thought of yours, and if you only whispered, I would hear it. I know everything, and about everything, even about the ocean which is so far off, and where the water is salt.

"There are two dances that I like, in which there are songs sung about me." Then he sang these songs and told them how to dance these dances.* He said, "Dance these dances and sing about me, calling me by name."

Then he said, "Brother, I want you to know that there is a tribe of your enemies getting ready to go on the warpath against you. I will let you know when they start, and all they do. Every move they make I will tell you of. They are coming from far up the Missouri River."

Two or three nights later *Pa-hu-ka'-tawa* appeared to his brother, and said, "They are coming. To-morrow night they will be here spying round the camp. Be ready for them. You must ask me to take pity on you, telling me what you want to do, and I will make you strong, so that you can succeed. If you want to strike two or three, ask me. If you want to kill two or three, tell me. You must call me grandfather."

---

* These dances afterward were practiced in two of the secret societies.

The next night they danced and asked him to take pity on them. One young man prayed, saying, "Let me strike nine, and at the tenth let me be wounded, but let me not die." A second young man prayed, saying, "I want to strike five and capture the biggest man in the party." Another man asked him, "Let me strike two, and then let me be killed." To each one who asked a favor of him, he said, "Let it be so." They did not see him, for there was no fire in the lodge: It was dark.

He said to them, "Be ready. To-morrow morning is the time when the enemy will attack you. I will send a fog from the north as a warning. They will come down toward the village, and you must go out on the plain in front of the village, and have a skirmish with them. Then draw off, and look toward the point of bluff which runs down into the plain on the east end of the battle field. Watch that point and you will see me. I will appear to you there. And this shall be a sign to you that it is I whom you see. When I come up over that point and turn around, facing to the north, the wind will change and will come from the south. And when the wind blows from the south, you make a charge on them."

So it was. The next morning the enemy made an
attack on them, and came down toward the village.
It was the very day he had said. The warriors went
out on the plain to meet them. They were wondering in what shape *Pa-hu-ka'-tawa* would appear to
them, how he would look. On that morning, before
the Sioux appeared, a white fog came down from
the north. Then the Sioux made the attack, and
the people began to look for *Pa-hu-ka'-tawa*. And
while they were looking toward the bluff, a great
white wolf came up over the point, and stood looking
first one way and then another, and then it turned
around and faced the north. And immediately the
wind changed and blew from the south. When the
wolf appeared, some of the braves doubted whether
it was *Pa-hu-ka'-tawa*, but when it turned round,
and the wind changed, then they knew that it was
he.

Then they made the charge, and each one of those
who had asked a favor received it. In every case
what *Pa-hu-ka' tawa* had promised came true. The
man who had prayed that he might strike nine and
at the tenth be wounded, struck nine and was
wounded at the tenth, but he did not die; the one
who asked to strike five, and to capture the biggest

man in the party, did so. He caught the prisoner,
and overcame him, and put a rope around his neck,
and led him into the village. And when he got him
to the village the women beat the captive with sticks
and clubs, and threw dirt at him, and had lots of fun
with him. The young man who had asked it, killed
two, and then was himself killed. All that *Pa-hu-
ka'-tawa* had promised came to pass.

The people killed many of the Sioux, and drove
them far, chasing and killing them all day long.
Then they came back to the village, bringing with
them the scalps and the weapons that they had
taken, the bows and the spears, the shields and the
war bonnets. They danced in the village, and sang
and rejoiced. Every one was glad because the
people had won a great victory.

The next night after the day of the battle, *Pa-hu-
ka'-tawa* came down to his brother's lodge, and told
him that he wanted to speak to him. His brother
awoke all his wives, and sent them out of the lodge,
telling them not to come back until he called them.
Then *Pa-hu-ka'-tawa* said to his brother, "Now, my
brother, you people have seen whether what I say to
you is true or not. You have seen what has happened, you can judge. Now, brother, I want you to

feel of me all over; nobody else but you to feel of me, my brother." His brother passed his hands all over his breast and arms and body and legs. *Pa-hu-ka'-tawa* said, "Now put your hands on top of my head, and feel there." He did so, and felt something soft. *Pa-hu-ka'-tawa* said, "Do you know what that is? That is the down feathers."

Then he told the story of his being killed. He said, "That time after I got killed, all kinds of *Nahu'rac* took pity on me. The flies and bugs, the fishes and birds, the deer and the wolves, all the animals took pity on me, and helped me to come to life again. They looked all over for my flesh and my bones, and brought them all together. One part of me, the top part of my skull, they could not find. The bugs crept through the ground looking for it, the fishes swam through the water and sought it, the flies buzzed about over the sand, and the deer and wolves hunted for it on the prairie, but they could not find this piece anywhere. Nor could they find my brains. Perhaps, when I was killed, the crows eat them out. When they had gathered the pieces all together, they laid each piece in its own place, so that they had the form of a man, and in place of the top of the skull and the brains they put the down feathers. After they had put all the pieces together, they stood around me, and prayed, and passed their paws over me, and danced and sang, and at last I breathed a little. Then they prayed again, and passed their paws over me, and at length I breathed regularly. Then I was not dead any more; I was alive again. Not as a person was I alive, but as a spirit.

"I am in every thing; in the wind, in the rain, in the grass. I go over the whole world. I am the wind, and I go everywhere all over the world. There is no one above me but *Ti-ra'-wa.* He is the only one I am under. He is the ruler of all. Whenever any human being on this earth, man woman or child, says anything about me, I hear it surely. You must tell all this to every one, and say to them that if they are sick or unfortunate, let them pray to me, and I will heal or help them.

"Now you know that I am living, but I am a spirit; and whenever you people have a fight with the Sioux, if you pray to me, and call me by name, and ask to be brave, and to be helped, I will hear you. If you wish to be brave, or if you wish not to be hurt in battle, even though the enemy be right upon you, and just striking or shooting at you, I will protect you. I shall live forever, as long as this world exists. So long as I come to you, I want you people to conquer the Sioux all you can, on account of what they did to me when they killed me and cut me in pieces. So long as the Sioux come down to attack you, I want you to conquer them every time.

"Now, brother, when I come down to see you, you must not get tired of me. I want to come down often to see you, and talk to you, to tell you what is going to happen, and to warn you whenever the Sioux are coming down to attack the Skidi. I go about everywhere, to the camps of the different bands of Sioux, and I know what the chiefs are saying in council; when they are talking of sending out war parties against you. If I come down to you often, do not get tired of seeing me."

He knew himself that his brother would some time refuse to listen to him, but his brother did not know it, and he said, "I will never get tired of you."

Some time after this, the Sioux came down again to attack the Skidi village. Two days before they came, *Pa-hu-ka'-tawa* came down to his brother and warned him, saying, "A big war party of Sioux will be here day after to-morrow to fight with you. But I am going to attend to them. On the morning of the second day from this, tell all the people to be ready, and to have their horses tied up close to the lodges, where they can get at them. Then, if you look up in the sky, you will see thick black clouds, as if you were going to have a great rain. When you begin fighting, do not be afraid of the enemy. Do not be afraid of them; go right up to them; they will not be able to shoot, their bowstrings will be wet, and the sinews will stretch and slip off the ends of the bows. They will not be able to hurt you."

On the morning that he had said, the Sioux came down, and the people went out to meet them. The sky above was black with clouds. When they began fighting, a heavy rain commenced to fall, but it did not rain everywhere, but only just where the Sioux were. The bowstrings of the Sioux got wet, so that they could not use them, for the sinews stretched, so that when they bent their bows the strings slipped off the ends of the bows, and there was no force to their arrows. The Skidi overcame the Sioux and drove them, and the Sioux ran far. The rain followed the Sioux, and rained over them, but nowhere else, and the Sioux fled, and the Skidi won a great victory.

Soon after this, *Pa-hu-ka'-tawa* came down and

visited his brother, and said to him, "My brother, whenever you have a feast or a council of old men, you must smoke to me and say, 'Father, we want you to help us.' Then I will hear you. At the same time you must pray to *Ti-ra'-wa.* There is one above us who is the ruler of all. I do not wish to be talked about commonly or by common men, but that whenever you have a feast you should call in the young men and tell them about me and let them hear." He did not want his name used irreverently, nor wish that the story of what he had suffered and done should be told commonly or for mere amusement. It is sacred and should be told only at solemn times.

Some time after this talk with his brother, he came down again to see him. Another man was living in his brother's lodge, and on this night his brother was not there, he was sleeping somewhere else. *Pa-hu-ka'-tawa* asked this man where his brother was. He answered, "He is not here to-night, he is sleeping somewhere else." *Pa-hu-ka'-tawa* said, "Go over and tell him that I am here, and that I want to see him." The man went and gave the message to the brother, who said, "I do not want to go. Tell him I am asleep." The man went back and told *Pa-hu-*

ka'-tawa that his brother could not come. He said, "He is asleep." *Pa-hu-ka'-tawa* sent him back again, to get the brother. The man went, and said to the brother, "He wants to see you very much." The brother said, "Tell him I can't come; I want to sleep to-night." The man returned and said, "He does not want to come, he is sleeping." He was sent back for the brother the third time, to tell the brother he must come, he was wanted. He sent word back that he could not, he was too sleepy. Then *Pa-hu-ka'-tawa* said, "Very well. Go back and tell him to sleep now, to sleep all he wants. I told him before that he would get tired of me at last. Let him sleep all he wants, I will come to him no more. I can go to some other tribe. This is the last time I will come. Tell him to sleep. I will trouble him no more. I am going off, but tell the people not to forget me; to talk of me sometimes, and to pray to me, and I will help them and care for the tribe."

So *Pa-hu-ka'-tawa* went away to the Rees, and the people knew him no more; after that he never came down to see them. When the people learned this, they felt very badly, and were angry at his brother who would not see him. There was living not long ago, among the Rees, an old woman, who, when she was a girl, had seen and talked to *Pa-hu-ka'-tawa*.

NOTE.—This is a Skidi story. The Rees have a story of what *Pa-hu-ka'-tawa* did after he had come to them. The Lower Village tribes have a story of a hero of this same name, which is quite different from that of the Skidi.

LONE CHIEF—SKIDI.

THE BOY WHO WAS SACRIFICED.

THERE was a time, far back, when some people thought that it was good to sacrifice to *Ti-ra'-wa* whatever they had that was most precious to them. The sacrifice of the animal, the burnt offering, has always been made by all the Pawnees; that is one of the things handed down from the ruler. It is very old. The Skidi have always performed the sacrifice of the captive. Each one of these is sacred and solemn, but it is not like giving up something that belongs to you, and that you love. It is a sacrifice, but it does not cost much.

Many years ago, in the Skidi village on the Loup, there lived a man, who believed that if he sacrificed his son to *Ti-ra'-wa*, it would be a blessing to him. He thought that if he did this thing, perhaps *Ti-ra'-wa* would speak to him face to face, and that he could talk to him just as two people would talk to one another, and that in this way he would learn many things that other people did not understand. His child was a nice boy about ten years old, strong, growing up well, and the man loved him. It made him feel badly to think of killing him. He meditated long about this, but the more he thought about it, the more he believed that this sacrifice would please *Ti-ra'-wa*. There were many things that he wanted to understand, and to do; and he thought if he gave up his son, these good things would come to him. So he resolved to make the sacrifice.

One morning he started out from the village, and took the boy with him. They went over to the Platte. When they got to the river, as they were walking along, the man took his knife from its sheath, and caught the boy by the shoulder, and stabbed him quickly, and cut him open. When the boy was dead, he threw the body into the river, and then went back to the village. When he got there, he went into his lodge and sat down. After a time he said to his wife, "Where is the boy?" The woman said, "He went out with you, when you went over to see the horses." The man answered, "No; I went out to where the horses are feeding, and looked at them, but he did not go with me."

The man went out, and looked for the boy all through the village, but he could not find him. At night when the boy did not come home, they began to get frightened, and for two days they hunted for the boy, and at last they got the old crier to call out for him from the top of the lodge, and ask if any one had seen him, but none of the people knew what had become of the boy. Now the mother was mourning, and the father pretended to feel very badly. They could not find the boy; and soon after this the tribe started on the summer hunt, and the father and mother went with them. The village made a good hunt, killing plenty of buffalo, and made much dried meat.

After the boy had been thrown into the river, he floated down with the current, sometimes turning over and over in the swift water, and sometimes grounding for a little while on a sand bar, and then being floated off again, and being carried further down. At length he came near to the place where the whirlpool is, under the bluff at *Pa-hŭk'*, where is the lodge of the *Nahu'rac*. There were two buzzards sitting on the bluff, just above this place, and as they sat there, one of them stretched out his neck and looked up the river, and after he had looked, he

said to the other, "I see a body." Then both the
buzzards flew down to where the boy was floating in
the water, and got down under him, and raised him
on their backs, and lifted him up out of the water,
and flew up to the bluff, carrying the boy on their
backs, and placed him on the ground on top of the
bluff over the big cave, which is the home of the
Nahu'rac. In this lodge were all kinds of animals,
and all kinds of birds. There were bears, and mountain lions, and buffalo, and elk, and beaver, and
otter, and deer; all kinds of animals, great and small,
and all kinds of birds.

There is a little bird, smaller than a pigeon. Its
back is blue, and its breast white, and its head is
spotted. It flies swiftly over the water, and when it
sees a fish, it dives down into the water to catch it.
This bird is a servant or a messenger for the *Nahu'rac.*
Such a bird came flying by just as the buzzards put
the body on the ground, and he stopped and looked
at it. When he saw how it was—for he knew all
that had happened—he flew down into the lodge
and told the *Nahu'rac* about the boy. The bird
said, "There is a boy up here on the hill. He is
dead, and he is poor, and I want to have him
brought to life again." Then he told the *Nahu'rac*

all the things that had happened. When the messenger bird had done speaking, the *Nahu'rac* earnestly counselled together for a long time to decide what should be done, and each one made a speech, giving his opinion about the matter, but they could not make up their minds what ought to be done.

The little bird was coaxing the *Nahu'rac*, and saying, "Come, now, we want to save his life." But the *Nahu'rac* could not decide. At last the chief of the *Nahu'rac* said, "No, messenger, we cannot decide this here. You will have to go to the other council lodges, and see what they say about it." The bird said, "I am going," and flew swiftly out of the lodge and up the river, till he came to the *Nahu'rac* lodge near the Lone Tree. When he got there, he told them all about the boy, and said that the council at *Pa-hŭk'* could not decide what should be done. The *Nahu'rac* here talked, and at last they said, "We cannot decide. The council at *Pa-hŭk'* must decide." Then the bird went to the lodge on the Loup, and the *Nahu'rac* there said that they could not decide. Then he went to *Kitz-a-witz-ŭk*, and to *Pa-hŭr'*; and at each place the *Nahu'rac* considered and talked about it, and then said, "We cannot decide what shall be done. The council at *Pa-hŭk'* must decide for themselves."

At last, after he had visited all the council lodges of the *Nahu'rac*, the bird flew swiftly back to the lodge at *Pa-hŭk'*, and told them there what the animals at the other lodges had said. In the council of the *Nahu'rac* at *Pa-hŭk'*, there were four chiefs, who sat there as judges to determine such matters as this, after they had all been talked over, and to decide what should be done. When the messenger bird came back, and told the *Nahu'rac* what the other councils had said, these judges considered for a time, and then spoke together, and at length the chief of the judges said to the bird, "Now, messenger, we have concluded that we will not decide this question ourselves. You decide it, and say what shall be done."

The messenger was not long in deciding. He did not hesitate. He said, "I want this boy brought back to life." Then all the *Nahu'rac* stood up, and went to where the boy lay, and stood around him and prayed, and at last the boy breathed once, and then after a little while he breathed again, and at last he came to life and sat up. He looked about and saw all these animals standing around him, and he wondered. He said to himself, "Why, my father stabbed me, and killed me, and now here I am among this great crowd of animals. What does this mean?" He was surprised.

The *Nahu'rac* all went back into the lodge, and took the boy with them. When all were seated in the lodge, the four judges talked to each other, and the chief one stood up, and said, "Now, my people, we have brought this boy back to life, but he is poor, and we must do something for him. Let us teach him all we know, and make him one of us." Then the *Nahu'rac* all made a noise. They were glad. Then they began to sing and they danced. They taught the boy all their secrets, and all their ways. They taught him how to cut a man open and cure him again, and how to shoot an arrow through a man and then cure him, and how to cut a man's tongue out and then to put it back, and how to make well a broken leg, and many other things. After they had done all these things, they said to the boy, "Now we have brought you back to life, and have taught you all these things, so that you are one of us. Now you must stop with us one season. Your people have gone off on the summer hunt. You must stay with us until the autumn. Then you can go back to your people." So the boy stayed with the *Nahu'rac* in their lodge.

At length the Skidi had returned from the hunt with plenty of dried meat. Soon after this, the *Nahu'rac* said one day to the boy, "Your people have got back from the hunt. Now you can go back to the village. Go back and get a lot of nice dried meat, and bring it back to us here, and we will have a feast."

The boy went home to the village. He got there in the night, and went to his father's lodge, and went in. There was a little fire burning in the lodge. It was nearly out, and gave only a little light, but he knew the place where his mother slept. He went up to her, and put out his hand and touched her, and pushed her a little. She awoke, and sat up and looked at him, and he said, "I've come back." When she saw him, and heard him speak, she was very much surprised, and her heart was glad to see her boy again. She called to his father, and he woke up. When he saw the boy he was afraid, for he thought it was a ghost. The boy told them nothing of what had happened, or where he had been. He just said, "I have come back again."

In the morning all the people were surprised to

hear that he had come back, and to see him, and they stood around looking at him, and asking him questions, but he said nothing. The next day the people still questioned him, and at last the boy said, "I have been all summer with friends, with people who have been good to me. I should like to take them a present of some nice dried meat, so that we can have a feast." The people said that this was good. They picked out four strong horses, and loaded them with dried meat, the nicest pieces. The boy's father gave some of it, and all the other people brought pieces and put them on the horses, until they had big loads. They sent two young men with the boy, to help him load and drive the horses, and they started to go to the *Nahu'rac* lodge at *Pa-hŭk'*.

When they had come pretty near the place, the boy sent the young men back to the village, and he went on alone, driving the pack-horses before him. When he reached the home of the *Nahu'rac*, he unloaded the horses, and turned them loose, and then went into the lodge. When he went in, and when the *Nahu'rac* saw him, they all made a hissing noise. They were glad to see him. The boy brought into the lodge all the dried meat, and they had a great feast. After the feast they had a doctors' dance, and the boy was made a doctor, and again was taught all that the *Nahu'rac* knew. After that he could do many wonderful things. He could sometimes go to a man that had been dead for a day, and then bring him back to life.

No one ever knew what the father had done, for the boy never told any one. He knew that he could never have learned all these wonderful things unless his father had sacrificed him.

FLESHERS.

THE SNAKE BROTHER.

ONE time, long ago, a big party of Pawnees went on the warpath down to the south. They could find no enemies anywhere, and they went a long way south. In this party were two brothers, poor boys, and one day as they were traveling along, apart from the others, in a piece of woods where it was very thick, they got lost. When they found that they were lost, they tried to go back to the camp, but they could not find the others, and at last gave up looking for them and started to go back north to their home. They had no food with them, and were looking about for something to kill, so that they might eat. As they were going along, they came upon a dead buffalo that had been killed some time, and there was nothing of it left but the bones, so they took some of the marrow bones, and carried them along with them, until they made a camp.

Not far beyond here they stopped to rest. There was a tree growing near where they stopped, and as they looked up into it, they saw a squirrel run up the tree. One of the brothers caught up his bow and arrows, and the other said, "Oh, kill him, kill him, quick." The boy shot and killed it, and they skinned it, and roasted it over the fire. While they were cooking it the elder brother said, "I wonder if it is good to eat the marrow and the squirrel together." The younger said, "No, it is not good to do so. This is not real meat.*" The elder thought the two kinds of food would be good together, and they disputed about this for some time. The elder brother kept coaxing the younger to eat the squirrel and the marrow together, but the younger said, "Oh, brother, I do not like to do this. To me it does not seem good. But if you wish to do it, why don't you?" The elder said, "I think I will do so;" and he did so, taking a bite of squirrel, and then a bite of marrow. He said, "It is nice, you had better take some." But the younger brother would not. He ate only the marrow. After they had eaten they did not go on further, but slept there.

About the middle of the night, the elder brother

* Like buffalo meat, or elk or deer.

felt a noise in his feet, and he sat up and felt of his legs and feet, and he found that his feet were stuck together, and were beginning to get round, like a snake, and had a rattle on the end of them, and that his legs were round and like the tail of a great big rattlesnake. He reached over, and put his hands on his brother, and shook him, and said to him, "Get up. There is something the matter with me." The younger brother woke up, and felt of his brother, and found how it was; as if he was changing into a snake, beginning at his feet. When he saw this he felt very badly. Then the older brother began to talk to the younger, and to give him good advice, for he felt very sad.

He said, "Now I am going to die, and leave my young brother here alone on this prairie. He is so young, he will not be able to find his way home, and he must die, too. Surely this has happened because I ate the marrow and the squirrel together." While he was talking, the change had moved up to his waist.

After a little while he got more hopeful, and he said, "Now, brother, I know that you will get home safely. I will protect you. I know that I am going to be a snake, and I shall stay right here. You see that hole," and he pointed to a hole in the bank.

"When I have changed into a snake, take me in your arms, and carry me over to that hole. I am going to stay there forever. That will be my home, for that is the house of the snakes. When you go back home, you must tell our father and mother how it was, and whenever you want to go on the warpath, take a big party and come down this way, and come right here, to this very place, and you will see me, for I shall be here. Now, brother, when you go back home, some time after you have reached home, I want you to come back all alone; come right here. You know what I told you; do not be afraid of me. I believe this was to happen to me, and I could not help it. After you have once come all alone, then the second time you may bring some others with you, but the first time come alone." So he talked to his brother, and as he spoke the change kept going on. While it was moving up his body, until it got to his head, he was still like a man in his mind, but all his body was like a great big snake. Then he spoke to his brother, and said, "Now, brother, cover up my head with the robe, and after a little while take it off again." The younger brother did as he was told, and when, after a while, he took the robe off, there he saw an immense snake's head as broad as his two hands. The elder brother had completely changed into a snake.

The young man took the snake in his arms, and carried him over to the hole, and put him on the ground by it. He felt very sad to go away and leave his brother here. Before he started, he spoke good words to the snake, and said, "Now, brother, I am going home, and I ask you to take pity on me, and to protect me. I do not know the country I am going through, and you must take care of me. Do not forget the promises you have made me." After he had spoken he did not wait to see the snake go into the hole, but started on his journey, and went off toward his home.

When he reached the village, he told all these things to his father and his mother. He said to all his relations, "Do not mourn for him. He is alive and he is well. The only trouble is, that he is in the shape of a snake." After he had been home ten days, he told his mother to make for him five pairs of moccasins, that he was going on the warpath for himself. His mother did so, and he stuffed them full of parched corn, and took a little sack of pounded buffalo meat on his back, and started back to see his brother.

It took him seven days fast traveling to get to where he left the snake. When he had come near the place, he saw there the hole where he had left his brother. He went up close to the hole and began to speak. He said, "Brother, I am here. I have come on the warpath, and I am here to see you. You told me to come, and to come alone. I have done what you bade me, and am here. Now, brother, remember to keep your promises. I want to see you this afternoon."

He stood there a little while, and then there began in the hole a rattling and a rustling and scraping noise, and presently dust began to roll out, and then out of the hole came this great big snake, which was his brother. First came out this great snake, and after him many other large ones came out, and crept all about, but the great snake, his brother, lay just outside the hole. The boy went up to the big snake and took it in his arms, and hugged it, and spoke to it, and the snake put out its tongue, as if it were kissing him. Then the boy put it down on the ground, and all the other snakes came back, and went in the hole, and after them all, last, the big snake went in the hole.

Then the boy left this place, and went on a little

further, and about sunset he came to a little creek, and here he lay down and slept. In the night he dreamed of his brother, who spoke to him and said, "Now, brother, I am glad that you have come down to see me, as I told you to. And now I say to you, be brave. Have courage. To-morrow morning when you awake, dress yourself up as if you were going to fight. Paint your face, put feathers in your head, make yourself ready to fight."

The next morning the boy woke up, and as the snake had told him in the dream, so he did. He painted his face and tied feathers in his head, and dressed himself up for the fight. Then he started on. Pretty soon he came to a little hill, and as he looked over it, he saw people coming toward him; people and many horses. He thought they were Sioux, and when he saw them, he went back a little, to find a place where he could hide. He went back to the little creek where he had slept, and there he sat down in the brush. When he had hidden himself in the brush, he waited; and the people came straight toward where he had hidden himself, and camped just below where he was. After a little while he raised himself up and looked at them, and saw only two persons, and presently he saw that one of them was a woman. He watched for a long time, looking about to see if there were any more, but he could see only these two. Then he considered what he should do. While he was thinking, it came to him what the snake brother had said to him in the night, and then he knew what to do.

He crept slowly along through the brush toward their camp, and when he got close to them, about twenty yards distant, he raised up his head and looked. He saw the woman cooking, and there were hanging on a little tree the man's bow and arrows and shield and spear, but the man he could not see. He was lying down asleep somewhere near by. The boy waited and watched. He was excited, and his heart was pounding against his ribs. After a little while, the woman left the fire and walked away toward the horses. Perhaps her husband had said to her, "The horses are going off, you had better go and turn them back." When she went toward the horses, the boy was going to run up to the man and kill him, but before doing so he changed his mind; for he thought, "If I kill him, perhaps the woman will get on a horse, and ride away, driving the other horses with her." So he waited until the woman had come back. When she had returned to the fire, he ran up toward her, and she heard him coming, and ran to wake her husband; but just as she got to him, the boy was by her side. He shot two arrows into the man and killed him and counted *coup* on him, and captured the woman. He took the whole scalp of his enemy's head.

Then he took the woman and went down to where the horses were, and they got on two of them, and rode back to where his brother, the snake, lived, driving the horses before them. Just before they got to the hole, the boy took his lariat and caught a nice spotted horse and a mule, and tied them up to the tree, and called up the woman, and tied her up against the tree as tight as he could tie her. When he had done this, he went up to the hole and began to talk. He said, "Oh, my brother, I see now that what you have promised me comes true. I did what you told me. Now here are these two animals and the woman; I give them to you for being good to me. They are yours. I am glad for what you have done for me this day." When he had finished saying this he spoke again, saying, "Now, brother, I want to see you once more. I am going off, and I want to see you before I go." After a little while he heard again the rattling sound in the hole, and

saw the dust coming out of it, and then his brother
came out of the hole, and then afterward the smaller
snakes; and these all went down to the tree and
climbed up into it. The tree was thick with them.
Then the boy did as he had done before. He went
close to the hole, and took his brother up in his arms
and hugged him, and the great snake thrust out his
tongue, as if kissing him. Then the boy spoke again
and said, "Now, brother, I am going away, and I
give you these two animals and this woman to keep.
They are yours." Then he started for his home,
and after a long time he arrived at the village.

After a time, he determined to start off again on
the warpath, and this time he took a party with him.
He had told the whole tribe what had happened, and
how his brother had protected and helped him; and
he said to those warriors who were going with
him, "Let each one of you take a present with you
for my brother; some beads or eagle feathers or
some tobacco as an offering, so that he may help
you." They started south to go to the place where
his brother lived. When they got there, the young
man said to the others, "Now you must, each one of
you, give something to my brother. Call him by his
kin name, and ask him to help you, and to make you

successful; and leave the things before the hole." They did as he said, and when they had made their presents, they went by. They saw nothing, for the brother did not call out the great snake.

Two or three days after they had passed the place, they found a camp of Sioux, and took a lot of horses and killed some of the enemy. Then they went back, and when they came to the snake's home, they took a horse and led it up near the hole and killed it, and gave it to him, and left the scalps at the mouth of the hole as presents to him. When they reached the village, there was great joy and a good time. They had all kinds of dances, for they were glad that the war party had killed some Sioux.

After that another war party started out, and the brother said to them, "Go straight to my brother, and make him a present, and ask him to give you good luck, and you will be successful." And it happened as he had said.

The brother was always fortunate in war. He became a chief and was very rich, having many horses. Ever after that time, when he took the lead of a war party, all the poor men would come and say, "I want to go with you." They knew that his brother was a snake, and would give him good luck.

O'RE-KA-RAHR.

A LONG time ago, as the tribe were on their summer hunt, a man and his wife got to quarreling. They had a child, a boy about ten months old. It was while they were traveling along, going from one camp to another, that they began to quarrel. At length the wife became very angry, and threw the baby to the man, saying, "You take that baby. It belongs to you, for it is a man child. I am not going to nurse it for you any longer." Then she went away.

The man took the child and carried it along with him. He felt very badly, both on his own account and on account of his child. He was so unhappy that he almost wanted to kill himself. He was so poor-minded because it was a disgrace that he, being a man, should be obliged to take care of his child until it was grown up, and he had no female relatives to whom he could turn it over to be reared. So he was very unhappy, and determined to leave the tribe and wander off alone, far from his people.

He did so. He carried the child on his back, as a woman does. When it cried for its mother's milk, he had none to give it. He could only cry with it. He hated to kill the child, or to leave it behind to die on the prairie. He wandered off to the south. He traveled on for a time, until he came near to where the buffalo were. By this time, the child had changed from a very fat baby to a very thin one, because it had not been nursed. When he got to the buffalo, he killed a cow, and took its udder, and while it was fresh he let the child suck it, until it became sour. Then he killed another cow, and did the same thing. In every way he did the best he could to nourish the child. Sometimes he would get a slice of meat, and half cook it, and let the child suck the juice. The child began to improve, and to get a little stronger. In this way he supported it for quite a long time, and it did pretty well, and at last it got used to this food, and became strong and well. By this time he had gone a long way.

At length he found that the child could sit up

alone. Then he began to give it all sorts of playthings, so that it could amuse itself. First he made for it a little bow and some arrows, and taught it how to use them. He made other things for the child to play with, and at last it got to be contented playing alone. Then the father would leave the child for a few minutes, and go off a little way, perhaps to the top of a hill near by, to look off over the country, but he would look back at the child every few steps to see that it was all right. When he would come back he would find the child safe, playing, well contented. After a while he got so that he would leave it for about an hour, and when he came back, find it safe and contented, playing. By this time the child had begun to walk. Finally the father went off once for half a day, and when he came back, he found the child playing about safe. It did not seem to mind much about the father being absent. About this time he killed a buffalo cow, and made some dried meat, and put it in a certain place, and told the child when it was hungry to go there and get a a piece.

He now went off and was gone a whole day, and when he came back at night the child was safe. Finally he made his preparations and went off to stay over night, and be gone two days. He did so, and when he came back, the boy was asleep. A second time he went away and was absent for two days, going quite a long distance. When he came back he found that the child was painted with white clay. The father thought this was strange. He said to himself, "Something must have come and talked to my child, and is taking care of him while I am gone."

When he came back the third time after a two days' journey, he found that the child had about his neck a string of *pa'hut.** The fourth long journey he took lasted three days, and when he returned, he found his boy still wearing this same string of beads, and with a feather tied in his head. Now his father knew that something was looking after his child while he was away, and when he went off, he would pray for the child. He would say, "*No'-a,* whatever it is that is taking pity on my child, also take pity on me."

The child had now grown so large that it could talk with him, and one day it said, "Father, you go away, and you be gone for four days; I will be all right here. When you come back you will find me safe."

* Wild currants strung like beads.

The man went. He started to go way down south, to be gone for four days. After he had been gone two days and two nights, he saw a signal smoke and went toward it. As he raised up his head and peeped over a hill before crossing it, he saw, far off, a lot of people and horses coming toward the river which lay between him and them. He lay on the hill a long time, watching to see where they would camp. When they had made camp, he went into a ravine, and crept down close to the camp, until he could see that it was just one lodge, and that about it were a whole herd of horses. He waited until evening, and then went over to the lodge. It was after dark when he went. The lodge was all surrounded by horses; everywhere nothing but horses, there were so many. He crept close to the lodge, and looked in through an opening by the door, and saw lying down opposite the door a great big man, and on either side a woman; only three persons in all. As he looked at these persons, he thought he recognized one of the women. He kept looking at her, and at last he remembered who she was, and that she had been captured long ago from the Pawnees. Her people were still living. The man was a Comanche.

While the Pawnee was watching, the man inside
the lodge asked for something, and the captive
woman stood up to go out of the lodge, and the
Pawnee stepped to one side, out of sight. The
woman came out into the darkness, and went out
among the horses. The Pawnee stepped up behind
her very softly, and put his hand on her shoulder,
and said to her in Pawnee, "Friend, do you belong
to my tribe?" The woman started to scream, but
he put his hand on her mouth, and said to her, "Be
quiet. Keep still. Do not call out." She answered
him, "Yes, I belong to your tribe." Then she said
in a very low voice that shook, for she was afraid,
"Do you belong to my tribe?" The man said,
"Yes." Then he asked her, "Who is that other
woman that I see in the lodge?" She answered
him, "She also belongs to our tribe, and is a prisoner." Then the man said, "You just wait and keep
still. I am going to kill that man." The woman
said, "That is good. That is good. This man is
the biggest man of all the Comanches. He has
come first to this place, and all the rest of the
Comanches are coming here to meet him. I am
glad that my people are living, and that I am going
back to see them once more. Do not fail to kill

him. I will tell the other woman to be ready, that our friend is here, and we will wait and watch."

When the woman went into the lodge, she whispered to the other woman, and said, "Be ready. A friend who belongs to our tribe is here. Take your hatchet, and be prepared to help to kill our husband."

The two women waited, and the Pawnee made ready to shoot the Comanche with his bow and arrow. The woman had said to him, "Push aside the door a little and be ready." He made a little bit of an opening by the door, just big enough to let an arrow pass through, and when the time came he let it go. *U'-ra-rish!* the arrow flew straight, and pierced the Comanche through the heart. So he died, and the Pawnee counted *coup* on him and took his scalp.

The women felt so glad to meet a friend that they put their arms around the man and patted him. They were going back home to see their relations. They asked him, "How many of you are here?" He answered, "I am alone." They were surprised.

They took down the lodge, and packed everything on the horses, and drove off the herd, leaving the dead body of the enemy in the camp. All night they traveled, and all the next day; and as they were

going, he told them how it came about that he was
alone.   They told him that there were about three
hundred head of horses in the herd that they had
with them.   When they had come pretty close to
where he had left the child, he told them about
the boy being there all alone; and the women just
ran their horses to get to the boy; whichever got
there first, he should be hers.   When they came to
the boy, they took him in their arms and petted him,
and took him as their own.

Now the father was no longer sad.   He had recovered two captured women, had killed his enemy,
and had taken a lot of horses.

They went on, and traveled far, and at length,
one night, they came to the Pawnee tribe, and
camped with them.   The horses just surrounded the
lodge, you could just see the top of it over their
backs.   The next morning all the people wondered
who these strangers could be.   They found out that
the man and child, who were lost, had returned,
and with them two women, captured long ago by
the Comanches.   So there was great joy in the tribe.
Then the man gave his relations many horses.   In
those days the Pawnees had not many horses, and it
seems that this man brought good luck in horses to

the tribe. Ever since that time they have had many horses. The mother of the child came to see it, she was so glad it was alive, but she was whipped out of the lodge.

The child grew to be a man, and was wealthy. After he had grown up, he told his father that ever since he could remember anything, a buck deer had talked to him, and taken care of him; that it had saved them, and brought them good fortune. In order that the *O're-ka-rahr* might be remembered, he established a dance, called the deer dance, which has been kept up to this day.

Many wonderful things happened to this same young man. Once he went on a war party against the Cheyennes, and stole some horses from them. The Cheyennes followed and overtook them, and they had a great fight. The first man killed was this young man. He was very brave, and the Cheyennes cut him up into small pieces, but that night it lightened and thundered and rained, and soon after the storm was over, the young man came walking into camp alive. He was all scarred over, where he had been cut up, but he had come to life because the deer had looked after him. He lived long to show the scars of the battles he had been through.

THE GHOST BRIDE.

IN a place where we used to have a village, a young woman died just before the tribe started on the hunt. When she died they dressed her up in her finest clothes, and buried her, and soon after this the tribe started on the hunt.

A party of young men had gone off to visit another tribe, and they did not get back until after this girl had died and the tribe had left the village. Most of this party did not go back to the village, but met the tribe and went with them on the hunt. Among the young men who had been away was one who had loved this girl who had died. He went back alone to the village. It was empty and silent, but before he reached it, he could see, far off, some one sitting on top of a lodge. When he came near, he saw that it was the girl he loved. He did not

know that she had died, and he wondered to see her
there alone, for the time was coming when he would
be her husband and she his wife. When she saw
him coming, she came down from the top of the
lodge and went inside. When he came close to her,
he spoke and said, "Why are you here alone in the
village?" She answered him, "They have gone off
on the hunt. I was sulky with my relations, and
they went off and left me behind." The man wanted
her now to be his wife, but the girl said to him, "No,
not yet, but later we will be married." She said to
him, "You must not be afraid. To-night there will
be dances here; the ghosts will dance." This is an
old custom of the Pawnees. When they danced they
used to go from one lodge to another, singing, dancing and hallooing. So now, when the tribe had gone
and the village was deserted, the ghosts did this.
He could hear them coming along the empty streets,
and going from one lodge to another. They came
into the lodge where he was, and danced about,
and whooped and sang, and sometimes they almost
touched him, and he came pretty near being scared.

The next day, the young man persuaded the girl
to go on with him, and follow the tribe, to join it on
the hunt. They started to travel together, and she

promised him that she would surely be his wife, but not until the time came. They overtook the tribe; but before they got to the camp, the girl stopped. She said, "Now we have arrived, but you must go first to the village, and prepare a place for me. Where I sleep, let it be behind a curtain. For four days and four nights I must remain behind this curtain. Do not speak of me. Do not mention my name to any one."

The young man left her there and went into the camp. When he got to his lodge, he told a woman, one of his relations, to go out to a certain place and bring in a woman, who was waiting there for him. His relative asked him, "Who is the woman?" And to avoid speaking her name, he told who were her father and mother. His relation, in surprise, said, "It cannot be that girl, for she died some days before we started on the hunt."

When the woman went to look for the girl she could not find her. The girl had disappeared. The young man had disobeyed her, and had told who she was. She had told him that she must stay behind a curtain for four days, and that no one must know who she was. Instead of doing what she had said, he told who she was, and the girl disappeared because she was a ghost. If he had obeyed the girl, she would have lived a second time upon earth. That same night this young man died in sleep.

Then the people were convinced that there must be a life after this one.

INTERIOR OF DIRT LODGE.

THE BOY WHO SAW A-TI'-US.

MANY years ago the Pawnees started on their winter hunt. The buffalo were scarce, and the people could get hardly any meat. It was very cold, and the snow lay deep on the ground. The tribe traveled southward, and crossed the Republican, but still found no buffalo. They had eaten all the dried meat, and all the corn that they had brought with them, and now they were starving. The sufferings of the people were great, and the little ones began to die of hunger. Now they began to eat their robes, and *parfleches*, and moccasins.

There was in the tribe a boy about sixteen years old, who was all alone, and was very poor. He had no relations who could take care of him, and he lived with a woman whose husband had been killed by the Sioux. She had two children, a boy and a girl; and she had a good heart, and was sorry for the poor boy. In this time of famine, these people had scarcely anything to eat, and whenever the boy got hold of any food, he gave it to the woman, who divided it among them all.

The tribe kept traveling southward looking for buffalo, but they had to go very slowly, because they were all so weak. Still they found no buffalo, and each day the young men that were sent out to look for them climbed the highest hills, and came back at night, and reported that they could only see the white prairie covered with snow. All this time little ones were dying of hunger, and the men and women were growing weaker every day.

The poor boy suffered with the rest, and at last he became so weak that he hardly could keep up with the camp, even though it moved very slowly. One morning he was hardly able to help the old woman pack the lodge, and after it had been packed, he went back to the fire, and sat down beside it, and watched the camp move slowly off across the valley, and up over the bluffs. He thought to himself, "Why should I go on? I can't keep up for more than a day or two longer anyhow. I may as well stay here and die." So he gathered together the ends of the sticks that lay by the fire, and put them on the coals, and spread his hands over the blaze, and rubbed them together, and got warm, and then lay down by the fire, and pretty soon he went to sleep.

When he came to himself, it was about the middle of the day, and as he looked toward the sky he saw two spots there between him and the sun, and he wondered what they were. As he looked at them they became larger and larger, and at last he could see that they were birds; and by and by, as they came still nearer, he saw that they were two swans. The swans kept coming lower and lower, and at last they alighted on the ground right by the fire, and walked up to where the boy lay. He was so weak he could not get up, and they came to him, one on each side, and stooped down, and pushed their shoulders under him, and raised him up and put him on their backs, and then spread their broad wings, and flew away upward. Then the boy went to sleep again.

When he awoke he was lying on the ground before a very big lodge. It was large and high, and on it were painted pictures of many strange animals, in beautiful colors. The boy had never seen such a fine lodge. The air was warm here, and he felt stronger than before. He tried to raise himself up, and after trying once or twice he got on his feet, and walked to the door of the lodge, and went in. Opposite the door sat *A-ti'-us.* He was very large and very handsome, and his face was kind and gentle. He was dressed in beautiful clothes, and wore a white buffalo robe. Behind him, from the lodge poles, hung many strange weapons. Around the lodge on each side sat many chiefs, and doctors, and warriors. They all wore fine clothes of white buckskin, embroidered with beautifully colored quills. Their robes were all of beaver skin, very beautiful.

When the boy entered the lodge, *A-ti'-us* said to him, " *Looah, pi-rau', we-tŭs sūks-pit*—Welcome, my son, and sit down." And he said to one of the warriors, "Give him something to eat." The warrior took down a beautifully painted sack of *parfleche,* and took his knife from its sheath, and cut off a piece of dried meat about as big as one's two fingers, and a piece of fat about the same size, and gave them to the boy. The boy, who was so hungry, thought that this was not very much to give to one who was starving, but took it, and began to eat. He put the

fat on the lean, and cut the pieces off, and ate for a
long time. But after he had eaten for a long time,
the pieces of meat remained the same size; and he
ate all that he wanted, and then put the pieces down,
still the same size.

After the boy had finished eating, *A-ti''-us* spoke to
him. He told him that he had seen the sufferings of
his people, and had been sorry for them; and then
he told the boy what to do. So he kept the boy
there for a little while longer, and gave him some
fine new clothing and weapons, and then he told one
of the warriors to send the boy back; and the warrior led him out of the lodge to where the swans
were standing near the entrance, and the boy got on
to their backs. Then the warrior put his hand on
his face, and pressed his eyelids together, and the
boy went to sleep. And by and by the boy awoke,
and found himself alone by the fire. The fire had
gone out, but the ground was still covered with snow,
and it was very cold.

Now the boy felt strong, and he stood up, and
started, running along the trail which the camp had
taken. That night after dark he overtook the camp,
for they traveled very slowly, and he walked through
the village till he came to the lodge where the woman

was, and went in. She was surprised to see him in his new clothes, and looking so well and strong, and told him to sit down. There was a little fire in the lodge, and the boy could see that the woman was cutting up something into small pieces with her knife.

The boy said to her, "What are you doing?"

She answered, "I am going to boil our last piece of robe. After we have eaten this there will be nothing left, and we can then only die."

The boy said nothing, but watched her for a little while, and then stood up and went out of the lodge. The door had hardly fallen behind him, when the woman heard a buffalo coughing, and then the breaking of the crisp snow, as if a heavy weight was settling on it. In a moment the boy lifted the lodge door, and came in, and sat down by the fire, and said to the woman, "Go out and bring in some meat." The woman looked at him, for she was astonished, but he said nothing, so she went out, and there in the snow by the side of the lodge was a fat buffalo cow. Then the woman's heart was glad. She skinned the cow, and brought some of the meat into the lodge and cooked it, and they all ate and were satisfied. The woman was good, so she sent her son to the lodges of all her relations, and all her friends, and told them all to come next morning to her lodge to a feast, "for," she said, " I have plenty of meat."

So the next morning all her relations and all her friends came, so many that they could not all get into the lodge, but some had to stand outside, and they ate with her, and she cooked the meat of the cow for them, and they ate until it was all gone, and they were satisfied. And after they had done eating, they lighted their pipes and prayed, saying, "*A-ti'-us, we'-tŭs kit-tah-we*—Father, you are the ruler."

While they were smoking the poor boy called the woman's son to him, and pointed to a high hill near the camp, and said, "*Looah, sūks-kus-sis-pah ti-rah hah-tūr*—Run hard to the top of that hill, and tell me what you see." So the boy threw off his robe, and smoothed back his hair, and started, and ran as hard as he could over the snow to the top of the hill. When he got there he shaded his eyes with his hand, for the sun shone bright on the snow and blinded him, and he looked east, and west, and north, and south, but he could see nothing but the shining white snow on the prairie. After he had looked all ways, he ran back as hard as he could to the village. When he came to the lodge, he went to the poor boy, and said to him, "I don't see anything but the snow." The poor boy said, "You don't look good. Go again." So the boy started again, and ran as hard as he could to the hilltop, and when he got there, panting, he looked all ways, long and carefully, but still he could see nothing but the snow. So he turned and ran back to the village, and told the poor boy again that he saw nothing. The boy said, "You don't look good." Then he took his bow in his hand, and put his quiver on his back, and drew his robe up under his arm so that he could run well, and started, himself, and ran as hard as he could to the top of the hill, and when he got there he looked off to the south, and there, as far as he could see, the plain was black with buffalo struggling in the deep snow. And he turned to the village, and signaled them with his robe that buffalo were in sight. In a few minutes all the Pawnees had seized their bows and arrows, and were running toward him, and the women fixed the *travois*, and took their knives, and followed. The boy waited on the hilltop until the warriors came up, and then they went down to the buffalo, running on the snow. The buffalo could not get away on account of the deep snow, and the Pawnees made a great killing. Plenty of fat meat they got, enough to last them until the summer hunt, and plenty of warm winter robes. They did not have to move any further, but stayed right here, killing meat and drying it until they were all fat and strong again.

And the poor boy became a great doctor in the tribe, and got rich.

Before this the Pawnees had always had a woman chief, but when the woman who was chief died, she named the poor boy as her successor, and the people made him head chief of the tribe.

FIRE-STICK.

HOW THE DEER LOST HIS GALL.

A LONG time ago, the deer and the antelope met upon the prairie. At that time both of them had dew-claws, and both had galls. After they had talked for a little while, each one of them began to boast about how fast he could run. Each one, the deer and the antelope, claimed that he could run faster than any other animal, and at length they became very angry in their dispute, and determined that they would have a race.

They staked their galls on the race, and it was run on the prairie. The antelope ran the faster, and won, and took the deer's gall. The deer felt very badly that he had lost it, and he seemed so miserable that the antelope felt sorry for him, and to cheer him up, he took off his dew-claws and gave them to him.

Since that time the deer has had no gall, and the antelope no dew-claws.

NOTE.—A story somewhat similar to this is current among the Blackfeet tribes of the northern country. In this tale the antelope won the deer's gall, as in the Pawnee story. Then the deer said, "You have won, but that race was not a fair one, for it was over the prairie alone. We ought to run another race in the timber to decide which is really the faster." They agreed to run this second race, and on it they bet their dew-claws. The deer ran the faster through the thick timber and over the logs, and beat the antelope, and took his dew-claws. Since then the antelope has had no dew-claws, and the deer no gall.

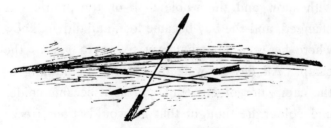

BOW AND ARROWS.

YELLOW FOX.

A LONG time ago, while the Pawnees were on their winter hunt, a young boy, *Kiwuk-u lah'-kahta* (Yellow Fox), went out alone to hunt, to see if he could kill a deer. When he left the camp in the morning, it was warm and pleasant, but in the middle of the day a great storm of wind and snow came up, and the flying snow hid everything, and it grew very cold. By and by the ground was covered with snow, and the whole look of the prairie was changed, and the boy became lost, and did not know where he was, nor what way to go to get to the camp. All day he walked, but he saw nothing of the camp, nor of any trail, and as it became colder and colder, he thought that he would surely freeze to death. He thought that he must die, and that there was no hope of his ever seeing his people

again. As he was wandering along, numbed and
stiffened by the cold, and stumbling through the
deep snow, he heard behind him a curious singing
sound, and in time with the singing was the noise
made by some heavy animal, running. The sounds
came nearer, and at last, close by the boy, ran a great
big buffalo bull. And as he ran near the boy, he
sang a song, and as he sang, the sound of his hoofs
on the ground kept time to the measure of the song.
This is what he sang:

> *A-ti-us ti-wa-ko Ru-ru! Teh-wah-hwa'-ko,*
> My Father says, Go on! He keeps saying,
>
> *Ru-ru-hwa'-hwa', Wi-ruh-rĕ.*
> Keep going on. It will be well.

The boy's heart became strong when he heard
that the Father had sent the bull, and he followed
him, and the bull led him straight to the camp.

NOTES ON THE PAWNEES.

NOTE.

THE notes on the origin, customs and character of the Pawnees, which follow, have been gathered during twenty years' acquaintance with this people. They are what they profess to be; not a history of the people, but a series of notes bearing on their mode of life in the old wild days, an attempt to give some clues to their habits of thought, and thus to indicate the character of the people. Such notes may be of use to some future historian who shall have the time and the inclination to trace out more fully the history of the Pawnees, and to tell, as it ought to be told, the story of a people who once were great. I could wish that it might be my privilege to undertake this congenial. task, but the constantly increasing pressure of other duties forbids me to hope that I shall be able to do so. I feel satisfaction, however, in being able to record the observations here set down.

In the collection of this material I had for years the assistance and coöperation of the late Major Frank North, who always placed at my disposal his great store of Pawnee lore. Luther H. North, his brother, has given me a vast deal of assistance, and last spring accompanied me to the Pawnee reservation. Without his aid this book would never have been written. Mr. John B. Dunbar has been most kind in reading over the chapter on the Pawnees, and has aided me with many suggestions, besides giving me help on certain linguistic points.

Nothing is said in this volume about the Pawnee language—a subject which is sufficiently important to deserve a volume by itself.

To every intelligent student of North American aborigines it must be a matter of keen regret that nothing is known of the language of this people. That a distinct linguistic stock like the Pawnee should pass away unrecorded would be a serious misfortune, and the Bureau of Ethnology of the Smithsonian Institution ought certainly to take some steps to preserve a record of the Pawnee language.

Major Frank North was undoubtedly more conversant with the spoken Pawnee tongue than any other white man has ever been. Since his death, there is no one who is so familiar with the language as Mr. John B. Dunbar, who has devoted much time to its study, and has made himself acquainted not only with its vocabulary, but also with its grammar. Born and reared among the Pawnees, familiar with them until early manhood, a frequent visitor to the tribe in later years, he is well fitted by interest and association to undertake the task of recording in permanent form the unwritten speech of this people. Add to this a long training as a student of language and history and a keen logical mind, and we have in Mr. Dunbar the man more than all others best fitted to undertake this difficult but most delightful task. The Director of the Bureau of Ethnology could not easily perform a greater service to aboriginal linguistics than to intrust to Mr. Dunbar the labor of preparing an extended work on the Pawnee language.

THE PAWNEES.

I. RELATIONSHIPS.

UNTIL within a few years the home of the Pawnees was in southern Nebraska and northern Kansas. This group of tribes may be called the main stock of the family; from them it took its name; they are its best and longest known members. In the earlier accounts of this people, the Pawnee Picts or Wichitas are often confounded with their more northern relatives.

The Pawnees proper consisted at one time of three bands or tribes, federated under a single head chief. These bands, in the order of their importance, were: The Chau-i, the Kit-ke-hahk'-i and the Pita-hau-erat. To these three was subsequently added—after the northern migration of the tribes, and their settlement in northern Kansas and Nebraska, but probably long anterior to the advent of the whites, and by conquest—the large, powerful and intelligent allied tribe, known as the Skidi or Pawnee Loups. These four have always been known in the writings of the earlier explorers in the West as respectively the Grand, the Republican, the Tapage and the Wolf Pawnees, and they constituted the Pawnee Nation.

The three tribes first named have always been together, and their Pawnee names, according to Major North, denoted the relative situations of the three villages. Thus Kit-ke-hahk'-i means "on a hill;" Chau-i, "in the middle;" Pita-hau-erat, "down the stream," or east; and in the olden times these were the relative positions of the different villages when the three bands were camping together. The Kit-ke-hahk'-i village was always the westernmost of the three, the Chau-i were next to them, and the Pita-hau-erat were furthest east. After the incorporation of the Skidi with the Pawnees, the village of that tribe was always placed furthest to the west, and it was spoken of as the Upper Village, while the other bands were termed the Lower Village Tribes.

Of the three original bands, the Chau-i has always been first in importance, and the head chief has been

GOOD CHIEF—KIT-KE-HAHK′-I.

chosen from it. The Kit-ke-hahk'-i band in numbers, importance and intelligence appear to rank about with the Chau-i, while, on the other hand, the Pita-hau-erat are regarded as less intelligent, responsible and worthy than the other bands.

The Skidi are usually looked upon as more intelligent than the Pawnees, and also as fiercer in their nature, and as making better soldiers. The Skidi traditions, though such testimony, of course, is not of much value, speak rather contemptuously of the prowess of the other bands in war, and the superiority of the Skidi is grudgingly acknowledged by the others. This is contrary to the view held by Mr. J. B. Dunbar, who speaks of the Skidi as more intelligent than the other bands, but as not being so good as warriors.

Besides this main group of tribes, the members of the Pawnee family, as given by Mr. Dunbar, are the Arickaras, known also as the Arickarees, Ricarees or Rees, the Caddos, the Huecos or Wacos, the Keechies, the Tawaconies, and the Wichitas or Pawnee Picts. To these may be added with some confidence the Tonkaways and the Lipans. The Caddos, Huecos, Keechies and Tawaconies are regarded by the Pawnees as closely connected with the

Wichitas. They had but one name, *Kiri-ku'ruks*, for all these tribes, and knew no distinction between them. There is no doubt that the Arickaras were recently—perhaps within a century—either a band of the Skidi tribe, or at least allied to them as closely as the Chau-i have always been to the Kit-ke-hahk'-i and the Pita-hau-erat. The relationship of the Tonkaways and the Lipans has only recently been discovered and has come to light through the removal of the Pawnees from their home in Nebraska to their present reservation in the Indian Territory.

In a note appended to his article on the Pawnees, published in the *Magazine of American History* for November, 1880, Mr. Dunbar says, "A friend, who has had much experience with the Indians of the Southwest, informs me that he is inclined to believe that the Lipans of Mexico are of Pawnee stock. They have, in times past, exchanged frequent hospitalities with the Wichitas, or Pawnee Picts, and the two understand each other's dialects readily. The name Lipans he explains as *li'panis*, that is, *the* Pawnees." While this suggestion is very interesting, so far as it goes, it scarcely furnishes sufficient ground on which to base a genetic connection of the Lipans with the Pawnee family. I have recently secured additional and more satisfactory evidence of such a connection

It is generally believed by the Pawnees, especially by those who are most intelligent, and have had most intercourse with the southern tribes, that the Lipans are allied to them, and that this relationship is traceable through the Wichitas and the Tonkaways. The evidence consists of (1) statements by the Wichitas and Tonkaways, (2) an alleged similarity of language and personal names, and (3) a similarity in the songs of the tribes. A Pawnee Indian, who has lived for seven seasons with the Wichitas, gave me the following story which he had gathered from that people. They say that long ago they did not know the Tonkaways, but that when the tribes met they found that they could understand each other's speech. Their languages were not the same, but they were not more unlike than were the tongues spoken by the Skidi and the three other Pawnee bands long ago; in other words, they were dialects of the same language. After that meeting, the Tonkaways and the Wichitas lived together for a time. But the Tonkaways had bad ways. They would eat human flesh. When they could find a Wichita boy out away from the camp, they would capture him, and strangle

and eat him. Sometimes they would kill a man of
the Wichitas, if they could catch him away off on the
prairie. Therefore the Wichitas drove the Tonkaways off south, and soon afterward moved up across
the Arkansas River, and into southern Kansas.
Since then the Wichitas and the Tonkaways have
never lived together. A Tonkaway chief named
Charlie told Ralph J. Weeks, an educated Pawnee,
"I have heard that my people are Pawnees, but that
we separated long ago." I am informed that the
personal names of the Tonkaways are the same as
those of the Pawnees, and are readily comprehended
by the latter. Ralph Weeks, while in a Tonkaway
lodge, heard a man call out to a girl, addressing her
as *Tsi-sah-ru-rah-ka'-ri-ku*, which means "Woman
Chief's House." Ralph inquired about this name,
and found that it was the same in sound as Pawnee,
and had the same meaning. The Tonkaways say
that some of the Pawnee words are the same as
those used by their relations to the south, the Lipans
and others. The songs of the Tonkaways are the
same as those of the Pawnees, and the latter at once
recognize them. The old songs of the Lipans are
the same as those of the Pawnees, according to both
Pawnee and Tonkaway testimony. Finally, the

Tonkaways and Lipans claim close relationship. They speak different dialects of the same language.

The Pawnees, however, say that they never knew of the existence of the Tonkaways until they came down into the Indian Territory, and, of course, never met them until after that time. Neither did they know the Caddos. As the Pawnees knew nothing of the Caddos and Tonkaways, so the Wichitas knew nothing of the Arickaras until recently, and were greatly surprised to learn that far to the north there was another tribe which spoke their language.

The Wichitas claim that they and the Caddos are one people. Their languages are said to differ somewhat, but only dialectically.

The southern members of the Pawnee family appear always to have lived on excellent terms with the other wild tribes which inhabited their country. They were allies of the Kiowas, Comanches, and Cheyennes, tribes with which the northern Pawnees were long at war.

II. ORIGIN AND MIGRATIONS.

The Pawnees came from the south. All the information bearing on their origin, which has as yet been secured, points to the conclusion that the primitive home of this family was in the south.

Although Mr. Dunbar has carefully traced out the later history of several of the members of this group, his researches carry us back scarcely further than the beginning of the present century, and we have no actual knowledge of the origin and early history of the Pawnees. Except the Arickaras, none of the tribes belonging to this family have ever dwelt much north of the Platte River, and in this we have an indication of their southern origin. The traditions of the tribe confirm this suggestion, and Mr. Dunbar has given other reasons, derived from his study of this people, which abundantly justify us in regarding them as migrants from the south.

There are still current among the Pawnees two traditions as to the region from which they came, but both of these are vague, and so lacking in detail as to be of little value except as suggestions which need confirmation before being accepted as having any solid basis of fact. The first of these traditions, now half forgotten, is known only to the very oldest men. It is to the effect that long ago they came from the far southwest, where they used to live in stone houses. This might point to an original home for the Pawnees in Old Mexico, and even suggests a possible connection with the so-called Pueblo tribes, who still live in houses made of stone, and entered from above.

Secret Pipe Chief, a very old Chau-i, the High Priest of the tribe, gave me the history of their wanderings in these words: "Long ago," he said, "very far back, all of one color were together, but something mysterious happened so that they came to speak different languages. They were all together, and determined that they would separate into different parties to go and get sinew. They could not all go in company, there were too many of them. They were so numerous that when they traveled, the rocks where their lodge poles dragged were worn into deep grooves. Then they were far off in the southwest, and came from beyond two ranges of mountains. When they scattered out, each party became a tribe. At that time the Pawnees and the Wichitas were together. We made that journey, and went so far east that at last we came to the Missouri

River, and stopped there for a time. When the season came round, we made out of the shoulder blade of a buffalo an implement to cultivate the ground. There we made our fields."

Another very old man, Bear Chief, a Skidi, said, "Long ago we were far in the southwest, away beyond the Rio Grande. We came north, and settled near the Wichita Mountains. One summer there we planted our corn. So we came from the south. After we left the Wichita Mountains, that summer we came north as far as the Arkansas River, and made our fields, and raised corn. Afterward we went to the Mississippi River where the Missouri runs into it. My father was born while we lived on the Mississippi." As Bear Chief must be nearly or quite eighty years old, it would seem likely that the Skidi, or some village of that tribe, may have been established on the Mississippi one hundred years ago, but this was not a permanent location.

The second of these traditions tells of a migration from the southeast. It states that the tribe originally came from somewhere in the southeast, that is from what is now Missouri or Arkansas. They started north after sinew—to hunt buffalo—and followed up the game, until they reached the northern country—the region of the Republican and the Platte rivers. They found this a pleasant country, abounding in game, and they liked it, and remained there. The Wichitas accompanied them part way on their journey, but turned aside when they had reached southern Kansas, and went south again.

All the traditions agree that up to the time of the journey which brought the Pawnees to their homes on the Solomon, Republican, Platte and Loup rivers, the Wichitas were considered a part of the Pawnee tribe. They agree also that after this separation, the two divisions of the tribe lost sight of each other for a very long time, and that each was entirely ignorant as to what had become of the other. We know that for a long time they were at war, and the difference of the dialects spoken by these two divisions of the family shows that the period of separation was a long one.

The tradition of the migration of the Pawnees from the southwest is evidently much older than the one which tells of their coming from the southeast. Most of the younger men know the latter; but for the account of the journey over the mountains from the southwest and across the Rio Grande, it is necessary to go to the very old men. It is quite possible that both stories are founded on fact; and, if this is the case, the migration from the southeast may have taken place only a few generations ago. Such a supposition would in part explain its general currency at the present time.

In the existing state of our knowledge of this people, we have no facts to go on, nothing in the nature of evidence as to their early history, and we can only speculate as to the probabilities in regard to their wanderings. It may be conjectured that the Pawnees came from somewhere in Old Mexico, and, either as a number of related tribes, or as a single tribe made up of different bands, they crossed the mountains and the Rio Grande in a body, and wandered eastward across what is now Texas. From this body it seems probable that the ancestors of the Lipans and the Tonkaways were the first to separate themselves. The main tribe perhaps gradually drifted further and further to the east until it had crossed Texas and reached northwestern Louisiana, and perhaps even the neighborhood of the Mississippi River. During this long journey, which must have occupied many years—perhaps many generations—we may imagine that the Huecos and possibly the Keechies dropped behind, and remained on the plains.

How long the Pawnees sojourned in Louisiana no one can say. They now found themselves in a country, which in climate, productions, and topography, differed widely from anything they had before known. Up to this time, these people had always inhabited the high, dry tablelands of Mexico, or the almost equally arid plains of Texas, and now they had come to a country having a heavy rainfall, abounding in swamps, and overgrown with deciduous timber. The traditions of both Skidi and Pawnees speak of a time when they lived in a country where grows the cane which the white men use for fishing poles. We may imagine that this forest country was a barrier to their further progress eastward, and that it turned their steps in a new direction.

When the Pawnees left Louisiana, the Caddos certainly, and perhaps the Keechies and the Tawaconies, were left behind, and for a very long time lived in and near what is now Caddo Parish, Louisiana, where they were at the time of the Louisiana Purchase. Geographical names in this region indicate that their residence there was a long one, and Caddo Lake, Caddo Fork, Caddo Gap and a town named Keatchie, still bear testimony of the former occupants of the soil. From there the Caddos moved up to the

Brazos River in Texas. They have always kept up a close intimacy with the Wichitas.

Perhaps it was during the sojourn of the Pawnees on the western borders of Louisiana and Arkansas, though it may have been much earlier, that the Skidi and the Arickaras, either as a single tribe, or as already divided into two separate bands, left the Pawnees and moved north and northwest. There appears to be reason for supposing that for a while this section of the tribe lived on the Red River, the Canadian and the Arkansas, and it is quite certain that sometimes they went as far east as the banks of the Mississippi near where St. Louis now is; but their permanent home, since they have been known to the whites, was on the Platte and the Loup rivers in Nebraska.

The Pawnees with the Wichitas moved northwest into what is now the Indian Territory and southern Kansas, where they separated, the latter turning off to the south, and living at various times on the Canadian and Red rivers and near the Wichita Mountains, while the Pawnees proper slowly continued their march northward and westward, residing for a time on the Arkansas and Solomon, the Republican and Platte rivers. Here they again met the Skidi.

It is impossible to conjecture when this settlement in the northern country took place, but it was certainly long ago. Mr. Dunbar has pointed out that "*O-kŭt-ut* and *oku'-kat'* signify strictly above and below (of a stream) respectively. Now their villages have usually been situated upon the banks of the Platte, the general course of which is from west to east. Hence each of these words has acquired a new meaning, *i. e.*, west and east." In the same way *Pŭk-tĭs'-tu*—toward the Omahas, has come to mean north; and *Ki'ri-ku'ruks-tu*—toward the Wichitas, to mean south. The coining of such words points to a long sojourn by the Pawnees in the region of the Platte. It is interesting to note that the Omahas have never in historic times lived north of the Pawnees, but always east of them, though we know that long ago they did live to the north.

These remarks on the movements of the Pawnees are, to be sure, very largely speculative, but speculation guided by the hints gathered from conversations with the older men. It is a surmise as to what may have been the wanderings of these people. If it were possible to talk with all the different tribes of the family, something more definite might be reached, but at this late day this seems hopeless. A study of the Lipans, and an investigation of their relationships with other southwestern tribes, might furnish us clues of the utmost importance in tracing the origin of the Pawnee family.

III. THE SKIDI.

Ranking high among the Pawnee bands, for their intelligence, energy and courage, stand the Skidi. Their past history is obscure, and we know little about it beyond the fact that it was different from that of the other bands. Although the relationship between them is perfectly well established, still both Pawnee and Skidi traditions agree that the two tribes were originally distinct, and that their first meeting took place long ago, but after the migration of the Pawnees to the northern country. We know, too, that the Arickaras were close neighbors and near relatives of the Skidi, and it is probable that they constituted a band, village, or division of that tribe.

It is believed by those who should be well informed, that the northward migration of the Rees took place not more than a century ago. One tradition of the separation runs in this way: The Skidi started out on a hunt, a part going ahead and the

others following later. The first party were killing
buffalo, when they were attacked by a large war
party of Sioux. These got between the two parties
of the Skidi, driving one of them back to the village,
while the other retreated northward. This retreat
continued until they had been driven some distance
up the Missouri River, where their enemies left them.
They remained there through the winter, and planted
their corn in the spring, nor did they apparently for
some time make any attempt to rejoin their tribe.
After some years, however, the two bands came
together on the Loup, and for a time lived together.
The Rees even went further south, to the neighborhood of the Wichita Mountains, where the Pawnees
at that time were living, but soon afterward they
went north again, and rejoined the Skidi on the
Loup, and lived near them there, and on the Platte
near Scott's Bluffs. It was not long, however, before a disagreement arose between the Rees and the
Skidi, and the Rees again moved off north. It is
probable that this quarrel may have originated in
the fact that the Rees wished to make war on the
whites, but there is some reason to believe that there
was also jealousy about the head chieftainship of the
two bands.

The testimony of men still living indicates that about one hundred years ago some of the Skidi lived on the Mississippi River, near the present site of St. Louis, and it is said that it was only the coming in of the white settlers in considerable numbers that caused them to move further westward. I am inclined to regard this location as only a temporary one, and to believe that their real home, prior to this, had been to the west, on the Platte and Loup rivers.

It is, of course, impossible to fix, even approximately, the time when the Pawnees and the Skidi came together, but it probably was soon after the Pawnees had settled on the Republican in their northward migration. It is said that their first meeting was friendly, and that they made a treaty, and smoked together. But no peace between two such warlike tribes could last very long, and there were frequent collisions and disagreements. There was a sharp rivalry between the Chau-i and the Skidi, and their disputes finally culminated in an unprovoked attack by the Skidi upon some Pawnees, while they were hunting buffalo, in which about one hundred of the latter were killed. The Pawnees made ready to avenge this injury, and marshaled all their forces. They made a night march to the vicinity of the Skidi village, which is said to have been on the north side of the Loup, distant from their own only about twenty miles, and just at daylight sent out about one hundred warriors, all mounted on dark colored horses, to decoy the Skidi from the village. These men, lying down on their horses, and covering themselves with their robes, represented buffalo, and rode over the hill in sight of the Skidi village. The ruse was successful. The Skidi at once started out to kill the buffalo, leaving their village unprotected. The disguised warriors fled, leading the Skidi further away, while the Pawnees who were in reserve rushed into the defenseless village, and captured it, almost without striking a blow. They took all the inhabitants back with them to their own village. The Skidi were forced to sue for peace; and for their breach of faith were heavily fined by the victorious Pawnees. They were incorporated into the tribe, and since that time have lived as a part of the Pawnee nation. This event was probably the culminating point of a series of petty fights and skirmishes, which must have been annoying to the Pawnees. This fighting went on within the memory of men now living, though there are but few who are old enough to remember it.

Curly Chief, who is about 65 years old, can remember a man who took part in these wars, and whose name was "The-Skidi-wounded-him-in-the-leg." Bear Chief, a very old and decrepit Skidi, and Secret Pipe Chief, an old Chau-i, have both told me that they can remember one or more fights between the Skidi and the other bands.

A rather interesting evidence of the feeling once existing between the Skidi and the other bands, and even now surviving among some of the oldest men, is the statement by Bear Chief that the three other bands were known as "Big Shields," the implication being that as they hid themselves behind these big shields they were not so brave as those who used smaller ones. The existence of such a feeling at the present day indicates that the final conquest of the Skidi and their incorporation into the Pawnee tribe took place not very long ago.

Mr. Dunbar sums up the traditions of the meeting of the tribes, their wars and subsequent union, in the following language: "The historic basis of this may be somewhat as follows: In the migration of the Pawnees from the south, the Skidi preceded the other bands perhaps by nearly a century. With them were the Arickaras. These two bands to-

gether possessed themselves of the region of the
Loup. When the other bands arrived they were
regarded as intruders, and hence arose open hostilities. The result of the struggle was that the two
bands were forced to admit the new comers, and aid
in reducing the surrounding territory. Subsequently
the Arickaras seem to have wandered, or more probably, to have been driven from the confederacy, and
to have passed up the Missouri. Later the Skidi, in
consequence of some real or fancied provocation,
attempted to retrieve their losses, but were sorely
punished, and henceforth obliged to content themselves with a subordinate position in the tribe."

It is said that in the olden time the Skidi were
very powerful. The tribe was made up of four
bands or villages, each of which numbered 5,000
people, or 20,000 for the whole tribe. This estimate,
which is founded merely on the statements of old
men now living, is probably excessive. There is no
doubt, however, that they were a large and powerful tribe, while their warlike habits and fierce natures
caused them to be feared and hated by all their
neighbors.

The four divisions of the Skidi tribe exist now
only in name, and the origin of these names is

almost forgotten. As the result of much effort and inquiry, I have secured the following list:

Names of the Skidi Bands.

1. *Tuhk-pah-huks-taht* — Pumpkin vine village. This name is said to have come from the fact that once, after planting time, this band went off on the summer hunt, and while they were away, the pumpkin vines grew so luxuriantly that they climbed up over the lodges, covering and hiding them.

2. *Skidi rah'ru*—Wolves in the pools (of water). The name originated in this way: Long ago one band of the Skidi were camped on the Loup River. It was winter, and the buffalo came to them in great numbers. They killed many and prepared great quantities of dried meat. The buffalo kept coming, and at length they had so much meat that they had room for no more. When they could no longer store dried meat, they stopped taking the flesh of the buffalo and took only the hides. The buffalo continued to come and to cross the river just below the camp, and the men on foot would chase the buffalo on the ice, where the great animals would slip and sprawl, so that the Skidi could run up

close, and stab them.   They would skin them there
and leave the carcasses on the ice.   From far and
near great numbers of wolves gathered to feed on
the carcasses, and as it was toward spring, and the
weather was growing milder, the ice began to melt
on top, and little pools of water stood on it.   About
this time, there came to this village a Skidi from
another band who were half starving, for they could
find no buffalo at all.   When the man saw that this
village had so much meat, he wondered at the
plenty, and asked how it was.   They took him out
from the village down to where the dead buffalo lay
on the ice, and pointed them out to him, and he saw
the wolves standing in the water and feeding on the
carcasses.   Then they took him back to the village,
gave him all the dried meat he could carry, and sent
him away to his home, heavily loaded.   When he
reached his own village he told the people there
how those in the other camp had plenty, and when
they asked him where it was, he told them, and said
that it was *Skidi rah'ru*—where the wolves stand in
the pools of water.

3. *Tuh-wa-hok'-a-sha*—Village on a ridge.   *Tuh*
—village, *wa*—the central roach on the head of a
man whose hair has been shaved on both sides, *hok'-*

a-sha—curving over. This village was on a ridge, reaching over on both sides of it.

4. *Tu-hi'ts-pi-yet*—Village on a point or peninsula. *Tuh*—village, camp, or band; *hits-pi-yu*—a point.

There are yet to be seen on the Loup Fork, in Nebraska, innumerable remains of Skidi villages, some of which are very ancient.

IV. NAME AND EMBLEM.

It is probable that the name Pawnee, as Mr. Dunbar has remarked, is an abbreviated form of the word *pa-ri'-ki*, which means a horn, and referred to the peculiar erect scalp lock which may once have been worn by this tribe. As Mr. Dunbar says, the name probably once embraced the Pawnee Picts or Wichitas, among whom this fashion of wearing the hair seems to have persisted long after it had been abandoned by the Pawnees. The same writer gives the name Arickara as from "*ŭr'-ik-i*, a horn; with a verbal or plural suffix, being thus simply a later and exact equivalent of *Pa'-ni* itself."

The name Pawnee Picts, so commonly applied to the Wichitas, appears to mean Pawnee Picked, or tattooed Pawnees; and refers to the markings upon the faces and breasts of these people, which are picked in with a sharp instrument. The northern Indians speak of the Pawnees as *Pa-na'-na*, while the southern tribes call them *Pi-ta'-da*, and the Dakotas call the Arickaras *Pa-da'-ni*. All these appear to be merely attempts to reproduce the name by which the Pawnees call themselve, *Pa'-ni*.

The English names of the four bands of the Pawnees are, as has been already stated, for the Skidi, the Wolf; for the Chau-i, the Grand; for the Kit-ke-hahk'-i, the Republican, and for the Pita-hau-erat, the Tapaje, Pawnees.

An old French trader, who has known these people for many years, states that the Skidi are called Wolf Pawnees from the river Loup, on which they lived; that Grand is an abbreviation for *Grandpas*, because the Chau-i were mostly tall men and took long steps; that the Kit-ke-hahk'-i were called Republican from the river of that name, and the Pita-hau-erat *Tapaje* (Fr. noisy), because they are noisy and restless, and are continually moving about from place to place. This explanation of these English names is not altogether satisfactory. Mr. Dunbar informs me that he believes that the Chau-i were called Grand from the appellation given them by the

Spaniards, who called them *Los Grandes*, referring to their physical stature.

In the chapter on the Skidi the names of the four bands of that tribe have been given, and their origin and derivation. The other tribes were divided into bands, or gentes, but these divisions have almost been forgotton. Of the Chau-i there is now said to be only one band; of the Kit-ke-hahk'-i three; the Great Kit-ke-hahk'-i, Little Kit-ke-hahk'-i, and Black-head Kit-ke-hahk'-i; while of the Pita-hau-erat there were two bands, the Pita-hau-erat proper and the Ka-wa-ra'-kish. This last-named division appears to have had some customs peculiar to itself, and quite different from anything known to the other Pawnees.

The Pawnees call the Wichitas and the other related southern tribes *Kiri-kur'uks*—Bear's-eyes. The reason for this appellation is obscure. The only explanation of it that I have been able to obtain, is that when the Pawnees first saw the Wichitas they thought they had eyes like a bear. As Mr. Dunbar has suggested to me, the allusion may have been to the ring sometimes painted or tattooed about the eyes of the Wichitas.

It is generally supposed that an Indian receives his personal name from some peculiarly memorable act that he has performed, or from some incident that has happened to him. This is not now commonly the case in the tribes with which I am best acquainted. Personal names formerly originated in this way among the Indians, but at the present day I question much if they are often given for such reasons. Most of the names borne by the warriors have been long known in the tribe, and I believe the coining of new names to fit a special set of circumstances to be now quite unusual. Children were named soon after they were born, and retained their childish names until well grown. *Ta'-ka*—white, was a common boy's name, as was *Ka-tit*—black; *Ki-ri'ki*—bright eyes, was often given to little girls. Nicknames referring to personal peculiarities were common.

Here is a list which will give some notion of the general character of the Pawnee names: Lucky Hawk, Good Fox, Turn-your-robe-hair-out, Chief of Men, Pipe Chief, Lone Chief, Leader, Brave Chief, Leading Fox, Still Hawk, Hunting Chief, Yellow Fox, Charging-the-camp, Angry Chief, Little Warrior, Good Bear, Eagle Chief, Sun Chief, White Horse, He-gives-away-many-horses-and-others-ride-them, Riding-up, Good Sky, Walking Bear, Proud

Eagle, Seven Stars, Sitting Bull, Big Mountain, Fancy Horse, Fox Chief, Good Sun, Curly Hair, Blue Hawk, Mad Wolf, White Elk, Young Hawk, War Chief, Good Chief, Curly Chief, Sitting Eagle, Running Eagle, Mad Bear, Walking Sun, See-the-eagle-flying, etc.

Mr. Dunbar states that "the tribal mark of the Pawnees in their pictographic or historic painting was the scalp lock dressed to stand nearly erect, or curving slightly backward something like a horn." I have never met a Pawnee who knew of this manner of dressing the hair in his own tribe, but all unite in stating that the Wichitas used to wear the lock in this manner. If this is the case, no doubt in ancient times it was common to the Pawnees as well, but with them it has become obsolete, and is now forgotten.

In books the sign for "Pawnee" is sometimes given as the forefinger of the right hand held at the back of the crown of the head, and pointing upward to represent this erect scalp lock, but I conceive that this sign is really that of the Pawnee Picts or Wichitas, who have been so constantly confused with the true or northern Pawnees.

The only sign for "Pawnee" that I have ever seen

employed among Indians in the West is that for
"wolf," which is the name under which the Pawnees
are, or at least were formerly, known to most other
tribes.   This sign is made in two ways, (1) by hold-

SIGN FOR PAWNEE.

ing the two hands, palm forward, the first and middle
fingers extended close together upward and a little
forward, thumb and other fingers closed, close to
the head, about opposite the temple; (2) the right
hand alone may be held palm forward at the height
of, and just in front of, the shoulder, the first and
middle fingers extended, separated and pointing
upward, the thumb and others closed; the hand is
then moved forward and downward from the wrist,

so that the extended fingers point almost to the front. Both these signs represent the pricked ears of a wolf, and, so far as my experience goes, are universally understood to mean " Pawnee." The one last described is now much the more common of the two. The first of these signs is shown in the frontispiece, which is copied from an engraving in the First Annual Report of the Bureau of Ethnology.

The Pawnees have always been called by their neighbors to the south "Wolves." It has been suggested that this term was applied to them by their enemies in contempt, but there seems no reason for believing this to have been the case, since it may be doubted that an Indian feels contempt for a wolf any more than he does for a fox, a rabbit, or an elk.

An Indian going into an enemy's country is often called a wolf, and the sign for " a scout " is made up of the signs " wolf " and " look." The Pawnees were most adroit scouts, warriors and stealers of horses; and it seems perfectly natural that they should have received from the neighboring tribes, who had such frequent evidences of their skill as scouts and horse takers, the appellation Wolf. The Pawnees themselves believe that the term was applied to them because of their great endurance, as well as of their skill in imitating wolves so as to escape detection by the enemy either by day or night. The Cheyennes, Wichitas and Comanches all testify that they call the Pawnees Wolves because they prowl like wolves; because, too, they have the endurance of wolves, and can travel all day, and dance all night, and can make long journeys, living on the carcasses they find on their way, or on no food at all.

The Pawnees, when they went on the warpath, were always prepared to simulate wolves. This was one of their regular practices, and this no doubt was one reason for their remarkable success in taking horses, for it enabled them to escape observation and to reconnoitre at close quarters without danger of discovery. Wolves on the prairie were too common to excite remark, and at night they would approach close to the Indian camps, and often venture into them. The Pawnee who was disguised as a wolf could trot up close to the village of his enemy, see where the horses were tied, and perhaps even hear what was being said, and lay his plans accordingly. The Pawnee starting off on the warpath usually carried a robe made of wolf skins, or in later times a white blanket or a white sheet; and, at night, wrapping himself in this, and getting down on his hands and knees, he walked or trotted here and there like a wolf, having thus transformed himself into a common object of the landscape. This disguise was employed by day as well. To escape observation when traveling in daylight, the Pawnee war party always chose the ravines and lower ground to march in. Sometimes, especially in a country where there was danger of coming unexpectedly on the enemy, it was important that a reconnoissance should be made from some commanding point. A man walking up to the top of a hill might be seen, and recognized as a suspicious object, a long way off, but no one would look a second time at a wolf. While the party remained hidden in some ravine or hollow, therefore, the man who was to ascend the hill would put his white robe over him and gallop to the top on all fours, and would sit there on his haunches looking all over the country, and any one at a distance who saw him, would take him for a wolf. It was acknowledged on all hands that the Pawnees could imitate wolves best. In one of the stories already given, an instance is mentioned in which two Pawnees in the United States service made use of this device to recover captured animals.

The name "Wolf," as given to the Pawnees, is probably merely a translation of the word *Skiri'ki*, meaning wolf, from which the name of the Skidi band may be supposed to be derived. Mr. Dunbar says: "The emblem probably originated from the Skidi band. They being in advance of the other bands in the northern migration, became known to the tribes about them as wolves; and as the other bands arrived the sign was naturally made to include them also, and in this enlarged use was at length accepted by the Pawnees themselves."

BUFFALO HORN LADLE AND SPOON.

PAWNEE CUSTOMS.

PAWNEE history goes back to a time when the tribe knew nothing of horses. In those early days they went on foot, and depended for animal food on their bows and arrows. At that time their bows did not differ from those recently in use, but the heads of their arrows were made of stone, and their knives were of flint. With this simple equipment they set out on the hunt.

Choosing a still day, they would surround a small bunch of buffalo, stretching out in a long line whose extremities would gradually draw together, as the hunters, perhaps disguised as wolves, stole from hill to hill, around the unconscious prey. When the circle was complete, some one man would shout and startle the buffalo, and then as they turned to run, another man would show himself before them, and call out, and turn them, and whichever way they ran, some one would appear before them, and turn them back. The buffalo, becoming each moment more frightened, would run now this way, now that, and gradually the Pawnees would close in on them, but would still keep the buffalo from breaking through the line by yelling, and by tossing their robes in the air. As the prey became more and more terror-stricken and confused, they would run here and there, and round and round within the ring of men; and as they grew more tired, the men would close in on them still more, and first one, and then another, would shoot an arrow, until at last the arrows were flying fast, and some of the great beasts were down, and others were staggering along with the blood pouring from their mouths; and soon the buffalo were so worn out that they could run no longer, and it was an easy matter for the Indians to dispatch them. Even those which were only slightly wounded were secured, for it is said that when the animals were hit by the arrows, even if it were only in the leg, they would soon swell up and die. This state-ment refers to a belief, which I find quite widespread among plains Indians, that the ancient stone arrow heads were peculiarly deadly, and possessed this property, that even a slight touch with them made a wound which was likely to be fatal. The Blackfeet Indians have often told me the same thing about the stone arrow heads which they used in early times.

Game, which inhabited the underbrush or the forest, was captured by a method similar to that employed to secure the buffalo. If the Pawnees discovered that deer or elk were in a piece of timber, they would surround it, and then alarm the game, and keep them from breaking through the line of men. The animals, frightened and confused, would run round and round in a circle until exhausted, when the Pawnees would close in, and kill them with their arrows.

It must be remembered in this connection, that in those days game animals were enormously abundant and comparatively tame, and also, that the Pawnees, from the necessities of their lives, were tremendously active, very swift runners, and as tireless as the wolves from which they took their name. Their endurance was something astonishing. In their long journeys on the warpath they often traversed on foot six or eight hundred miles of country, carrying, during a part of the time, very heavy loads. Instances are not uncommon where runners have traveled one hundred miles in twenty-four hours. I myself know of a case where two men ran over seventy miles in eleven hours. We may imagine that in the old days when the Pawnees made all their journeys on foot, and were thus constantly exercising, their speed and activity were greater, and their powers of endurance still more remarkable.

Although their ancient arrows were usually headed with flint, they sometimes used bone or the sharpened tine of a deer's horn. No one now alive can remember when these were in common use, but there are men who have heard their fathers and their grandfathers tell of them, and who say that these arrows were good for war and for the chase. "You could drive them through a thick shield," said Bear Chief. As soon as they began to trade with the whites, arrow heads of sheet-iron came into use. They say that, so long as the Pawnees used flint for making arrow heads, they used to find plenty of these stones lying on the prairie, but that when the whites brought them iron, *Ti-ra'-wa* said to himself, "The Pawnees no longer need these flint stones; I will make no more of them." This shows an odd confusion of ideas, for, of course, the reason that they did not find the stones was that they no longer looked for them, their use having been abandoned.

Although these stone arrow heads must have passed out of general use toward the end of the last century, yet some of them were preserved much later, and it is possible that there may even now be some among the Pawnees, hidden away in the sacred bundles. After they ceased to be used for general purposes, they took on a sacred character and were employed to slay the sacrifices; among the Skidi to kill the captive, and in the Lower Village tribes the buffalo and deer, for sacrifice. There was a time when it was deemed essential that the animals to be sacrificed to *Ti-ra'-wa*, should be killed by one of these ancient—and so sacred—arrows.

In the early days the Pawnees did not depend for food wholly—perhaps not even largely—on the flesh of the animals which they killed by hunting. They have always been an agricultural people, cultivating the ground, and raising corn, beans, pumpkins, and squashes. They also dug up many edible roots, and collected and dried various berries and other fruits. Besides this, they captured birds and smaller mammals by means of snares and traps. It is said that before they obtained horses, they killed but few buffalo, only enough to provide themselves with clothing and with sinew for sewing, backing bows, and other uses.

The Pawnees aver that they have cultivated the corn as far back as they can remember. They say also that this is their corn, that it is not the corn of the whites, but is different from it—which is true— and that they did not get it from the whites. It is their own. On this they insist strenuously. I have found it impossible to obtain any clue as to where the corn came from or how they obtained it. To all inquiries on this point, they reply that it must have been "handed down from above;" that it was given them by "the Ruler." Various stories are told about it, but none of them are very pointed or satisfactory.

They call the corn *a-ti'ra*, "mother." It has a sacred character, and plays an important part in many of their religious ceremonies. This name which they give it, the mother corn, no doubt refers to the fact that it nourishes and supports them; that by it they are made strong. I have also heard it said that it is called mother because it produces others; it has young ones like a woman; "you put it in the ground and it brings forth others."

The Pawnees cultivated their fields with hoes

made from the shoulder blade of the buffalo. Taking the ligament from the back of a buffalo's neck, they lashed a stick firmly to the articulation of the shoulder blade, nearly at right angles to the plane of the bone and to its length. Then, dipping the joint into hot water, the ligament would shrink, and bind the bone and the handle together as firmly as iron.

Years ago, on the sites of abandoned Pawnee villages, on the Loup, Fork and on the Platte, fragments of pottery used to be found among the débris of the fallen lodges. The manufacture of this pottery was no doubt abandoned long ago, and has probably not been practiced to any considerable extent since they met the whites. A man about fifty years of age stated to me that he had never seen these pots in use, but that his grandmother had told him that in her days they made and used them. He said that they were accustomed to smooth off the end of a tree for a mould. A hot fire was then built, in which stones were roasted, which were afterward pounded into fine powder or sand. This pounded stone they mixed with fine clay, and when the material was of the proper consistency, they smeared it over the rounded mould, which was perhaps first

well greased with buffalo tallow.   After the clay had
been made of even thickness throughout, and smooth
on the outside, they took a small, sharp stone, and
made marks on the outside to ornament it.   When
the material was sufficiently dry, they lifted it from
the mould and burned it in the fire, and while it was
baking, "put corn in the pot and stirred it about, and
this made it hard as iron."   This may mean that it
gave the pot a glaze on the inside.   In these pots
they boiled food of all kinds.   Mr. Dunbar informs
me that these pots were also made in later times
within a frame-work of willow twigs.   The clay,
made very stiff, was smeared on this frame, the inside
being repeatedly smoothed with the moistened hand,
and but little attention being given to the appearance
of the outside.   After they had been sun-dried, such
pots were baked without removing the frame, which
burned away in the fire, leaving the marks of the
twigs visible on the outside of the pot.

Corn was, and is still, crushed in wooden mortars,
hollowed out by fire, and the pestle is also of wood,
about four feet long, with an enlargement at the
upper end to give added weight.

Dishes and bowls were made of wood, or of large
gourds; spoons and ladles were fashioned from the

horns of the buffalo; mats were woven of rushes, ropes of buffalo hair, and lariats of rawhide.

Fire in the early days was obtained by means of fire sticks, the point of one being twirled on a hollow in the other, until the charred dust at first smoked and then ignited. It is said that sometimes it would take four men to make a fire, one relieving another as they grew tired. It was hard, slow work, but sometimes one man, if he was stout, could make a fire alone. The use of fire sticks on war parties has continued till within a short time, perhaps within twenty years.

As their clothing was manufactured wholly from skins, sewing occupied a considerable part of the time of the women. This was done by means of a bone needle—often the metacarpal or metatarsal bone supporting the accessory hooflets on the deer —and a thread twisted of sinews. Such sewing was extremely durable.

The other implements and utensils of the Pawnees did not differ materially from those of other plains Indians.

It is a long time since they first began to use articles and implements manufactured by the whites. Curly Chief related to me the story of what was perhaps the first official visits from the whites ever received by the Pawnees. He said:

"I heard that long ago there was a time when there were no people in this country except Indians. After that the people began to hear of men that had white skins; they had been seen far to the east. Before I was born they came out to our country and visited us. The man who came was from the Government. He wanted to make a treaty with us, and to give us presents, blankets and guns, and flint and steel, and knives.

"The Head Chief told him that we needed none of these things. He said, 'We have our buffalo and our corn. These things the Ruler gave to us, and they are all that we need. See this robe. This keeps me warm in winter. I need no blanket.'

"The white men had with them some cattle, and the Pawnee Chief said, 'Lead out a heifer here on the prairie.' They led her out, and the Chief, stepping up to her, shot her through behind the shoulder with his arrow, and she fell down and died. Then the Chief said, 'Will not my arrow kill? I do not need your guns.' Then he took his stone knife and skinned the heifer, and cut off a piece of fat meat. When he had done this he said, 'Why should I take your knives? The Ruler has given me something to cut with.'

"Then taking the fire sticks, he kindled a fire to roast the meat, and while it was cooking, he spoke again and said, 'You see, my brother, that the Ruler has given us all that we need; the buffalo for food and clothing; the corn to eat with our dried meat; bows, arrows, knives and hoes; all the implements which we need for killing meat, or for cultivating the ground. Now go back to the country from whence you came. We do not want your presents, and we do not want you to come into our country.'

"Afterward, however, a treaty was made. The first treaties were not to purchase land. The Government made presents, and bought the right to pass through the country. Roads were made up the Republican, the Platte and the Solomon rivers."

II. EVERY-DAY LIFE.

In these hasty remarks upon the ways of the Pawnees, which are in fact no more than a series of rough notes supplementary to Mr. Dunbar's fuller history of this people, I shall not attempt to give any general account of their habits. These can be learned by reference to the papers, so often quoted. My object is to give a picture of the Pawnee ways of thought rather than of their material life.

Their government was semi-republican. They were ruled by a head chief, in later times always the head chief of the Chau-i band; and this title was hereditary, but the chief, if he had not the requisite strength of character, might lose all his influence, and his position be practically, though not in name, held by a sub-chief or even warrior of his own or another band. As has been well said, "The office itself was hereditary, but authority could be gained only by acknowledged personal accomplishments." Each band was ruled as to its own affairs by four chiefs—a head chief, second chief, third and fourth chiefs—but often some warrior who held no office, and bore no title, might wield more power and influence than any of these. In minor matters, the chief gave his orders without consultation with any one, but more important affairs were usually discussed in council by chiefs, head men and warriors, and the opinion of the assemblage prevailed, even if it were opposed to the opinion of the chief. Among the Pawnees, as elsewhere, a man's personal character determined the position he should occupy and the influence he should wield. Bravery, wisdom, and personal popularity were the important factors in acquiring and retaining influence and authority.

Mr. Dunbar alludes to one matter which is little understood in general; that is the existence among the Pawnees of a class of servants. These were for the most part young men, or boys growing up, who had not yet acquired any special standing. They lived in the family of men of position and influence, from whom they received support, and for whom they performed many offices, which were almost menial. The relation which they held to the head of the family was not altogether unlike that of a page or a squire to his knight in mediæval times. These young men drove in and saddled the horses, made the fires, ran errands, and carried messages for the leaders whom they followed. The same menial offices were often performed by other, older men, who were too lazy and too worthless to make positions for themselves, and who were willing to continue to serve for their support. This relation of servant persisted even among the Pawnee Scouts after their enlistment, and, while among the privates in this body all were of course equal in name, it was yet common, as the camp prepared to start in the morning, to see the younger men saddling up the horses, and performing other duties for the chiefs and the proved warriors, whose military standing was no higher than those who were serving them.

The dress of the old-time Pawnee male consisted of a breech clout, leggings, fringed at the side, and reaching from ankle to thigh, and moccasins. Over all this, when the weather demanded it, was worn the buffalo robe, the hair side being turned in. The dress of the women consisted of a sort of sleeveless shirt, and a skirt of dressed buffalo cow skin, reaching to below the knee, with leggings of cloth or buckskin, laced above the knee, and moccasins. They also wore the robe or blanket. No head covering was used, though in war and on great occasions the men wore bonnets or chaplets of eagle feathers, and sometimes both men and women wove wreaths out of cottonwood or willow twigs, with the green leaves left on, to shade their eyes from the fierce rays of the sun. The children were at first scantily clad. The boy, after he was released from his board, went naked, except perhaps for a string of beads around his neck, until he was ten or twelve years old, though usually he assumed the breech clout before that age. Girls were clad in a shirt or smock almost as soon as they could walk.

At the present time but few of the Pawnees wear their hair cut in the ancient fashion, but twenty years ago a large proportion of the older men had the whole head shaved, except a narrow roach which ran from the forehead to the back of the head. This roach, on which the hair was usually left less than an inch long, was sometimes stiffened at the sides with grease and paint to make it stand up well. From this roach the scalp lock fell back in its natural position. At the present day many of the men cut their hair short, like the whites. The women usually wore their hair in two braids, one on each side, falling behind the ears, and the younger ones were careful in tending it.

All hair upon the face and on other parts of the body was usually plucked out, but I have seen a Pawnee with a heavy beard under his chin.

Paint was freely used in ornamentation, especially on the face and breast. Black, as is the case with most tribes, was the color for war. Red, white and yellow, were used merely for ornament.

As already indicated, the arms of the Pawnees were the bow and arrow, the lance, the club, and the hatchet. The bow was almost invariably made of the *bois d'arc*, and was backed with sinew, and had a string of the same material. The arrows were made with the greatest labor, care and exactness, and those manufactured by each individual were so marked that they could at once be distinguished from those of every other maker. It is well known that the arrows of each Indian tribe differed from those of every other tribe, but besides this, each man's arrows bore his private mark. The manufacture of the bow and arrows was a long, slow process, and after they had been completed they were carefully guarded and protected from injury. Although the Pawnees have long been accustomed to use firearms in war, yet the use of the bow and arrow in hunting persisted up to quite recent times, in fact up to the date of the disappearance of the buffalo. A reason for this is readily found in the fact that an arrow cost only time to manufacture, and the Indian has an abundance of time. For cartridges, or for powder and lead, he must pay money, or trade some of his possessions. An arrow, too, may be used over and over again, and may thus account for many head of game, whereas a cartridge can be used but once. In their secret war expeditions, too, the bow was a favorite weapon, because it was noiseless. An enemy found at a little distance from his camp, could be stealthily approached and silently shot down, without necessarily alarming persons in the neighborhood, when a rifle shot, ringing over the prairie and echoing among the bluffs, would call out every warrior in the village, to learn whence it came. I have been told, by warriors, that on their war parties, they left their rifles at home and carried only their bows, so that they might not be tempted by the sight of an enemy to fire a shot, which might bring themselves and their companions into danger.

The Pawnees were superb horsemen and owned many ponies. I can learn nothing definite as to when they first obtained these animals, nor from what source. A tradition exists, that up to the time of the tribe's advent into the northern country, their only beast of burden was the dog, which then carried their packs and hauled their *travois*. The story goes that the Pawnees obtained their first horses soon after their separation from the Wichitas. The three bands were traveling north together, when the scouts who had been sent ahead to overlook the country, hastened back and announced to the chiefs that they had discovered a camp of Indians. A council was at once held to determine whether they should attack this unknown village as enemies, or should approach them as friends. The majority declared for an attack, and it was so decided. Approaching under cover as near as possible, the horde of dusky footmen poured over the hills and down into the valley where stood the doomed village. The attack was sudden, fierce, and successful. They killed and captured many of the enemy, and took the camp, while the survivors fled in hopeless confusion. Among the plunder taken were a lot of horses; strange beasts then to the rude Pawnees, and at which they wondered greatly. A captive woman explained to the conquerors that these creatures were good to ride, and useful to pack on. Old men still tell, with a smile, of the ludicrous first attempts of the warriors to ride the horses. This occurrence is said to have taken place on the Smoky Hill River, in what is now Kansas, and the Indians from whom the horses were captured, are understood to have been Cheyennes.

The permanent habitations of the Pawnees were dirt or sod houses, often of very considerable size. The remains of the old medicine lodge of the Skidi, on the Loup, show it to have been two hundred and

COW SKIN LODGE.

ten feet in diameter. The lodges were circular in form, with walls seven or eight feet high, and the roof rose from these walls to the apex above the center of the lodge, where was the hole for the escape of smoke from the fire, which burned on the floor below. A covered passageway led to the entrance. Around the walls the inmates slept, the beds being partitioned off, and protected in front as well, by a curtain which might be a skin, or a mat woven of reeds or coarse grass. The cooking was all done over the fire in the middle of the lodge. Possessions were stowed away behind the beds, or hung up on the posts which supported the roof.

On their hunts or when traveling, the Pawnees used the ordinary cow skin lodge of the plains Indians. This was composed of neatly dressed buffalo hides, from which the hair had been removed, set up over a frame-work, made up, usually, of sixteen long slender poles. An opening at the top gave exit to the smoke; and wings, projecting at either side of the smoke hole, and so arranged that their positions could be changed by moving two additional poles on the outside of the lodge, served to regulate the draft, and keep the lodge free from smoke. The inmates slept close to the walls, and the fire, with the inevitable pot hanging over it, burned in the middle. These lodges were warm, and usually dry, and made good shelters. They were occupied for the greater part of the year, for the Pawnees, after the spring planting was fairly over, usually started at once on their summer hunt, from which they only returned in time to harvest their crops. At the beginning of winter, when the robes were at their best, they made the winter hunt, from which they did not return until toward spring. The planting over, they set out again on the hunt.

In their personal intercourse with each other, and with strangers, the Pawnees were kindly and accommodating. I have had little kindnesses unostentatiously done me by Pawnee men, such as I should never expect to receive from white persons not connected with me by ties of blood. In the village, the well-to-do gave freely to those who were poor, and all were very hospitable. They were a light-hearted, merry race, keenly alive to the ridiculous, and very fond of a joke. They were great chatterers, and had about them nothing of the supposed taciturnity of the Indian. Of modesty or delicacy in conversation, as we know it, they had none. Both sexes spoke freely to each other of matters which are never mentioned in civilized society, and much of their conversation, as well as many of their stories, could not well be printed.

III. A SUMMER HUNT.

It was in the month of July, 1872. The Pawnees were preparing to start on their semi-annual buffalo hunt, and only the last religious rites remained to be performed before the nation should leave the village for the buffalo range.

"*Eh, idadi, whoop,*" came from without the lodge; and as I replied, "*Ehya, whoop,*" the sturdy figure of *Le-ta-kats-ta'-ka* appeared in the doorway.

"*Lau, idad, tŭt-tū-ta-rik ti-rah-rēk*—Come, brother, they are going to dance," he said, and then he turned and went out.

I rose from the pile of robes on which I had been dozing, and, after rolling them up, strolled out after him. The village seemed deserted, but off toward the medicine lodge, which stood upon its outskirts, I could see a throng of Indians; and a low murmur of voices and of footsteps, the hum which always accompanies any large assemblage, was borne to my ears on the evening breeze. The ceremonies, which comprised the consecration of the buffalo staves and the buffalo dance, were about to begin. The great dirt lodge was crowded. I pushed my way through the throng of women and boys, who made up the outer circle of spectators, and soon found myself among the men, who made way for me, until I reached a position from which I could see all that was going on within the circle about which they stood.

For several days the priests and the doctors had been preparing for this solemn religious ceremonial. They had fasted long; earnest prayers had been made to *Ti-ra'-wa*, and sacrifices had been offered. Now the twelve buffalo skulls had been arranged on the ground in a half-circle, and near them stood the chiefs and doctors, reverently holding in their hands the buffalo staves and sacred bows and arrows, and other implements of the chase. For a little while they stood silent, with bowed heads, but presently one and then another began to murmur their petitions to *A-ti-us Ti-ra'-wa*, the Spirit Father. At first their voices were low and mumbling, but gradually they became more earnest and lifted their eyes toward heaven. It was impossible to distinguish what each one said, but now and then disjointed

sentences reached me. "Father, you are the Ruler
—We are poor—Take pity on us—Send us plenty of
buffalo, plenty of fat cows—Father, we are your
children—help the people—send us plenty of meat,
so that we may be strong, and our bodies may increase and our flesh grow hard—Father, you see us,
listen." As they prayed they moved their hands
backward and forward over the implements which
they held, and at length reverently deposited them
on the ground within the line of buffalo skulls, and
then stepped back, still continuing their prayers.

It was a touching sight to witness these men calling upon their God for help. All of them had passed
middle life, and some were gray-haired, blind and
tottering; but they prayed with a fervor and earnest-
ness that compelled respect. They threw their souls
into their prayers, and as a son might entreat his
earthly father for some great gift, so they plead with
Ti-ra'-wa. Their bodies quivered with emotion, and
great drops of sweat stood upon their brows. They
were thoroughly sincere.

After the last of the articles had been placed upon
the ground, their voices grew lower and at length
died away. A moment later a drum sounded, and a
dozen or twenty young warriors sprang into the cir-

cle and began the buffalo dance. This was kept up without intermission for three days, and as soon as it was over, the tribe moved out of the village on the hunt.

From the village on the Loup, we traveled southward; for in those days the region between the Platte and the Smoky rivers swarmed with buffalo. With the Pawnees were a few Poncas, Omahas and Otoes, so that there were about four thousand Indians in the camp. It was the summer hunt of the tribe. Twice each year the agent permitted them to visit the buffalo range. The meat which they killed and dried on these hunts, the corn and squashes which they grew on their farms, and the small annuities received from the Government, were all they had to subsist on from season to season. Thus the occasion was one of importance to the Indians. Perhaps only the older heads among them fully appreciated its economic interest; but for all it was a holiday time; a temporary escape from confinement. Life on the reservation was monotonous. There was nothing to do except to sit in the sun and smoke, and tell stories of the former glories of the nation; of successful fights with the Sioux and Cheyennes, and of horse stealing expeditions, from which the heroes had returned with great herds of ponies and much glory. Now, for a little while, they returned to the old free life of earlier years, when the land had been all their own, and they had wandered at will over the broad expanse of the rolling prairie. Now, for a time, it was as it had been before the cornfields of the white man had begun to dot their river bottoms, before the sound of his rifle had made wild their game, before the locomotive's whistle had shrieked through the still, hot summer air. Half a year's provision was now to be secured. The comfort—almost the existence—of the tribe for the next six months depended on the accumulation of an abundant supply of dried buffalo meat, and no precaution was omitted to make the hunt successful. It would not do to permit each individual to hunt independently. Indiscriminate buffalo running by six or eight hundred men scattered over the prairie, each one working for himself alone, would result in the killing of some few buffalo, but would terrify and drive away all the others in the neighborhood. This matter was too important to be trusted to chance. The hunting was systematized.

The government of the hunt was intrusted to the Pawnee soldiers. These were twenty-four warriors of mature age, not so old as to be unfitted for active work, yet with the fires of early youth somewhat tempered by years of experience; men whose judgment and discretion could at all times be relied on. These soldiers acted under the chiefs, but the practical guidance of the hunt was wholly in their hands. They determined the direction and length of each day's march, and the spot for camping. They selected the young men who should act as scouts, and arranged all the details of the approach and the charge when a herd of buffalo was discovered large enough to call for a general surround. All the men were under their control, and amenable to their discipline. They did not hesitate to exercise their authority, nor to severely punish any one who committed an act by which the success of the hunt might be imperilled.

The scouts sent out by the soldiers were chosen from among the younger men. They acted merely as spies, their office was to find the buffalo. They moved rapidly along, far in advance of the marching column, and from the tops of the highest hills carefully scanned the country before them in search of buffalo. If a herd was discerned, they were not to show themselves, nor in any way to alarm it. Having found the game, their duty was to observe its movement, learn where it was likely to be for the next few hours, and then to report as quickly as possible to the camp. The soldiers then determined what action should be taken. If the news was received late in the day, and the buffalo were at some distance, the camp would probably be moved as near as practicable to where the herd was feeding, and the chase would take place in the early morning. If, on the other hand, the scouts found the herd in the morning, the men would start off at once for the surround, leaving the women to follow, and make camp as near as possible to where the dead buffalo lay.

Day after day we traveled southward, crossing the Platte River, and then the Republican about due south of the present flourishing town of Kearney. South of the Platte a few scattering buffalo were found, but no large herds had been met with— nothing that called for a surround. At length we camped one night on the Beaver, a small affluent of the Republican, emptying into it from the south.

With the gray dawn of morning, the camp, as usual, is astir. By the time our little party have turned out of our blankets, some of the Indians have already finished eating, and are catching up their horses and preparing to ride off over the bluffs, leaving the squaws to take down the lodges, pack the ponies, and pursue the designated line of march. Before we are ready to "pull out," most of the ponies have been packed, and a long, irregular line of Indians is creeping across the level valley, and beginning to wind up the face of the bluffs. The procession moves slowly, proceeding at a walk. Most of those who remain with the column are on foot, the squaws leading the ponies, and many of the men, wrapped in their blankets, and with only their bows and arrows on their backs, walking briskly over the prairie, a little to one side. These last are the poorer Indians—those who have but few horses. They travel on foot, letting their horses run without burdens, so that they may be fresh and strong, whenever they shall be needed for running the buffalo.

Side by side, at the head of the column, walk eight men who carry the buffalo staves. These are slender spruce poles, like a short lodge-pole, wrapped with blue and red cloth, and elaborately ornamented with bead work, and with the feathers of hawks, and of the war eagle. These sticks are carried by men selected by the chiefs and doctors in private council, and are religiously guarded. Upon the care of these emblems, and the respect paid to them, depends, in a great measure, the success of the hunt. While borne before the moving column, no one is permitted to cross the line of march in front of them.

Close behind the staff bearers follow a number of the principal men of the tribe; the head chief, old *Pi'ta Le-shar*, and a dozen or fifteen sub-chiefs or head men, all mounted on superb horses. Behind them comes the camp at large, a fantastically mingled multitude, marching without any appearance of order. Here most of the individuals are women, young girls and children, for the men who accompany the camp usually march singly, or by twos and threes, a little apart from the mob. Most of those rich enough in horses to be able to ride at all times, are scattered over the prairie for miles in every direction, picking up the small bands of buffalo, which have been passed by the scouts as not large enough to call for a general surround. The hunters are careful, however, not to follow too close upon the advance line, whose movements they can readily observe upon the bare bluffs far ahead of them.

At the time of which I am writing, the Pawnees

had no wagons, all their possessions being transported on pack horses. The Indian pack pony is apt to be old and sedate, requiring no special guidance nor control. A strip of rawhide, knotted about the lower jaw, serves as a bridle, and is either tied up to the saddle or held in the rider's hand. In packing the animals a bundle of lodge-poles is tied on either side of the saddle, one end projecting forward toward the horse's head, the other dragging on the ground behind. This is the *travois*. Cross poles are often tied between these two dragging bundles, and on these are carried packages of meat and robes. Often, too, on a robe stretched between them, a sick or wounded Indian, unable to ride, is transported. The lodge-poles having been fastened to the saddle, the lodge is folded up and placed on it between them, and blankets, robes, and other articles are piled on top of this, until the horse has on its back what appears to be about as much as it can carry. The pack is then lashed firmly in position, and pots, buckets and other utensils are tied about it wherever there is room.

On top of the load so arranged one or two women, or three or four children, clamber and settle themselves comfortably there, and the old horse is turned loose. Each rider carries in her hand a whip, with which she strikes the horse at every step, not cruelly at all, but just from force of habit. If the pack is low, so that her feet reach down to the animal's sides, she keeps up also a constant drumming on his ribs with her heels. The old horse pays not the slightest attention to any of these demonstrations of impatience, but plods steadily along at a quiet walk, his eyes half closed and his ears nodding at each step. If the riders are women, each one holds a child or two in her arms, or on her back, or perhaps the baby board is hung over the end of a lodge-pole, and swings free. If the living load consists of children, they have in their arms a lot of puppies; for puppies occupy with relation to the small Indian girls the place which dolls hold among the white children. Many of the pack animals are mares with young colts, and these last, instead of following quietly at their mothers' heels, range here and there, sometimes before and sometimes behind, their dams. They are thus constantly getting lost in the crowd, and then they charge backward and forward in wild affright, neighing shrilly, until they have again found their proper place in the line of march. Many of the yearling colts have very small and light packs tied on their backs, while the two-year-olds are often ridden by the tiniest of Indian boys, who are now giving them their first lesson in weight-carrying. Loose horses of all ages roam about at will, and their continual cries mingle with the barking of dogs, the calls of women and the yells of boys, and make an unceasing noise.

The boys are boiling over with animal spirits, and, like their civilized brothers of the same age, are continually running about, chasing each other, wrestling, shooting arrows and playing games, of which the familiar stick game seems the favorite.

Whenever the column draws near any cover, which may shelter game, such as a few bushes in a ravine, or the fringe of low willows along some little watercourse, the younger men and boys scatter out and surround it. They beat it in the most thorough manner, and any game which it contains is driven out on the prairie, surrounded and killed. The appearance even of a jackass rabbit throws the boys into a fever of excitement, and causes them to shriek and yell as if in a frenzy.

All the morning I rode with the Indians, either at the head of the column, chatting as best I could with *Pi'ta Le-shar* and other chiefs, or falling back and

riding among the women and children, whom I never
tired of watching.   Frequently during the day I saw
at a distance, on the prairie, small bunches of buffalo
in full flight, hotly pursued by dark-skinned riders,
and occasionally two or three men would ride up to
the marching columns with heavy loads of freshly-
killed meat.   The quick-heaving, wet flanks of the
ponies told a story of sharp, rapid chases, and their
tossing heads and eager, excited looks showed how
much interest they took in the hunt.

The report of firearms was seldom heard.   Most
of the Indians hunted with the primitive weapon of
their forefathers—the bow and arrow.   For buffalo
running an arrow is nearly as effective as lead.   The
power of the bow in expert hands is tremendous.
Riding within half a dozen yards of the victim's side,
the practiced bowman will drive the dart so far
through the body of the buffalo that its shaft
may project a foot or more from the opposite side—
sometimes indeed may pass quite through.   Besides,
the bow can be used very rapidly and accurately.   I
have seen an Indian take a sheaf of six arrows in his
hand, and discharge them at a mark more rapidly
and with more certainty of hitting his target than I
could fire the six barrels of a revolver.

It was nearly noon, and I was riding along at the head of the column. I had but one horse, and did not care to wear him out by chasing around over the prairie, preferring to save him for some great effort. We were traveling along a smooth divide between two sets of ravines, which ran off, one to the east and the other to the west. *Pi'ta Le-shar* had just informed me by signs that we should make camp about two miles further on, by a stream whose course we could trace from where we then were. Suddenly, without the slightest warning, the huge dark bodies of half a dozen buffalo sprang into view, rising out of a ravine on our left not a hundred yards distant. When they saw the multitude before them, they stopped and stared at us.

They were too close for me to resist the temptation to pursue. As I lifted the reins from my pony's neck and bent forward, the little animal sprang into a sharp gallop toward the game, and as he did so I saw half a dozen Indians shoot out from the column and follow me. The buffalo wheeled, and in an instant were out of sight, but when I reached the edge of the bank down which they had plunged, I could see through the cloud of dust, which they left behind them, their uncouth forms dashing down the ravine.

My nimble pony, as eager for the race as his rider, hurled himself down the steep pitch, and sped along the narrow broken bed of the gully. I could feel that sometimes he would lengthen his stride to leap wide ditches, where the water from some side ravine had cut away the ground, but I never knew of these until they were passed. My eyes were fixed on the fleeing herd; my ears were intent on the pursuing horsemen. Close behind me I could hear the quick pounding of many hoofs, and could feel that one of the horses, nearer than the rest, was steadily drawing up to me—but I was gaining on the buffalo. Already the confused rumble of their hoof-beats almost drowned those of the horses behind me, and the air was full of the dust and small pebbles thrown up by their hurrying feet. But they were still ahead of me, and the gulch was so narrow that I could not shoot. The leading horseman drew nearer and nearer, and was now almost at my side. I could see the lean head and long, slim neck of his pony under my right arm, and could hear the rider speak to his horse and urge him forward in the race. My horse did his best, but the other had the most speed. He shot by me, and a moment later was alongside the last buffalo.

As he passed me the young Indian made a laugh-

ing gesture of triumph, slipped an arrow on his bow-
string, and drew it to its head; but just as he was
about to let it fly, his horse, which was but a colt,
took fright at the huge animal which it had over-
taken, and shied violently to the right, almost un-
seating its rider. At the same moment the buffalo
swerved a little to the left, and thus lost a few feet.
Truly, the race is not always to the swift. As I
passed the Indian, I could not restrain a little whoop
of satisfaction, and then swinging my rifle around,
I fired. The buffalo fell in its stride, tossing up a
mighty cloud of the soft yellow earth, and my pony
ran by him fifty yards before he could be checked.
Then I turned and rode back to look at the game.
The other Indians had passed me like a whirlwind,
and, close at the heels of the herd, had swept around
a point of bluff and out of sight. Only my rival
remained, and he was excitedly arguing with his
horse. The logic of a whip-handle, applied with
vigor about the creature's ears, convinced it that it
must approach the dead buffalo; and then the rider
dismounting, and passing his lariat about the animal's
horns, drew the pony's head to within a few feet of
the terrifying mass, and fastened the rope. When
he had accomplished this, he grinned pleasantly at

me, and I responded in kind, and in dumb show transferred to him all my right and title in the dead buffalo. At this he smiled still more cheerfully, and set to work "butchering."

The animal was a superb specimen, just entering his prime, and was fat, round and sleek. His horns were symmetrically curved and beautifully polished. Not a scratch marred their shining surfaces, nor a splinter was frayed from their sharp points. The sweeping black beard was long and full, and the thick curls upon his hump and massive shoulders were soft and deep, while the short hair of his sides and hips was smooth as the coat of a horse. His size was enormous. It seemed that he would have turned the scale at quite two thousand pounds. Certainly his weight exceeded that of both the fifteen-hand ponies that stood beside him.

A few moments later, I was again in the saddle, and riding on along the course taken by the remaining buffalo, for I was anxious to see what had become of them. On rounding the point of the bluff, where I had last seen them, my curiosity was satisfied. The valley here widened out until it was perhaps sixty yards across, and on either side rose vertical bluffs of yellow chalk to a height of forty feet. Scattered about over the little plain, lay half a dozen buffalo, over each of which bent one or two Indians busily plying the knife. At the foot of the bluff at one side of the valley stood four or five others, looking at a cow, perched on a narrow shelf ten feet below the top. I shall never understand how that animal reached the position it occupied. There was evidently no way of getting to it except by jumping up from below, which was obviously impossible— or down from above, which seemed out of the question. The shelf was so short that the animal could move neither backward nor forward, and was just wide enough for it to stand on. As I rode up and joined the little group below it, the head and shoulders of a middle-aged Indian appeared over the top of the bluff, above the cow. He lay down flat on his breast, and holding in both hands an old-fashioned muzzle-loading pistol, attempted to shoot the cow from above, but his old arm would not go off. He snapped it half a dozen times, and then, discouraged, called out something to us below. One of the boys turned to me, and said very slowly and distinctly, "He say, you shoot." I therefore dismounted, and fired at the cow, which responded by shaking her head angrily, and whisking her short tail. Another call came from the old fellow on top of the bluff, and the young man said to me, "He say, you hit her; right spot." A moment later, the cow bent forward and fell on her knees, and the Indian above dropped down on her back.

Turning my horse's head in the direction from which I had come, I rode up through a side ravine on to the high prairie. A mile away I could see the column of marching Indians, plodding along at their old slow pace. Here and there, over the rolling hills, dark forms were visible, some of them in rapid motion, others apparently stationary. Often it was impossible to determine whether these figures were horsemen or buffalo, but sometimes, far away, I could see a mimic chase in which pursuer and pursued appeared no larger than ants.

As I came up with the Indians, they were just descending into the stream bottom, where camp was to be made. The small boys had, as usual, dispersed themselves over the valley and among the underbrush. Many of the squaws, leaving the ponies and packs to their sister-wives or children, were hurrying up or down the stream to gather wood. Already the leading ponies were being relieved of their loads. Suddenly, from the mouth of a little ravine coming down into the stream bottom, rose a chorus of shrill yelps and shrieks from childish throats, and a gang of wild turkeys were seen, running rapidly through the high grass toward the hills. A moment later, with a loud *quit-quit* of alarm, they took wing, but not before several of their number had fallen before the missiles of the boys. Most of them went up or down the creek, but one inexperienced bird took its course directly over our heads.

Those who have seen the Indian only on dress parade, talk of his stolidity, impassiveness, and his marvelous control over his countenance and his emotions. This demeanor he can and does assume, and when he is with white men, or among strangers, he is usually all that he has been pictured; but take him by himself, and he expresses his feelings with as little restraint as a child. So it was now. No grave chief, nor battle-scarred warrior, nor mighty worker of *ti-war'-uks-ti* (magic) was too dignified to express his interest at the appearance of this great bird sailing laboriously along, thirty or forty feet above him. It was as if the turkey had flown over a great company of schoolboys, and the utter abandonment of the excited multitude, the entire absence of restraint, the perfect naturalness of the expression of feeling, had in them something very delightful and infectious. Every Indian, who held in his hand anything that was light enough to throw, hurled it at the bird, and a cloud of whips, sticks, hatchets, fleshers, and arrows, rose to meet it as it passed along. One missile knocked from its tail a few long feathers, which drifted slowly down on the heads of the people. It kept on, but before it had passed beyond the long line of Indians extending back over the plain, its strength became exhausted, it came to the ground, and was at once dispatched by those nearest to it.

Almost before the turkey's fate had been decided, many of the lodges had been pitched, and now the slender gray columns from a hundred camp-fires began to climb up through the still air toward the blue above. The women were hard at work cooking, or spreading out freshly killed robes, or putting up drying scaffolds, while the men lounged in the shade and smoked or chatted. Our wagon was halted at one side of the camp, and the tired horses and mules stripped of saddles and harness, and picketed near at hand. The Indian pack ponies were collected and driven off on the upland in charge of several boys.

We had invitations to eat meat at several lodges that day. Usually we did not accept these freely proffered hospitalities, because we had no means of returning them, but one of these invitations came from a particular friend, and to-day we broke through our rule. We feasted on roast ribs, *ka'wis*, and dried meat, and really had a delightful time. It was about three o'clock when we finished the meal, and we were lounging about the lodge, smoking and chatting, in lazy after-dinner fashion, when we were startled by a series of yells and shouts, among which I distinguished the words "*Cha'-ra-rat wa-ta'*—The Sioux are coming." Our Indian companions snatched up their arms, and rushed out of the lodge, and we were not slow in following. "*Sūks-e-kitta-wit wĭs-kūts*—Get on your horses quick," shouted our host. The camp was in a state of wild excitement. Naked men were running to their horses, and jerking their lariats from the picket pins, sprang on their backs and rode hard for the hills; while women and boys rushed about, catching horses, and bringing them in among the lodges, where they were securely fastened. Less than a mile away, we saw the horse herd dashing along at top speed, and a little to one side of it a horseman

riding in circles, and waving his blanket before him.
It was evident that the Sioux were trying to run off
the herd. We ran as hard as we could to the wagon,
caught up rifles and cartridge belts, and buckling
on the latter as we ran, kept on to the horses. There
was no time to saddle up. We looped the ropes
around their jaws, sprang on their naked backs, and
were off. As we rode up on the prairie, the herd of
ponies thundered by, and swept down the bluffs to
the camp. The rolling expanse before us was dotted
with Indians, each one urging forward his horse to
its utmost speed. Many of them were already a
long way in advance, and were passing over the
furthest high bluff, which seemed to rise up and
meet the sky. Hard as we might push our ponies,
there was little hope that we would be in time to
have any hand in the encounter—if one took place
—between the Pawnees and their hereditary foes.

We kept on until we reached the crest of the high
bluff. From here we could see far off over the plain,
dozens of black dots strung out after one another.
Nearer at hand, other Indians, whose steeds, like
ours, had proved too slow for the swift pursuit, were
riding back toward us, showing in their faces the
disappointment which they felt at being left behind.

With these we turned about, and rode toward the camp. Among them was one of the herd boys, for the moment a hero, who had to repeat his story again and again. He had been sitting on top of a hill, not far from the horses, when he discovered several Sioux stealing toward them through a ravine. Signaling his comrades, they succeeded in getting the herd in motion before the robbers had approached very close to them. Eight of the slowest horses had dropped behind during the flight, and had no doubt fallen into the hands of the enemy.

One by one, the Indians came straggling back to camp during the afternoon and evening, but it was not until late that night that the main body of the pursuers came in. They had ten extra horses, two of which they had taken in turn from the Sioux. They had no scalps, however, for they had been unable to overtake the enemy.

Long we sat that night by the fire in *Pi'ta Le-shar's* lodge, talking over the exciting event of the afternoon; and as we rose to go to our wagons, and said good night, the old man, who had been silently gazing into the coals for some time, looked up at me and smiled, saying, " *Wa-ti-hes ti-kōt-it ti-ra-hah*— To-morrow we will kill buffalo."

When we turned out of our blankets the next morning, a heavy mist hung over the prairie. This was unfortunate, for so long as the fog lasted it would be impossible for the scouts to see far enough to discover the buffalo. The first few hours of the march were uneventful. Once or twice the huge bodies of a small band of buffalo loomed up through the white mist about us, their size and shape greatly exaggerated and distorted by its deceptive effect. As the sun climbed toward the zenith, the air grew brighter, and by mid-day the fog had risen from the ground, and though still clinging in white cottony wreaths about the tops of the higher bluffs near us, we now could see for quite a long distance over the prairie. A little later the sun burst forth, and the sky became clear. Soon after noon we went into camp.

We had but just begun our dinner, when a runner was seen coming at full gallop down the bluffs. It was one of the scouts. He dashed through the village, and did not check his pony's speed until he had reached old *Pi'ta Le-shar's* lodge. Here he stopped, and bending from his horse spoke a few words very earnestly, gesticulating and pointing back over the prairie in the direction whence he had

come. As he rode on and past us, he called out,
"*Te-co'di tŭt-tu-ta-rik ti-ra-hah*—I saw many buffalo,"
and we shouted back to him, "*Tū-ra-heh*—It is good."

At once the women began to take down the lodges
and pack the ponies. Buffalo had been discovered
about fifteen miles to the southwest, and orders had
been issued to move the village to the creek on
which they were feeding, while the men should go on
at once and make the surround. Our teamster, to
whom the Indians had already, from his occupation,
given the name "Jackass Chief," was directed to
move with the camp; and leaving everything save
guns and ammunition belts in the wagons, we joined
the crowd of men who were riding out of the village.

The scene that we now beheld was such as might
have been witnessed here a hundred years ago. It
is one that can never be seen again. Here were
eight hundred warriors, stark naked, and mounted
on naked animals. A strip of rawhide, or a
lariat, knotted about the lower jaw, was all their
horses' furniture. Among all these men there was
not a gun nor a pistol, nor any indication that they
had ever met with the white men. For the moment
they had put aside whatever they had learned of
civilization. Their bows and arrows they held in

their hands. Armed with these ancestral weapons, they had become once more the simple children of the plains, about to slay the wild cattle that *Ti-ra'wa* had given them for food. Here was barbarism pure and simple. Here was nature.

A brief halt was made on the upper prairie, until all the riders had come up, and then, at a moderate gallop, we set off. A few yards in advance rode the twenty-four soldiers, at first curbing in their spirited little steeds, till the horses' chins almost touched their chests, and occasionally, by a simple motion of the hand, waving back some impetuous boy, who pressed too close upon them. Many of the Indians led a spare horse, still riding the one that had carried them through the day. Often two men would be seen mounted on the same animal, the one behind having the lariats of two led horses wound about his arm. Here and there a man, with his arm over the horse's neck, would run along on foot by the side of the animal which was to serve him in the charge.

As we proceeded, the pace became gradually a little more rapid. The horses went along easily and without effort. Each naked Indian seemed a part of his steed, and rose and fell with it in the rhythmic swing of its stride. The plain was peopled with Cen-

taurs. Out over each horse's croup floated the long
black hair of his rider, spread out on the wings of
the breeze. Gradually the slow gallop became a fast
one. The flanks of the horses showed here and there
patches of wet, which glistened in the slanting rays
of the westering sun. Eight, ten, a dozen miles had
been left behind us, and we were approaching the
top of a high bluff, when the signal was given to halt.
In a moment every man was off his horse, but not a
pony of them all showed any sign of distress, nor
gave any evidence of the work he had done, except
by his wet flanks and his slightly accelerated breathing. Two or three of the soldiers rode up nearly to
the top of the hill, dismounted and then peered over,
and a moment later, at another signal, all mounted
and the swift gallop began again. Over the ridge
we passed, down the smooth slope, and across a wide
level plain, where the prairie dogs and the owls and
the rattlesnakes had their home. Through the dog
town we hurried on thundering hoofs, no doubt amaz-
ing the dogs, and perhaps even arousing some slight
interest in the sluggish, stupid snakes. Bad places
these to ride through at such a pace, for a little care-
lessness on your horse's part might cost him a broken
leg and you an ugly tumble. But no one took much

thought of dog town or horse or possible accident, for the minds of all were upon the next high ridge, behind which we felt sure that the buffalo would be found.

And so it proved.   Just before reaching it we were again halted.   Two of the soldiers reconnoitered, and then signaled that the buffalo were in sight.   The tired horses were now turned loose and the extra ones mounted.   As we rode slowly up over the ridge, we saw spread out before us a wide valley black with buffalo.   Two miles away, on the other side, rose steep ragged bluffs, up which the clumsy buffalo would make but slow progress, while the ponies could run there nearly as fast as on level ground.   It was the very place that would have been chosen for a surround.

At least a thousand buffalo were lying down in the midst of this amphitheater.   Here and there, away from the main herd on the lower hills, were old bulls, singly and by twos and threes, some of them quietly chewing the cud, others sullenly pawing up the dust, or grinding their battered horns into the yellow dirt of the hillsides.   Not the slightest notice was taken of us as we rode down the slope at a pace that was almost a run, but still held in check by the soldiers.

The orders for the charge had not yet been given. Our line was now much more extended than it had been; each man pressing as far forward as he dared, and those on either flank being so far ahead of the center that they were almost on a line with the soldiers. We had covered perhaps half the distance between the hilltop and the buffalo, when some of the outlying bulls seemed to observe us, and after looking for a moment or two, these started in rapid flight. This attracted the attention of the herd, and when we were yet half a mile from them, they took the alarm. At once all were on their feet. For a moment they gazed bewildered at the dark line that was sweeping toward them, and then, down went every huge head and up flew every little tail, and the herd was off in a headlong stampede for the opposite hills. As they sprang to their feet, the oldest man of the soldiers, who was riding in the center of the line, turned back toward us, and uttered a shrill *Loo'-ah !* It was the word we had waited for.

Like an arrow from a bow each horse darted forward. Now all restraint was removed, and each man might do his best. What had been only a wild gallop became a mad race. Each rider hoped to be the first to reach the top of the opposite ridge, and to turn the buffalo back into the valley, so that the surround might be completely successful. How swift those little ponies were, and how admirably the Indians managed to get out of them all their speed! I had not gone much more than half-way across the valley when I saw the leading Indians pass the head of the herd, and begin to turn the buffalo. This was the first object of the chase, for in a stampede, the cows and young are always in the lead, the bulls bringing up the rear. This position is not taken from chivalric motives on the part of the males, but simply because they cannot run so fast as their wives and children. Bulls are never killed when cows and heifers can be had.

Back came the herd, and I soon found myself in the midst of a throng of buffalo, horses and Indians. There was no yelling nor shouting on the part of the men, but their stern set faces, and the fierce gleam of their eyes, told of the fires of excitement that were burning within them. Three or four times my rifle spoke out, and to some purpose; and one shot, placed too far back, drew on me a quick savage charge from a vicious young cow. My pony, while a good cattle horse, was new at buffalo running, and his deliberation in the matter of dodging caused me an anxious second or two, as I saw the cow's head sweep close to his flank. It was far more interesting to watch the scene than to take part in it, and I soon rode to a little knoll from which I could overlook the whole plain. Many brown bodies lay stretched upon the ground, and many more were dashing here and there, closely attended by relentless pursuers. It was sad to see so much death, but the people must have food, and none of this meat would be wasted.

Before I turned my horse's head toward the camp, the broad disk of the setting sun had rested on the tops of the western bluffs, and tipped their crests with fire. His horizontal beams lit up with a picturesque redness the dusky forms which moved about over the valley. Up the ravines and over the hills were stringing long lines of squaws, leading patient ponies, whose backs were piled high with dark dripping meat, and with soft shaggy skins. Late into the night the work continued and the loads kept coming into the camp. About the flickering fires in and before the lodges there was feasting and merriment. Marrow bones were tossed among the red embers, calf's head was baked in the hot earth, fat ribs were roasted, *ka'-wis* boiled, and

boudins eaten raw. With laughter and singing and
story telling and dance the night wore away.

Over the plain where the buffalo had fallen, the
gray wolf was prowling, and, with the coyote, the
fox and the badger, tore at the bones of the slain.
When day came, the golden eagle and the buzzard
perched upon the naked red skeletons, and took their
toll.   And far away to the southward, a few frightened buffalo, some of which had arrows sticking in
their sore sides, were cropping the short grass of the
prairie.

THE PAWNEE IN WAR.

I. ENEMIES AND METHODS OF WARFARE.

THE Pawnees were a race of warriors. War was their pleasure and their business. By war they gained credit, respect, fame. By war they acquired wealth.

On their long journey from their primitive home in the far southwest, they must have met, fought with and conquered many tribes. By conquest—so says tradition—they obtained their first horses, captured no one knows how long ago, in an attack on a Cheyenne village.

They were brave men, but brave after their own peculiar fashion. Their courage was not displayed in the same way as that of the white man. They thought it folly to expose themselves unnecessarily. An enemy was to be surprised, and killed, while asleep if possible, or shot through by an arrow from behind. To meet him in what we call fair fight, when there was a chance to kill him from an ambush, would have seemed an insane or desperate proceeding. And yet, as has been shown by some of the stories already narrated, they often faced death with a calmness and an indifference which indicated the highest physical courage.

It has been very well said that the purpose of the Indian in his warfare was to inflict the greatest amount of injury on his enemy with the least possible risk to himself.

In the old time wars, the participants exercised the greatest prudence and caution. They took no risks, where risks could be avoided. It was more glorious for a war party to kill a single enemy without receiving a wound, than to kill a dozen, if thereby they lost a man. The warrior, who led out a war party, and brought it back without loss, received credit. His skill as a leader was praised, and his influence grew. A leader, who lost men, lost also prestige; the chiefs withdrew their confidence from him, the young men might decline after that to join his party.

When the Pawnees came into the northern

country they found it occupied by the Poncas, the
Omahas and the Otoes. According to their custom,
they attacked these tribes, and, after a resistance
more or less prolonged, conquered them. The Poncas appear to have made the most stubborn fight
against the invaders, and it is related that they made
an alliance with the Sioux against their common
enemy. From time to time there would be a cessa-
tion of hostilities, and peace would be made, but this
never endured long.

There still exists among the Pawnees a triumph
song, composed after a treacherous attack on the
Pawnees by the Poncas during a time of peace. Mr.
Dunbar's remarks on this song are so interesting
that I quote them in full. He says, "The Pawnee
has a song, constituting the finest satirical production in the language, relating to an attempt that the
Poncas are said to have once made to recover their
independence. Their warriors in a body, so the
account states, made a pretended visit of peace to
the village of Chau-i, at that time the head band
of the Pawnees. After lulling to rest, as they supposed, the suspicions of the Chau-i, according to a
preconcerted plan, they made an attack on them, but
were signally discomfited. In commemoration of

the victory then achieved, the Pawnees composed this song, and the presumption is that such a remarkable production would not have originated and maintained its position permanently in their minds without a good historic basis." This is the song:

A,   Li-hit!   *Ku's-ke-har-u,*   *Kŭr-ŭ-u-ras,*
Aha, you Ponca!   It was (pretended) peace.   Did you find

    id-i, tŭs-ku-ra-wŭsk-u?   *Laŭ-i-lŭk-u-ru-tŭs.*
What you were laughing at me about?   You meant fight.

"The keen satire of the interrogation is exquisite. It conceives of the Poncas as quietly laughing in their sleeves, during their ostensibly amicable visit, in anticipation of the summary retribution that they expected to inflict upon their oppressors."

At last the Poncas, Omahas and Otoes were effectively subjugated, and were permitted to live on the borders of the Pawnee territory, and under the quasi-protection of that tribe.

In the old days before the coming of the whites the Pawnees had no enemies near at hand. They had conquered all surrounding nations, and claimed and held the country from the Missouri River to the Rocky Mountains, and from the Niobrara, south to the Arkansas River or to the Canadian. Then, when they wished to go to war, they were forced to journey either to the Rocky Mountains to fight the Utes, or up the Missouri to attack the Crows, or down into Mexico to plunder the Spaniards, or into Texas to steal horses from the Comanches, the Wichitas and other southern tribes. Then the war parties were great bodies—sometimes one thousand men—and all on foot. Afterward, as settlements approached them and other tribes were driven into their country, and the different Pawnee bands were crowded together, their campaigns diminished in importance, the war parties became smaller and smaller, until at last only half a dozen men would start out, and sometimes a single individual would go off by himself to steal horses.

The Pawnees were true Ishmaelites. They had no friends upon the prairies save those whom they had conquered and held by fear. Foes swarmed about them. To the north were the different bands of the Dakotas and the Crows; to the west the Utes, with the Arapahoes, the Kiowas and the Cheyennes; and to the south the Comanches, Cheyennes, Kiowas, Kansas, Osages, and their relations the Wichitas. With these last they were long at war; for the Pawnees and Wichitas had forgotten each other's existence, or rather each tribe was wholly ignorant as to

what had become of the other. Only a tradition of
the old relationship still remained. The kinship was
rediscovered within the last thirty years, when some
Kaws came north on a visit to the Pawnee village,
and brought with them a Wichita, who had been
visiting at the Kaw agency. The Pawnees found
that this man spoke a language nearly like their own,
and at length discovered that the Wichitas were a
part of their own people. Attempts were made to
establish a peace, and to renew their old friendly relations, but the fact that the Wichitas were so closely
allied to the Comanches, Kiowas and Cheyennes
made it very difficult for the tribes to come together
on a friendly footing. Hostilities still continued
therefore, nor was a lasting peace made until the
visit of *Wi-ti-ti le-shar'-uspi*, already described.

As a result of this well nigh universal hostility, the
Pawnees were constantly being attacked, and were
constantly losing men, women and children. Mr.
Dunbar, who has taken pains to collect some facts
bearing on this point, says:

"Probably, not a year in this century has been
without losses from this source (warfare), though
only occasionally have they been marked with considerable disasters. In 1832 the Skidi band suffered

a severe defeat on the Arkansas from the Comanches. In 1847 a Dakota war party, numbering over seven hundred, attacked a village occupied by two hundred and sixteen Pawnees, and succeeded in killing eighty-three. In 1854 a party of one hundred and thirteen were cut off by an overwhelming body of Cheyennes and Kiowas, and killed almost to a man. In 1873 a hunting party of about four hundred, two hundred and thirteen of whom were men, on the Republican, while in the act of killing a herd of buffalo, were attacked by nearly six hundred Dakota warriors, and eighty-six were killed. But the usual policy of their enemies has been to cut off individual or small scattered parties, while engaged in the chase or in tilling isolated corn patches. Losses of this kind, trifling when taken singly, have in the aggregate borne heavily on the tribe. It would seem that such losses, annually recurring, should have taught them to be more on their guard. But let it be remembered that the struggle has not been in one direction against one enemy. The Dakotas, Crows, Kiowas, Cheyennes, Arapahoes, Comanches, Osages and Kansas have faithfully aided each other, though undesignedly in the main, in this crusade of extermination against the Pawnee

It has been in the most emphatic sense, a struggle of the one against the many. With the possible exception of the Dakotas, there is much reason to believe that the animosity of these tribes has been exacerbated by the galling tradition of disastrous defeats which Pawnee prowess had inflicted upon themselves in past generations. To them the last seventy years have been a carnival of revenge."

Mr. Dunbar regards the constant warfare against their many enemies as one principal cause of the rapid diminution in numbers of the Pawnees, and, no doubt, it was a cause; but a far more important one was the sapping of the tribe's vitality by contact with the whites. Their villages lay almost directly in the path of trans-continental emigration, and it was the introduction of spirits and the special diseases contracted from the whites which weakened the tribe, and made the tough and sinewy Pawnee a ready prey to sickness and death.

Although so ferocious to people of their own color, the Pawnees have ever been at peace with the whites. Bad men among them have, no doubt, sometimes stolen horses, but the tribe has never carried on an organized war against the Government. While they have often been provoked by wanton outrages inflicted on them, yet they have always borne themselves peaceably and mildly, and sought redress by legal or persuasive, rather than by hostile measures.

There is one instance on record which, while it shows their ferocity, exemplifies also their natural justice, and deserves to be repeated. This is the story of the Rawhide.

In the year 1852, among a small party of emigrants, who were crossing the plains on their way to California, was a man who had frequently asserted that he would kill the first Indian he saw. While the train was camped on a small creek flowing into the Elkhorn, a young squaw was seen, who belonged to the neighboring Pita-hau-erat village. Some accounts say that she came to the camp to beg, others, that she was going to the stream for a bucket of water. At all events, she was seen by the emigrants, who bantered the young man to carry out his boast that he would kill the first Indian he saw. He shot and killed the woman. The train moved on during the night. On the following day the tribe learned of this wanton butchery. They pursued the train, and surrounding it, demanded the murderer. He was at once given up, and a council was held, at which his fate was decided. The train was ordered back to the scene of the murder, and there, in the presence of his horrified companions, the Pawnees proceeded to flay the murderer alive. After this had been done, the emigrants were permitted to proceed on their journey. The stream on whose banks this act of grim justice took place is still known as Rawhide Creek.

Not only have the Pawnees never been at war with the whites, but, for the past twenty-five years, they have been their allies in every serious Indian war which has taken place east of the Rocky Mountains.

The Pawnee was taught to deal in ambuscades and surprises, yet he could fight in the open, too, if necessity demanded. Sometimes they had pitched battles with their foes, but their weapons were very primitive, and such combats were—in view of the numbers engaged on either side—comparatively bloodless. Between the years 1860 and 1870 such battles frequently took place near the Pawnee village, when the Sioux, who were far more numerous than the Pawnees, would come down from the north to try to destroy the village. Many a time I have heard from the lips of grizzled warriors the stories of these battles. Sometimes the enemy would come down in small parties, and steal horses, or kill squaws who were working in the corn patches, but at other times large bodies of warriors would approach the village without any attempt at concealment.

About sunrise the Sioux would ride up over the hills in a line fronting toward the village. They appeared mounted on their best ponies, clad in their most elaborate war costume, and wearing long war bonnets of the feathers of the war eagle, which almost swept the ground as their horses curveted along to the music of the monotonous but thrilling war chant. At the instant of their appearance the Pawnee village would begin to stir like a disturbed ant hill. The shouts of command by the men, the piercing calls from women, the alarmed and excited shrieks of the children, the neighing and heavy hoof-beats of the horses, the barking and howling of the dogs, as they were kicked out of the way, made a very Babel of sounds. The men snatched their arms, and springing on their horses rode out on to the plain to meet the enemy, while the women and children, after the horses had been secured, mounted to the tops of the dirt lodges to watch the fight. The Sioux, when they had come into full view, stopped, and sat there on their horses, proud of their brave

attire, and courting admiration.   The Pawnees, too,
if time permitted, would don their finest war dresses,
though often they fought naked, and elaborately paint
themselves and their horses.   As the Pawnees rode
toward their enemy, the Sioux slowly advanced
toward them, both with extended front.   Each party
chanted its songs of war, and uttered yells of defi-
ance.   While they were still six or seven hundred
yards apart they halted, and stood facing each other.
After a short wait, a warrior from one side or the
other rode out before the line and addressed his
party.   He opened his speech with some remarks
derogatory to the foe, and in praise of his own people.   From these generalities, he passed to a consideration of his own excellent qualities, told of what
he had done in the past, and what he now intended
doing, and when he had finished speaking, he bent
low over his horse's neck, and rode furiously toward
one end of the enemy's line.   When he had come
within easy bowshot, he usually turned his horse's
head, and rode as hard as he could down along the
line, leaning down, half hidden by his horse, and dis-
charging arrow after arrow at the enemy.   They also
shot at him, as he flew by, and as he rode along,
those whom he had passed dashed out in pursuit,

until the whole party were riding after him as hard
as they could go. If he passed along the line without injury, he turned his horse toward his own party,
and rode back, his pursuers following him but a
short distance. If, however, he was wounded by the
arrows shot at him, and fell from his horse, or if his
horse was hit and disabled, or if, on account of the
greater speed of their ponies, it seemed likely that
the enemy would overtake him, the whole body of
his tribe made a headlong charge to rescue and
bring him off. The enemy were as eager to take his
scalp as his own people were to save it, and the
opposing warriors came together in a hot melee.

There was little twanging of bow strings, and not
much thrusting of lances; for the most part the
fighting was at quarters too close for this, and the
combatants pounded at each other's heads with
hatchets, war clubs, whip handles, bows and *coup*
sticks. Bruises were given and received, sometimes
a few men were gashed with hatchets and lances,
and occasionally a man was killed. If the man about
whom the struggle was taking place was scalped, his
party at once drew off, leaving his body, which had
now ceased to have any interest for them, in the
hands of the enemy. If, however, he escaped scalp-

ing, his friends and foes soon separated and withdrew to their former positions. Then, after a breathing spell, a man of the other party rode forward, and made his speech, and the charge and general attack might be repeated.

Occasionally a very daring or desperate man, instead of riding down the opposing line, would charge through it, and as he reached it would let fly an arrow at some particular man, and count *coup* on, and scalp him as he dashed by. He would at once be surrounded by foes, who did their best to kill him, while his own tribesmen would charge upon them, and for a short time the struggle would be very fierce. A brave man, killed and scalped, was mutilated in all conceivable ways by the enemy, and was often cut up into small pieces.

In this way the battle might go on for the greater part of a day with varying fortunes, but without the loss on either side of more than a man or two, until at last one party or the other would become discouraged, and would break and run.

The Sioux in their attacks on the Pawnee village were never the victors. They were always defeated and driven back, and often, in the pursuit, two or three times as many men were killed as in the actual battle. It was but natural that the Pawnees should have been successful in this defense of their village, for in such fights they felt that they must conquer. Defeat to them there meant the loss of all that they possessed, the slaughter of their women and children, and the destruction of their village. Besides, if defeated, they had no place to retreat to. They would fight to the death.

Their fierce courage and their fighting qualities were well shown on one famous occasion. The tribe had gone off south on the buffalo hunt, and there were left in the village only some of the sick, the old men, and a few boys, women and children. Among the sick who remained was *Ska-di'ks* (Crooked Hand), a Skidi brave, recognized as a leader in battle, and one of the bravest warriors in the tribe. The Sioux had learned of the departure of the Pawnees with all the fighting men, and had planned to come down, kill all the people left at home, and destroy the village.

One morning, to the dismay of those who had been left behind, six hundred of the very best of the Sioux warriors rode slowly into view over the hills, and down on to the plain above the village. They made no charge, for it was unnecessary to hurry

about killing the few women, the old men and the
sick who were to be their unresisting victims. They
wished to prolong the agony of these wretched Pawnees, whose scalps were already theirs, and whose
village would soon be only a few heaps of smoking
ruins. As they rode slowly down the hill there was
no clink of steel nor rattle of harness, only the soft
rustling of the prairie grass under the unshod hoofs
of their spirited war ponies, but this sound was
drowned by the ominous music of their triumphant
war song, which, now loud, now low, was faintly
borne on the breeze to the fated village. Very
deliberately they came on, singing as they marched,
proudly, like conquerors, while the sun glittered on
polished lance-head and gleaming hair plate, and the
wind blew out the fringes of their white war shirts,
or gaily tossed the streaming plumes of their superb
war bonnets.

The news of their appearance was brought to
Crooked Hand, where he lay sick in his lodge. At
once he threw aside the robe in which he was
wrapped, and as he rose to his feet, he cast away
from him by the same motion his sickness. His
orders were quickly issued, and as promptly obeyed.
The village must fight. Tottering old men, whose

sinews were now too feeble to bend the bow, seized their long disused arms and clambered on their horses. Boys too young to hunt, whose bodies had never been toughened by the long journeys of the warpath, whose hearts had not been made strong by the first fast, grasped the weapons that they had as yet used only on rabbits and ground squirrels, flung themselves on their ponies, and rode with the old men. Even squaws, taking what weapons they could —axes, hoes, mauls, pestles—mounted horses, and marshaled themselves for battle.

The force for the defense numbered two hundred; superannuated old men, boys and women. Among them all were not, perhaps, ten active warriors, and these had just risen from sick beds to take their place in the line of battle. But then this little force had a leader. Crooked Hand, mounted on a superb war pony, was as cool and unconcerned as if he were about to ride out to a band of buffalo, instead of leading a force of old men and children against six hundred of the best warriors that the Sioux could muster.

At that time the Pawnee village was encompassed by a high sod wall, and some of Crooked Hand's people wished to await the charge of the Sioux behind this shelter, but their leader would not permit this. He said to them, "We can conquer the Sioux anywhere." So *Ska-di'ks* led his forces out to meet the attack in fair open combat on the plain, on the same ground where so many times the Pawnees had routed their enemies. As the Pawnees passed out of the village on to the plain, the Sioux saw for the first time the force they had to meet. They laughed in derision, calling out bitter jibes, and telling what they would do when they had made the charge; and, as Crooked Hand heard their laughter, he smiled, too, but not mirthfully. He knew what perhaps the Sioux had forgotten, that his people were single-minded, and that they would fight until they died. Their strokes would be for their homes and lives.

The battle began. It seemed like an unequal fight. Surely one charge would be enough to overthrow this motley Pawnee throng, who had ventured out to try to oppose the triumphal march of the Sioux. But it was not ended so quickly. The fight began about the middle of the morning, and, to the amazement of the Sioux, these old men with shrunken shanks and piping voices, these children with their small white teeth and soft round limbs, these women clad in skirts, and armed with hoes, held the invaders where they were; they could make no advance. A little latter it became evident that the Pawnees were driving the Sioux back. Presently this backward movement became a retreat, the retreat a rout, the rout a wild panic. Then, indeed, the Pawnees made a great killing of their enemies. Many an old man, whose feeble legs had long refused to bear him on the warpath, again quavered his war cry, again counted *coup* upon his enemy. Many a boy, who had never shed the blood of any creature larger than a prairie chicken, that day struck his enemy, and with shrill childish voice shouted his whoop of triumph, as he tore away the reeking scalp. More than one woman, used only to pounding corn and dressing robes, that day counted her *coup*, and when the tribe returned, told what she had done, and changed her name like a warrior.

To the Pawnees that day was like the day of Thermopylæ to the Greeks.

Crooked Hand, preëminent among the heroes of that fight, with his own hand killed six of the Sioux, and had three horses shot under him. His wounds were many, but he laughed at them. He was content; he had saved the village.

The same indomitable spirit here shown has char-acterized the Pawnees always. For generations they fought as their fathers had fought, in their own way, with their native enemies, but when they were enlisted in the Government service, and trained in the white man's ways of war, they adapted them-selves readily to their new conditions.

A body of men braver than the Pawnee Scouts, under Major Frank North and his brother Luther, never rode on horses. They were far better than any white soldiers that ever fought on the plains; for, besides their natural courage, they had at their finger ends all the wonderful wisdom of the savage. They could tell, as it seemed by instinct, where a trail would lead, where the enemy that they were pursuing would camp, what were his plans. They had the endurance of their prototype, the wolf. No labor was too severe, no journey too long, if its end was a battle with their foes. Their courage, their discipline, their knowledge of the plains, their ac-quaintance with the habits of their enemies, their endurance, made them superb soldiers; but, perhaps, more than all this, and yet a part of all this, was the absorbing devotion and trust which they felt for *Pa'-ni Le-shar*, their white leader. Through all the

years that they followed him, he never led them but
to victory; through all these years he never lost a
man in battle, and the belief of the Pawnees in his
ability and his success was like the devotion felt by
the *Grande Armée* for Napoleon.

II. PA'-NI LE-SHAR AND HIS SCOUTS.

No account of the Pawnees' warfare would give
any just impression of their prowess if it omitted
to mention *Pa'-ni Le-shar* and the forces which he
commanded. The Pawnee Scouts, under the gal-
lant and able leadership of Frank North, did splen-
did service against hostile Indians. They saved
hundreds of lives and millions of dollars' worth of
property, and in their campaigns wiped out in blood
the memory of many an injury done to their race by
the Sioux, the Cheyennes, the Arapahoes and the
Kiowas.

Frank North was born in Ohio, March 10, 1840.
When about fifteen years of age he accompanied his
family westward to Council Bluffs, and a little later
across the Missouri River into Nebraska. At about
this time, his father, who was a surveyor, was lost in
a snow storm, and the responsibility of caring for his

family fell in large measure on the boy. Soon after this he obtained employment as clerk in the trader's store at the Pawnee agency, and thus made the acqaintance of the tribe. His strong character early brought him to the notice of their principal men, and almost before attaining manhood he had become a person of influence in the councils of the Pawnee Nation.

In the year 1864 Frank North was authorized to enlist a company of Pawnee scouts to be employed against the bands of hostile Indians, whose depredations were at that time becoming very troublesome. The command was organized that autumn, and did some service along the old emigrant trail. It was not until the summer of 1865, however, that it saw any serious fighting. In that year General Connor of California commanded a large expedition to the Powder River country, and the Pawnee scouts accompanied him and rendered brilliant service.

Later, during the building of the Union Pacific Railway, the depredations of the hostile Sioux, Cheyennes and Arapahoes became so serious along the line of the road that the Government authorized Mr. North to enlist a battalion of scouts from the Pawnee Nation, and offered him the command with the rank of major. Several companies of these scouts were so enlisted, and for years the battalion did good service on the plains and in the mountains in Nebraska, Kansas and Wyoming, serving under Generals Auger, Emory, Carr, Royal, Mackenzie and Crook, some of the most successful Indian fighters in that Department. The Pawnee scouts were everywhere, and at all times brave men, good soldiers and victorious warriors. The amount of property saved to the Government, the settlers and the railroad through the efforts of Major North's command can scarcely be computed. In all his service of almost constant fighting, extending over a period of more than ten years, he never lost a man on the battle field, and this caused him to be regarded by the Pawnees as divinely favored.

It is impossible within the limits of a few pages to give even a sketch of the services performed by Frank North and his scouts. Two or three isolated episodes in his career will show something of the constant danger and hardship of the life he led, and of the courage, coolness and determination of the leader and his men.

Such an episode, memorable alike for its danger, the completeness of the victory gained, and the fact that it won for him the title by which he was ever after known among the Pawnees, marked his first campaign. It was in the Powder River country, and Captain North had started with a detachment of his scouts in pursuit of a party of Indians, whose trail he had found. For some weeks his men had been hard worked; and at this time their horses were so jaded that although they had come within sight of the Cheyennes, they were unable to overtake them and force them to a fight. Captain North, who was mounted on a fresh horse, rode far ahead of his men, who were constantly falling further and further behind. At length, realizing the futility of continuing the pursuit, North dismounted, fired a parting shot at the Indians, and was about to ride back toward camp, when the fleeing Cheyennes, about twenty-five in number, turned and charged him. He then discovered that he had outridden all his men. Not one of them was in sight. Hastily dismounting, he prepared to receive the enemy, and firing as they advanced killed one. The rest sheered off, and rode out of rifle shot, and then formed again for another charge. Feeling for a cartridge to reload his rifle, North made the startling discovery that he had but three left, all the others having been lost during his rapid ride. He found, too, that his horse had been wounded by a ball from the Cheyennes, and was in no condition for running; indeed, it could not be ridden. His situation seemed well nigh hopeless, but he prepared to make the best of it, by retreating on foot, leading his wounded horse as a shelter, from behind which to fight. When the Cheyennes charged him he would face about, raise his gun to his shoulder, as if about to fire, and the Indians, who had already tasted the quality of his lead, would drop down behind their horses, and sheer off, never coming so close to him as to make it necessary for him to use one of his precious cartridges. After a long weary walk of twelve or fifteen miles, during which his moccasin-shod feet were cruelly lacerated by the thorns of the cactus, over which he walked, his pursuers left him, and he reached his command in safety. No sooner had he arrived at the camp than, taking a fresh horse and ordering out a well-mounted detachment of his men, he set out in pursuit of the enemy. All that afternoon they rode hard, and when night fell, dismounting a couple of Pawnees to follow the trail on foot, the pursuit was still kept up. Just after daylight, as they rode out into a little park in the mountains, a tiny column of blue smoke rising from a clump of cottonwood trees showed where the hostiles were camped. The Pawnees rode steadily forward in double file in military fashion; and the Cheyennes, supposing that they were white soldiers, jumped on their horses and rode out on to the open hillside where they formed a line of battle to meet the enemy. The Pawnees rode quietly onward until they were quite near the Cheyennes, and then loud and clear their ringing war whoop broke out upon the morning air. When the Cheyennes heard this war-cry, which told them that the attacking party were Pawnees, their hearts became like water, and they turned and fled. Already, however, seven of their number had fallen before the Pawnee bullets, and the fresher horses of the Pawnees easily overtook the tired ones ridden by the pursued. Of that party of Cheyennes not one escaped, and with twenty-seven scalps, and all the plunder, the victorious Pawnees returned that afternoon to their command.

Among the captured property were thirty-five horses and mules, some of which had been taken from a party of fifteen soldiers, killed to a man by these Cheyennes but a few days before; there were also the scalps of these soldiers, and wearing apparel belonging to white women and children, which justified the belief that they had recently massacred a party of emigrants.

It was on the occasion of the scalp dance which followed this victory, and when the Scouts were changing their names, as was the custom after a successful encounter with the enemy, that the Pawnees gave to Major North the title *Pa'-ni Le-shar* (Chief of the Pawnees), a name which has been borne by only one other white man, General John C. Fremont, the Pathfinder.

The story of the killing of Tall Bull, and the fight with Turkey Leg's band of Sioux, illustrate the readiness and the daring of Major North in battle. Tall Bull was a chief who commanded a large village of renegade Sioux and Cheyennes, who had given great trouble by their depredations. Major North, with his Pawnees and some white United States troops, had been looking for this village for some time, and at length succeeded in surprising it near Summit Springs. The village was captured in the charge and many of the hostiles killed. Others fled or concealed themselves in the ravines and washouts, which seamed the prairie, and made a desperate fight. The Pawnees were scattered about in little parties, killing the Indians thus concealed, when Major North and his brother came riding rapidly along, side by side, over the open prairie. They had approached within fifty or sixty yards of a narrow steep-walled ravine, of the existence of which they were ignorant, when an Indian raised his head above its side and fired. The ball whistled between the heads of the two riders; Major North threw up his hands and reeled in the saddle as if about to fall, and the Indian's head disappeared from sight. Springing from his horse, the Major handed his bridle rein to his brother and directed him to ride away at a gallop. The tramp of the two horses sounded more and more faintly on the hard ground, and the Indian, thinking that the whites were riding off, raised his head to note the effect of his shot. North's rifle was already leveled at the spot where the head had disappeared, and as the black hair came into view the finger pressed the trigger more and more closely, and as the eyes appeared above the ground, a ball pierced the brain of Tall Bull. A hundred yards up the ravine was found his war pony, stabbed to the heart, and by it sat his squaw, awaiting with Indian patience whatever fate might come to her.

During one of the summer hunts, on which Major North accompanied the Pawnees, they were one day scattered out over the prairie running buffalo, when all at once North heard the whistle of rifle balls and saw the dirt thrown up about his horse by the bullets. He called to a Pawnee near him to tell those boys to be more careful about shooting. The Pawnee looked in the direction from which the balls were coming, and after an instant called back, "They are Sioux, you had better run." It was a large party of Sioux under the Chief Turkey Leg.

North and the Pawnee rode for the bluffs near at hand, and before reaching them were joined by C. D. Morse, his brother-in-law, and half a dozen Pawnees. The little party was surrounded by the Sioux and took refuge in a shallow washout at the head of a ravine, where they were somewhat sheltered from the enemy's fire by the sunflower stalks and the low edges of the bank. Their horses were at once killed, and the Sioux, who were numerous, became very bold, charging up to the edge of the washout, and shooting down into it.

They were led by an Indian, apparently of some importance, who was conspicuous by a large American flag which he carried. This man was constantly

exhorting his men, and would lead them part way on
the charge, turning off, however, before coming within range of the washout, where North and his brother-
in-law, with the seven Pawnees, were lying concealed. After each charge he would ride to the top
of a hill near at hand, and make a speech to his warriors. It occurred to Major North that if he could
kill the man who carried the flag the other Sioux
might lose some of their courage. As they were re-
tiring from a charge, therefore, he crept cautiously
down the ravine, concealed by the long grass which
grew in its bed, until he had come within rifle range
of the hill from which the leader was making his
speech, and by a careful shot killed him and regained
the shelter of the washout without injury.

Disheartened by the fall of their leader, the Sioux
made no further attempt to kill the besieged company,
but after a little desultory long-range firing drew off,
so that North and his little party regained the main
village in safety.

The Pawnee Scouts were last called out in 1876,
when General Mackenzie fought the hostile Cheyennes in the Powder River country; and, led by Major
North and his brother, they made that famous charge
on the village which inflicted on the hostiles the

crushing blow from which they never recovered. How *Pa'-ni Le-shar* held his men under fire that day, when the bullets were raining on them from the hillsides, was told in a letter written to me by a participant in the fight. "For cool bravery," it ran, "he beats anything that you ever saw. Why, at one time we were under such hot fire that even our scouts wanted to run, and to tell you the truth, I felt sort of that way myself; but Frank just straightened himself up on the old black horse and said, very quietly, 'The first one of *my* men that runs I will kill.' They didn't run."

If the full story of Major North's life were written it would constitute a history of the Indian wars in Nebraska and Wyoming from 1860 to 1876—a history so complete that there would be little left to add to it. Wherever the hostile Indians were worst there Frank North was to be found at the head of his Pawnee Scouts, doing the hardest of the fighting, and accomplishing work that could have been done by no other body of men.

From his long service in the army Major North was known to all officers who have ever been stationed in the field where his operations were conducted, and by all of them he was admired and respected. He was closely connected with the growth of the State of Nebraska. Several times he represented Platte county in the Legislature, and the strength and uprightness of his character won the confidence of all who knew him. He died at his home in Columbus, Nebraska, March 14, 1885, aged forty-five years.

His was a singularly lovable nature. If the stronger manly points of his character inspired respect and admiration, not less did his gentleness and consideration for others win the deepest affection. He was modest almost to diffidence, and it was with difficulty that he could be induced to speak of his own heroic achievements. And yet his face told the story of the power within the man.

The secret of Major North's success in commanding the Pawnees, who loved him as much as they respected him, lay in the unvarying firmness, justice, patience and kindness with which he treated them. He never demanded anything unreasonable of them, but when he gave an order, even though obedience involved great peril, or appeared to mean certain death, it was a command that must be carried out. He was their commander, but at the same time their brother and friend. Above all, he was their leader. In going into battle he never said to them, "Go," but always "Come on." It is little wonder, then, that the devotion felt for him by all the Pawnee Nation, and especially by the men who had served under him in battle, was as steadfast as it was touching.

III. WAR PARTIES.

It has already been said that the highest ambition of the Pawnee young man was to be successful in war. His whole training, all his surroundings, caused him to believe that this success was the only thing worth living for. Life at best he regarded as hard enough, and only the fame to be acquired by the performance of brave deeds could sweeten it so as to make it endurable. To convey a notion of the way in which these war parties were originated, and of the manner in which they were led, I give here stories told me by three brave men who in the old days led out many war parties. The three stories were taken down from the lips of the narrators. Only one who is familiar with scenes in an Indian camp can conceive how much these stories lose by being put into cold type. As heard from the lips of the Indian, they have accessories of surroundings, voice and gesticulation, which add tremendously to their vividness and their interest. Your Indian is a real actor, and in telling a story he throws himself into his tale, and helps out his vocal speech with a sign vocabulary which almost tells the whole story to one who is ignorant of the language.

In the middle of the lodge the fire is burning, and over it hangs the pot which is ever bubbling. At the back of the lodge, opposite the doorway, sits the host, and above him to the lodge poles are tied the sacred bundles, their buckskin coverings black with the smoke and wear of years, perhaps of centuries. To the left of the host are the most important guests, and the other inmates of the lodge are scattered about here and there, the women being nearest the door. The host hands the pipe to some young man, who carefully fills it, and soon it is passing around the circle. Then a few remarks are made by the older men, and some question is asked which starts discussion. After that comes a pause, and then a middle-aged warrior begins a story. He is They-know-that-Leader, and he tells how he took the horses:

"They tell me that my father was a warrior, and in his time led out many war parties. In my young days I went out with war parties as a volunteer many times.

"In my trips with warriors I had closely watched their ways and movements. I had learned from them how to shoot and how to travel so as to escape discovery. I made three trips as leader. I resolved one time, just as we were setting out on the summer hunt, that during the hunt I would lead a party off on the warpath. I made my plans, but I waited first to make the sacrifice. At that time we did not go far; we came back to the village because the Sioux were about us on the hunt.

"On a certain day I played all day the stick game (*Satsa-wi-kah-tūsh*). In the afternoon I had lost everything I had. Late in the afternoon I called a few of the young men to sit down with me. When they had come and sat down with me, there were only a few. I said to them, 'I have called you together to let you know that I am poor in mind. I want to find out if *Ti-ra'-wa* will take pity on me and help me. I intend that you and I shall go off somewhere on the warpath. Make your preparations to start in two days. Get your moccasins filled with food, get your awls and sinews, your arrows and your bows.'

"On the day I had set, in the night, we went out from the village, having with us the old man who had performed the ceremonies of the sacred things that I was to have with me.   On the outskirts of the village, we stood in a row, and the old man prayed for our success.   Then we were ready to start.

"Different war parties had gone out before I started, but I considered to see if there was not some way in which I could beat them.   I made a plan by which I got ahead of them.   We traveled fast, and went up to Grand Island to get some arrows—for my young men had but few arrows—and also to get some provisions.   The next morning we again started, and went as far as we could that day.   At night I performed ceremonies, as I had been directed.   I filled a pipe and smoked to *Ti-ra'-wa*, as we have always done.   That is the first thing we have to do.   Then I told some of my young men to build a fire, and others to go off to a distance to watch.

"On a war party some one was always taken along who could shoot well.   This time we had no one except myself.   The next day I killed an antelope, but I did not sacrifice then, because those are not animals which we sacrifice.   We had been gone three nights more before I killed anything more. The fourth day I killed a buck deer, and I sacrificed it. From that day on I never killed anything.

"After I had been out nine days I stole the horses. It was not always the same about stealing horses. It was not always done in the same way. It was day-time when my scouts discovered that there were people about; they saw signs of a village. They told me afterward that they had heard reports of guns during the day. They had not come back to tell me of this, but had gone by. I was coming on behind with the young men, when all at once I heard the report of a gun. As soon as I heard it I stopped, and sent two spies out to see what it was, and whether a camp was near. They wandered about in the timber, and came back and said that they saw nothing. I told my men that we would go off to a distance and wait there during the night. We waited there until morning, and when the sun got up we heard the report of guns in different directions, and some-times coming toward us. We went to a cañon, and hid in the plum brush, and ate plums. Of course we were afraid, but we ate the plums. We thought that this might be the last time we would ever have any plums. They were shooting all about us, and seemed to be coming closer. In the afternoon, the shots stopped, and they went on to their camp.

"While we were hiding here, many of the party feared that we had been seen. They wanted to start back as soon as it grew dark, but I deceived them. I told them that I was very thirsty, and that we would have to go down to a certain place near the river, and get a drink of water. After night we started, and as we were going along, we heard a dog bark. We stopped and sat down, and I told my companions that two men, whom I called by name, were to go and steal horses. 'But,' I said, 'I am going with them to look after them.' I told them to pull off their leggings and moccasins, because the brush was dry and caught on them, making a noise. We went together to a certain place near the village, and then these young men told me that they had been there the day before and had been discovered. Then they turned around and went back to where the party were hiding, but I went on to the village.

"When I came close to the village everything was still; the people were asleep. Where I entered the camp, there was a little timber growing, and here I stopped. While I was considering what I should do, a girl came out of a lodge, but she went away from

me. If she had come toward me I should have killed her, for she would have discovered me. After the girl had entered a lodge, I went into the camp to where there were some horses. I drove them out of the camp. Six went back, and I drove nine to where I had left my party. The two that I had ordered to steal horses for me were there. When I came to the place, and found all my men there, I said to them, 'This is very good. I have stolen some horses for you. Now I will go back and get the rest of them for you. One of the other men persuaded me not to go again, but to let him go. He did so, and brought the six other horses.

"It was the custom, if it was very difficult or dangerous to go to a place to steal horses, for the leader himself to go and do the work.

"After two nights on the return journey I divided the horses among the men. It used to be the custom after a party had been successful and brought back the horses for them to change their names. After this trip my name was changed to They-know-that-Leader.' It was the custom among the Pawnees if they brought in horses to make an offering. We felt that we owed something to *Ti-ra'-wa*, and we gave a horse to the priest, the old man who had performed the ceremonies. I was gone but thirteen days, and returned to my tribe."

After him follows *A-ka-pa-kish*—Pities-the-Poor He, too, tells his story, and explains why one of his war parties was unsuccessful:

"My father told me, if I should ever want to go off on a war party, to humble myself, and not to let a day pass without praying to *Ti-ra'-wa* by my smokes. I must always remember to pray to *Ti-ra'-wa* to give me a strong will, and to encourage and bless me in my worship to him. Even when I was eating I must always remember to pray to him. This I must do for some time before starting out.

"At one time I felt that I was poor, and I resolved to go off on the warpath. A warrior, whom I knew, went out and took a lot of horses. He had been as poor as I. I believed that this man had got his horses because he had prayed to *Ti-ra'-wa*, and I thought, 'If I pray to *Ti-ra'-wa*, why may I not do the same. So I prayed. No one else knew what I intended. After I had made up my mind, I selected another man, one whom I could trust, and called him to tell him of my resolve. I made him sit by me in the lodge, and said to him, 'I want you to sit by me to-day, and smoke, and learn my intention.' After we had smoked, I said to him, 'My friend, I want you to know that we are on the warpath. We are going out to look for some horses.' After he had smoked, the other man replied, saying, 'Brother, it is well. Let us ask *Ti-ra'-wa* to take pity on us, to help us on our war trip, and to let us bring home many horses.' We two were the leaders.

"Some time after we had talked together, and made up our minds what we would do, we selected certain young men that we could depend on, and told them that we were on the warpath. This was done in this way. We selected a pipe with which to have a sacred smoke, filled it and smoked. Then we called together into the lodge the others, who did not know our purpose. After they had assembled, I filled the pipe, and said, 'We are going on a war party. We have filled this pipe, and must decide what is to be done.' Then I passed the pipe to the man who sat next to me. If he wished to join us he smoked, and passed it to the next man. It was not allowed for any one to smoke unless he would go with this party. Some might refuse the pipe, saying, 'I have decided to go with another party.' The smoking of the pipe was a promise that the leader could depend on the man who smoked.

"They used to have a certain ceremony to follow before starting out on the warpath. It was something handed down, a special manner of praying to *Ti-ra'-wa* that he would bless them in their warfare.

"At last everything was ready for the start. The young men had their packs made up. They carried cooked pounded corn, and pounded buffalo meat mixed with tallow; and sometimes the loads were heavy. Some would carry ten pairs of moccasins, each one stuffed full of corn, or pounded buffalo meat. They were well fed. The loads were so heavy that at first we would only make short marches. The leaders had to see that the young men were not overworked.

"When all was ready, the priest who performed the ceremonies met us. He brought with him the sacred bundle which we were to take with us. At night when it was all still, after every one was asleep, the ceremonies were performed. We smoked and worshiped to the east and west, and to the north and south, and prayed for success.

"On that night we started, and went as far as we could; and the next day, toward evening, when we

stopped, we dug out a fire-place, like the one in a
lodge, and we two leaders sat by it, facing the east,
while before us were the sacred things. The leader
has to be a good orator, he has to speak to his young
men, and advise them well, encouraging them to be
strong-hearted. He would speak to them and say,
'We have but a short time to live, so while we are
on this trip let us determine to be single-minded.
Let us all look to *Ti-ra'-wa*, who is the ruler over
all things, and ask him to take pity on us, and bless
our warpath. We must respect the animals that the
ruler has made and not kill any of them; no birds,
nor wolves, nor any creeping things.' Not a night
passed but that, after we were seated in a circle,
I would talk to the party, and pray, and hope that
Ti-ra'-wa would bless us and take pity on us, and
that we might be the party that would have good
success. On my war parties I had to watch at all
times, even when I was resting, to see that my young
men should, before they slept, pray to *Ti ra'-wa*
that they might dream something good, and that it
might come to pass.

"The old priest who had performed the ceremonies, and had let me take the sacred things, had told
me to kill a particular kind of animal, a deer, and

sacrifice it. I sent some spies ahead to look over the country, and a messenger came back from them, saying that they had seen some animals. He did not describe them, and I ordered the messenger to have the hunter kill them. I heard the report of a gun. The hunter with two shots killed three. They were antelope. When the hunter came to me he told me what he had done, and described the animals which he had killed. They were not the animals I had been directed to kill for the sacrifice. I hesitated, for I did not know what to do. I did not wish to eat these animals before the sacrifice had been made. To do this is bad. It troubled me. I was troubled, because if we ate them it would look as if we cared nothing for *Ti-ra'-wa.* Finally we ate what had been killed, and made no sacrifice. Afterward we killed two more and ate them, and still made no sacrifice.

"One night I dreamed that the hunter had shot a buffalo. It fell, but as we went up to it, it got up and ran off. We went on for eight days, and had made no sacrifice to *Ti-ra'-wa.* One day my scouts saw a man sitting on a hill. Some of them wanted to shoot at him, but the others said 'no.' They came back to tell me about it, and when they had returned to the place where they had seen him, the man was gone. The man had seen my spies. Not far off was a village, and the warriors in it came to look for us, but we ran away. They hunted for us, but we had got out of their sight. After this we came back home."

Curly Chief, second chief of the Kit-ke-hahk'-i band, is the last, and he tells how he sacrificed a scalp:

"It was in the fall, before the winter buffalo hunt was made, that I thought I would go on the warpath. Every little while I would call a few men to sit down with me, and would tell them that I had it in mind to go on the warpath.

"The people went out on the winter hunt and killed buffalo, and while they were on their way back to the village, I started on the warpath with a number of young men. From the camp we went south to the Arkansas River. When we reached that river, it began to snow, and the snow fell six feet deep. We stopped in one place eleven days, till the snow got less deep. From there we went on to the sandhills by the North Canadian. One day as we were going along, we saw far off three Indians on foot. They

were Kiowas.   Probably they had been on the warpath and had lost their horses.   We attacked and
killed them.   They did not fight.   We killed them
like women.   Then, indeed, we divided the scalps,

CURLY CHIEF—KIT-KE-HAHK'-I.

and made many of them.   From there we started
home, and found the tribe camped on the Solomon
River.   When we reached home there was great joy,
and we danced the scalp dance.

"I sacrificed a scalp to *Ti-ra'-wa.*   I felt that he

had given me the victory over my enemies, and for this reason I wanted to give him something, I wanted to make an acknowledgment of his goodness to me. He had taken pity on me and helped me. It was a sacrifice greater than the sacrifice of the buffalo meat. Not many men have made it, but once in a while you see some one who has been noticed by the Ruler. It is our aim, after we have been helped, to give thanks."

PAWNEE DIRT LODGE.

RELIGION.

IT is generally believed that, among the Indians of North America, the priests and the shamans, "medicine men," or doctors, are the same. This is not the case with the Pawnees. Among them the priestly office was entirely distinct from that of the doctor, and had nothing in common with it. The priest was in a sense the medium of communication with *Ti-ra'-wa;* he prayed to the deity more efficaciously than could a common person, acted, in fact, as an intercessor; he knew the secrets of the sacred bundles, and when he asked anything good for the tribe, or for an individual, it was likely to be granted. His education and the power given him from above brought him into specially close relations with *Ti-ra'-wa*, who seemed to watch over him and to listen to him when he interceded for the tribe. He was an intermediary between *Ti-ra'-wa* and the people, and held a relation to the Pawnees and their deity not unlike that occupied by Moses to Jehovah and the Israelites.

The office of the "medicine man," shaman or doctor, had to do only with sickness or injury. He was the healer. Disease was caused by bad spirits, and it was the doctor's part to drive off these evil influences.

In the lodge or house of every Pawnee of influence, hanging on the west side, and so opposite the door, is the sacred bundle neatly wrapped in buckskin, and black with smoke and age. What these bundles contain we do not know. Sometimes, from the ends, protrude bits of scalps, and the tips of pipe stems and slender sticks, but the whole contents of the bundle are known only to the priests and to its owner—perhaps, not always even to him. The sacred bundles are kept on the west side of the lodge, because, being thus furthest from the door, fewer people will pass by them than if they were hung in any other part of the lodge. Various superstitions attach to these bundles. In the lodges where certain of them are kept it is forbidden to put a knife in the fire; in others, a knife may not be thrown; in others, it is not permitted to enter the lodge with the face painted; or again, a man cannot go in if he has feathers tied in his head.

On certain sacred occasions the bundles are opened, and their contents form part of the cere-monial of worship.

No one knows whence the bundles came. Many of them are very old; too old even to have a history. Their origin is lost in the haze of the long ago. They say, "The sacred bundles were given us long ago. No one knows when they came to us." Secret Pipe Chief, one of the very oldest men in the tribe, and its High Priest, said to me:

"All the sacred bundles are from the far off coun-try in the southwest, from which we came long ago. They were handed down to the people before they started on their journey. Then they had never seen anything like iron, but they had discovered how to make the flint knives and arrow points. There was nothing that came to us through the whites. It all came to us through the power of *Ti-ra'-wa*. Through his power we were taught how to make bows and stone knives and arrow heads.

"It was through the Ruler of the universe that the

sacred bundles were given to us. We look to them, because, through them and the buffalo and the corn, we worship *Ti-ra'-wa*. We all, even the chiefs, respect the sacred bundles. When a man goes on the warpath, and has led many scouts and brought the scalps, he has done it through the sacred bundles. There were many different ceremonies that they used to go through. The high priest performs these ceremonies.

"The high priestship was founded in this way: The black eagle spoke to a person, and said to him, 'I am one of those nearest to *Ti-ra'-wa*, and you must look to me to be helped; to the birds and the animals—look to me, the black eagle, to the white-headed eagle, to the otter and the buffalo.'

"The black eagle sent the buzzard as a messenger to this person, and he gave him the corn. The secrets of the high priestship and the other secrets were handed down at the same time. The buzzard, because he is bald, stands for the old men who have little hair. The white-headed eagle also represents the old men, those whose hair is white. These are the messengers through whom *Ti-ra'-wa* sends his words to the people. The Wichitas also had these secrets, and so have the Rees."

The Pawnees believe that they were created by *Ti-ra'-wa*, but that there had been people on the earth before them. They say, "The first men who lived on the earth were very large Indians. They were giants; very big and very strong. The animals that lived then were the same that we know now, and of the same size. These giants used to hunt the buffalo on foot. They were so swift and strong that a man could run down a buffalo, and kill it with a great stone, or a club, or even with his flint knife. Then, when he had killed it, if it was a big buffalo bull, he would tie it up, throw it over his back, and carry it into camp, just as a man to-day would carry in an antelope. When one killed a yearling, he would push its head up under his belt, and let its body swing by his side, just as we would carry a rabbit.

"These people did not believe in *Ti-ra'-wa*. When it would thunder and rain, they would shake their fists at the sky and call out bad words. In these days all people, wherever they live—all Indians, all white men, all Mexicans and all black men—when they smoke up, speak to *A-ti'-us Ti-ra'-wa*, and ask that he will give them the right kind of a mind, and that he will bless them, so that they may have plenty to eat, and may be successful in war, and may be made chiefs and head men. When we smoke toward the earth we say, 'Father of the dead, you see us.' This means that this is *Ti-ra'-wa's* ground. It belongs to him, and we ask him that he will let us walk on it, and will let us be buried in it. We believe that after we are dead we will live again with *Ti-ra'-wa* up in the sky. We fear nothing after death worse than we know now. All will live again with *Ti-ra'-wa* and be happy. A thief, one who steals from others in the camp, one who is bad, dies, and that is the end of him. He goes into the ground, and does not live again. One reason why we believe that there is a life after death is that sometimes, when asleep, we dream and see these things. We see ourselves living with *Ti-ra'-wa.* Then, too, we often dream of our people whom we have known, and who have died. We dream of being dead ourselves, and of meeting these people and talking with them, and going to war with them.

"Now, these giants did not believe in any of these things. They did not pray to *Ti-ra'-wa*, and they thought that they were very strong, and that nothing could overcome them. They grew worse and worse. At last *Ti-ra'-wa* got angry, and he made the water rise up level with the land, and all the ground became soft, and these great people sank down into the mud and were drowned. The great bones found on the prairie are the bones of these people, and we have been in deep cañons, and have seen big bones under ground, which convinces us that these people did sink into the soft ground.

"After the destruction of the race of giants, *Ti-ra'-wa* created a new race of men, small, like those of to-day. He made first a man and a woman. They lived on the earth and were good. To them was given the corn. From this man and this woman the Pawnees sprung, and they have always cultivated the corn from the earliest times."

There can be no doubt as to the belief of the Pawnees in a future life. The spirits of the dead live after their bodies have become dust. The stories of the Ghost Bride and the Ghost Wife, already given, are examples of this belief. Secret Pipe Chief told me of himself:

"I was dead once. Just as I died, I found my way leading to an Indian village. I entered it, and went straight to the lodge of my friends and my relations. I saw them, and when I saw them I knew them again. I even knew my old relations,

whom I had never looked on when I was alive. I
went into a lodge, but I was not offered a seat, and
I thought that I was not welcome. I came out of
the lodge, and went out of the village toward the
west. Then I came back to life again. In the
morning I had died, and I came to life in the afternoon. That must be the reason that I still live, and
am getting old. I was not welcome yet. They did
not receive me. From this I am convinced that
there is a life after we are dead."

Sometimes ghosts appear to them, but more often
they merely speak to them; only a voice is heard.
They believe that the little whirlwinds often seen in
summer are ghosts. The reason for this is that
once a person shot at a whirlwind with his arrow.
The arrow passed through it, and it all disappeared
and came to nothing. Then the man was convinced
that it was a ghost, and that he had killed it.

The different bands of the Pawnees had not all
the same beliefs. Thus the Skidi band offered up
the human sacrifice—a captive taken in war—to the
morning star. This is thought to have been a pro-
pitiatory offering to avert the evil influences exerted
by that planet. At the present day the Indians
speak of the sacrifice as having been made to *Ti-*

ra'-wa. None of the other tribes had this form of worship, and in this fact we have another indication that the separation of the Skidi from the Pawnees had been a long one. The *Ka-wa-ra-kish* band of the Pita-hau-erat, are said to have been "the only ones of the Pawnees who did not worship *Ti-ra'-wa.* They worshiped toward the west."

Mention has been made of the *Nahu'rac,* or animals, which possess miraculous attributes given them by *Ti-ra'-wa.* The Pawnees know of five places where these animals meet to hold council— five of these *Nahu'rac* lodges. One of these is at *Pa-hŭk',* on the south side of the Platte River, opposite the town of Fremont, in Nebraska. The word *Pa-hŭk'* means "hill island." Another animal home is under an island in the Platte River, near the town of Central City. It is called by the Pawnees *La–la–wa–koh–ti–to,* meaning "dark island." The third of these sacred places is on the Loup Fork, opposite the mouth of the Cedar River, and under a high, white cut bank. It is called *Ah-ka-wit-akol,* "white bank." Another is on the Solomon River, *Kitz-a-witz-ŭk,* "water on a bank;" it is called *Pa'howa* sometimes. This is a mound, shaped like a dirt lodge. At the top of the mound, in the middle, is a round hole, in which, down below, can be seen water. At certain times, the people gather there, and throw into this hole their offerings to *Ti-ra'-wa*, blankets and robes, blue beads, tobacco, eagle feathers and moccasins. Sometimes, when they are gathered there, the water rises to the top of the hole, and flows out, running down the side of the mound into the river. Then the mothers take their little children and sprinkle the water over them, and pray to *Ti-ra'-wa* to bless them. The water running out of the hole often carries with it the offerings, and the ground is covered with the old rotten things that have been thrown in. The fifth place is a hard, smooth, flinty rock, sticking up out of the ground. They call it *Pa-hūr'*, "hill that points the way." In the side of the hill there is a great hole, where the *Nahu'rac* hold councils. This hill is in Kansas, and can be seen from the Burlington & Missouri River Railroad. It is known to the whites as Guide Rock.

II. CEREMONIES.

To describe satisfactorily any considerable proportion of the religious ceremonials of the Pawnees,
would require a more extended space than is here at
my command. Several of the special ceremonies,
however, may be mentioned in general terms.

Like some other tribes of the plains Indians, the
Pawnees had a certain special worship at the time of
the first thunder in the spring. This first thunder
warned them that winter was at an end and that the
time of the planting was drawing near.

Of this worship a Chau-i said to me: "We all believe in *Ti-ra'-wa*. We know that there is a power
above that moves the universe, and that he controls
all things. In the old days when they had buffalo
meat, they used to make a sacrifice at the time of
the first thunder in the spring. The next day after
it had thundered, all the people would go into the
sacred lodge, where the sacred bundles were kept at
that time. When they had all come together, the
priest would open the bundles and take out the
sacred things, among which were Indian tobacco and
some little pieces of scalp tied to a stick. Through
these sacred things we worshiped, and the sacrifices

were made to the Ruler above. This seemed to be a help to us, and we used to live, increase and grow strong. Up north, when we worshiped at the time of the first thunder, we never had cyclones. Down here, now that this worship has been given up, we have them."

There is no doubt that the most important of the religious ceremonials of the Pawnees were the burnt offering of the animal and of the scalp. These two, though different, had yet the same meaning. In each the sacrifice was an offering to *Ti-ra'-wa*. Perhaps next in importance to these were the buffalo dance and the corn dance, which were special ceremonies to implore a blessing on the hunt and on the harvest.

The first animal killed on the hunt was sacrificed. It was necessary that this animal should be either a deer or a buffalo; the first one killed on the hunt of these two kinds. They were not permitted to kill any other sort of an animal, save only these two, until after the sacrifice had been made.

When this first animal had been killed, it was brought into the camp, and taken to the sacred lodge, and there the priests themselves went through the secret ceremonies. Then they divided the meat, and took a part of it to the southeast end of the village. There they built a fire of sticks, and placed the meat on it. As the fire burned the flesh, the whole tribe marched slowly and reverently by the fire, and grasped handfuls of the smoke, and rubbed it over their bodies and arms, and prayed, saying, "Now, you, *Ti-ra'-wa*, the Ruler, look at your children, and bless them; keep them and have mercy upon them, and care for them." If any could not understand, such as little children, their elders, who did understand—their relations—prayed for them. The sick were carried out to the place, and prayed, and the smoke was rubbed over them. The young men would run races, starting from a certain place, and going around the village until they came to the place where the smoke of the sacrifice rose.

The sacrifice, by burning of the scalp, was a very elaborate performance, and occupied a whole day. The high priest faced the east and prayed, and sang twelve times. Descriptions of it given me in general terms indicate that this ceremony was extremely interesting. It was rather unusual, but was performed once in 1877.

The sacrifice of the captive has not been practiced by the Skidi for a long time, perhaps forty or fifty years. Bear Chief told me that he had witnessed it six times; Eagle Chief, who is, perhaps, between fifty and sixty years old, says he has seen it once. The old Skidi described the ceremony as follows:

"The Skidi alone of the Pawnees sacrificed human beings to *Ti ra'-wa.* When they had returned home from war successful, bringing captives with them, they selected one of these for the sacrifice. The others were adopted into the tribe, but this one, who must be young and stout, one who would fatten easily, was kept apart, eating by himself, fed on the best of food and treated with the greatest kindness. No hint of the fate in store for him was given until the day of the sacrifice. For four nights before that day the people danced; and for four days they feasted. Each day after they had got through feasting, the dishes were taken to their especial place. Each woman, after she got through eating, rose, and said to the prisoner, 'I have finished eating, and I hope that I may be blessed from *Ti ra'-wa;* that he may take pity on me; that when I put my seed in the ground they may grow, and that I may have plenty of everything.'

"At the end of the four days two old men went, one to each end of the village, and called aloud, directing every male person in the village to make a bow and an arrow, and to be ready for the sacrifice. For every male child that had been born a bow and an arrow was made; for the little boys small bows that they could bend and small arrows. The arrows must be feathered with the feathers of the eagle, or of some bird of prey, a hawk, an owl or an eagle. They must not cut the feathers nor burn them to make them low.

"The next day, before daybreak, every one was ready. All of the warriors, who had led parties on the warpath, took from their sacred bundles their collars, made from the feathers of the bird they wore,* and put them on their backs and tied them about their necks. They held their pipes in their left hands, to signify that they were warriors. Every male carried his bow and arrow. Every woman had a lance or a stick. Just before daylight they all went out to the west end of the village, and stood there looking for the prisoner to be brought. Here two stout posts had been set up, one of ash and the other of hackberry, and between these had been tied four cross-poles, the three lower ones to aid in climbing up to the highest of the four.

* The Purple Martin, *Progne subis.*

"As day broke, the people, looking back toward the village, could see the captive being led toward them, bound hand and foot. Behind him, as he was led along, followed a warrior carrying the heart and tongue of a buffalo; after him came another, carrying a blazing stick, then one with a bow and arrow, and last a warrior with the stuffed skin of an owl.

"They led the naked captive to the posts, and lifting him up, tied first the left hand and then the right to the top cross-pole, and afterward tied the feet below. Every one stood there silent, looking, waiting; the men holding their weapons and the women their sticks and lances. On the ground under the sacrifice was laid the wood for a great fire, which was now lighted. Then the man with the blazing stick stepped forward, but before he reached the captive, the warrior with the bow and arrow, he who had taken the captive, ran up close to the victim and shot him through from side to side, beneath the arms, with the sacred arrow, whose point was of flint, such as they used in the olden time. After the blood had run down upon the fire below, the warrior who carried the buffalo tongue and the heart, placed them on the fire beneath the body. When this had been done the man who carried the owl ran up, and seized the burning stick and burned the body, once under each arm, and once in each groin, in all four times. Then, at a given signal, the males all ran up, and shot their arrows into the body. If any male children were not large enough to shoot, some one shot for them. There were so many arrows that the body was stuck full of them; it bristled with them.

"A man chosen for this purpose now climbed up, and pulled out all the arrows from the body, except the one which was first shot through the side of the sacrifice, and placed them together in a pile on the ground, where they were left. After pulling out the arrows, this man took his knife and cut open the breast of the captive, and putting his hand in the opening, took out a handful of blood, and smeared it over his face, and then jumped to the ground, and ran away as fast as he could. Each of the four men, after he had done his part, ran away very fast, and went down to the river and washed himself. When this had been done the women came with their sticks and spears and struck the body and counted *coup* on it. Even the little children struck it. After they had done this, they put their sticks together on the ground in a pile, and left them there. By this time the fire was burning up high and scorching the body, and it was kept up until the whole body was consumed. And while the smoke of the blood and the buffalo meat, and of the burning body, ascended to the sky, all the people prayed to *Ti-ra'-wa*, and walked by the fire and grasped handfuls of the smoke, and passed it over their bodies and over those of their children, and prayed *Ti-ra'-wa* to take pity on them, and to give them health, and success in war, and plenteous crops. The man who had killed the captive fasted and mourned for four days, and asked *Ti-ra'-wa* to take pity on him, for he knew that he had taken the life of a human being.

"This sacrifice always seemed acceptable to *Ti-ra'-wa*, and when the Skidi made it they always seemed to have good fortune in war, and good crops, and they were always well.

"After the sacrifice was over, then came the old women to rejoice over what had been done. They would act as the warriors used to do, when coming back from a war party. They carried the mother corn. They went to the body and counted *coup* on it, and then went back to the village. Some of them would take the large hollow stalks of the sunflower,

and put dust in them, and then blow it out, pretending to shoot, the puff of dust standing for the smoke
of a shot.   They would go up to the secret lodge,
and standing outside of it, would tell the story of
how they came to go on their pretended war party,
and what they did while they were gone, and what
enemies they struck—the whole long story.   The
people meanwhile would stand about and laugh at
them as they did these things.   Imitating the warriors, the old women changed their names also.
One of the leading old women once took the name
'Mud on the Meat,' another, 'Skunk Skin Tobacco
Pouch,' another 'Sitting Fish Old Man,' another
'Old Man Stepping on the Heart.'   The old men
standing about would joke with the old women, and
these would joke and make fun of each other."

The different acts of this sacrifice appear to have
been typical of the deeds and necessities of warfare.   Thus the feathers of the eagle used on the
arrows shot into the captive represented success in
war.   Their use was a prayer to *Ti-ra'-wa* that, as
these birds were fierce and successful when making
an attack, so those who shot might be fierce in war
and always conquerors.   The burning of the body of
the captive with the blazing stick, perhaps, typified

the lighting of the sacred pipe, which could only be done by one who had sacrificed a scalp. The shooting arrows into the body by the males and the striking it by the women typified the killing of and counting *coup* on the enemy. The cutting open the belly was the first act in the sacrifice of the animal, the burnt offering.

It will be noted that this account differs in many particulars from that given by Mr. Dunbar in his papers on this people, but I think it worth recording, as being an independent relation by a very old man, who, I have no doubt, has been an eye-witness of more than one of these remarkable sacrifices.

I know of no satisfactory and detailed account of any of the sacred dances of the Pawnees. There were many of these, among them the corn dance, the buffalo dance, the wild horse dance, the deer, bear, dog dances and so on. I give below an account of the corn dance, as detailed to me by Curly Chief, who said:

"The windy month [March] was the one in which *Ti-ra'-wa* gave us the seed to cultivate. The first moon of April is the one during which they had a special worship about the corn. Until these ceremonies had been performed no one would clear out the patch where they intended to plant the crop. Everybody waited for this time.

" The Kit-ke-hahk'-i was the only tribe in which this special ceremony was handed down. The Chau-i and Pita-hau-erat worshiped with them. The preparations for this dance are always made by a woman. She has to think about it a long time before she can make up her mind to undertake it. In making ready for the dance, she must furnish the dried meat made from the whole of a buffalo, fat and lean, every part of it. The sack which holds the heart she dries, and fills it with all the kinds of corn—the five colors, the blue corn, which represents the blue sky, the red corn, which stands for the evening sunset, the yellow corn, which typifies the morning sunrise, the white corn, which stands for a white cloud, and the spotted corn, which represents the sky dotted with clouds. All these she puts in the bag, placing in the sack three grains of each at a time. On the special day which has been fixed for the dance, she must offer these things to *Ti-ra'-wa.* The people are all gathered together, the women standing on the outside of the circle behind, and the men on the inner side of the circle in front. This is a woman's dance, and yet the men are there in front of the women.

These men are the leading warriors of the tribe. They have been off on the warpath, and in time of corn have gone to the enemy. They have been successful in war, and therefore they are with the women. They stand about the circle holding their pipes in their left hands, showing that they are leaders of war parties, and each with the skin of a particular bird * tied on top of the head, showing that they are warriors.

"The floor of the lodge must be hard, and swept as clean as it can be. On the left hand side as you look toward the door is a buffalo skull.

"When the day has come all the people are gathered together and are standing about the lodge. The high priest stands at the back of the lodge with the sacred bundles of the three bands before him. Then this leading woman comes forward, and presents to the high priest the dried meat and the sack of corn, and two ancient, sacred hoes, made from the shoulder-blade of a buffalo, bound to a handle by the neck ligament. She places them on the ground before the sacred bundles, the corn in the middle, and the two hoes on either side. With these things she also presents a sacred pipe, filled and ready for light-

* A Martin, *Progne.*

ing, taken from a sacred bundle. Then she steps back.

"The old high priest must well know the ceremonies to be performed. He prays to *Ti-ra'-wa* and lights the sacred pipe, blowing smoke to heaven, to the earth, and to the four points of the compass. While the ceremonies are going on, the buffalo skull is taken to the sacred place in this lodge, and put in a particular position. Then the leading woman steps forward again, followed by two others. She takes the bag of corn, and the other two women take the hoes, and they stand in front of the high priest. He sings and prays. The leading woman stands in a particular position, as directed by the high priest, holding the bag of corn up to the sky in both her hands; and as he sings, she raises and lowers it in time to the music of the song.

"After these ceremonies the women come forward, holding their hoes in their hands, and dance about the lodge one after another in single file, following the leading woman. Four times they dance about the lodge. She cannot pass the priest the fifth time. These ceremonies and the songs and prayers were to ask for a blessing on the hunt and on the corn, and to learn whether they would be blessed in both.

After the women had danced and gone back to their places, everybody looked on the floor of the lodge to see whether there were any buffalo hairs there. If they saw them, they all said, 'Now we are going to be successful in our hunt and in our corn.' Everybody said, 'We are blessed.'

"Then when they would go out on the hunt they would find plenty of buffalo, and the messenger sent back to the village from the hunt would return to the camp and say, 'We have plenty of corn.' If they saw a great many buffalo hairs they would get many buffalo; if but few they would get some buffalo.

"The next day after these ceremonies every one would begin to clear up their patches and get ready to plant corn. The leading woman who prepared the dance is respected and highly thought of. After that she is like a chief.

"This ceremony is the next principal thing we have after the burnt offering of the animal and of the scalp. We did not invent this. It came to us from the Ruler, and we worship him through it. He gave us the corn and blessed us through it. By it we are made strong.

"We are like seed and we worship through the corn."

III. MEDICINE AND MYSTERY.

It has been said that the "medicine men" or doctors among the Pawnees occupied a position by themselves. Their guild was entirely distinct from that of the priests. A priest might be a doctor as well, but not because he was a priest.

The doctors were primarily healers. Their function was to fight disease. Like many other savage nations, the Pawnees believed that sickness was caused by evil spirits, which had entered into the patient and must be driven out if he was to recover. In their treatment of injuries the doctors were often singularly successful. Major North has cited for me a number of instances, in which men, whose hurts had refused to yield to the treatment of the United States Army surgeons, had been cured by Pawnee doctors. Some of these have been detailed elsewhere. As might be imagined, however, the Pawnee treatment of disease was less efficacious. Simple ailments were often treated with success by means of the familiar sudatory, or "sweat house;" but in the case of more serious complaints, the dancing and rattling, which constitute so large a part of the doctor's treatment, tend to aggravate rather than to check the disease. I have not space to discuss the very interesting subject of the system of therapeutics practiced by the Pawnee doctors. Mr. Dunbar has gone into this matter quite fully, and the reader is referred to his papers for an account of their practice.

As the doctors had to fight evil spirits, it is not surprising that they should have summoned magic to their aid; but this magic probably served its more important purpose in impressing the other Indians with a belief in the doctors' powers. Some of the performances which took place at the doctors' dances were very marvellous, and most of them were quite inexplicable to those who saw what was done. That they should have imposed on the Indian spectator is perhaps not surprising; but it is further to be noted that clear-headed, intelligent white men, whose powers of observation have been highly trained, have confessed themselves wholly unable to explain these startling performances, or to hazard a guess as to the means by which they were accomplished. That these things happened as detailed is well authenticated by the testimony of many perfectly credible witnesses.

Other masters of mystery are provided with mechanical aids of one kind or another—some apparatus which assists them in imposing on their audiences, by concealing certain objects, or certain acts, by means of which they cause things to appear different from what they really are. The Pawnee doctors had nothing of this. Their dances were conducted by naked men in a ring surrounded by spectators. The floor of bare earth, packed hard and worn smooth by the tread of many feet, afforded no apparent opportunity for concealment or trickery. Under such conditions were performed their mysteries, a few of which I will mention as they appeared to watchful spectators, distant not more than twenty-five or thirty feet, and often much nearer.

The simplest performances were the swallowing of spears and arrows. These feats were merely mechanical, and were no doubt really as they appeared, the arrows and the spears being driven down the gullet to the distance of a foot or eighteen inches. Instances occurred where men who had swallowed arrows died from the injuries received in the operation. Bear Chief, himself a doctor, and tattooed with a bear on the right side, told me that it was much harder and more painful to swallow an arrow than a spear.

Among the more remarkable performances witnessed and vouched for by my friend, Captain L. H. North, are the following:

Several men, representing elk, came into the ring, and trotted about, so as to be seen by every one, imitating the movements of those animals. To their heads were tied branches to represent horns, and each wore an elk skin thrown over his back. A doctor came into the ring, and handed to the spectators his arrows, which they examined, and found to be ordinary arrows with the usual sheet-iron points. On receiving back the arrows from those who had examined them, the doctor pretended to hunt the elk, and at length shot at them, striking them in the sides or on the legs. The arrows, instead of penetrating the flesh, bounded back, some of them flying fifteen or twenty feet in the air. They appeared to be shot with the full force of the bow, and when picked up and handed to the onlookers, the sheet-iron points were found to be doubled back as if they had been shot against a plate of iron, and the shafts of some of them were split. The elk trotted away and out of the ring without injury.

A man, representing an enemy, came into the ring on foot. A doctor followed, armed with a hatchet, which he passed to the spectators for examination.

It was an ordinary hatchet of the tomahawk form. On receiving back the hatchet, the doctor started in pursuit of the enemy, who fled. The doctor overtook him, and with a vigorous blow, sunk the hatchet up to the handle in the enemy's skull, leaving it there. The wounded man staggered on, passing within five or six feet of the ring of spectators, who plainly saw the blood from the wound running down the man's face, and dripping from his hair behind. They saw also the gray brain-matter oozing from the wound. The wounded man was taken from the ring into the doctor's lodge. A few days later he was seen about, and in his usual health.

A small boy, six or eight years of age, was led into the ring quite naked. He was placed upon the ground, and two men sat upon him, one on his chest, the other on his legs. With a knife an incision was made in his belly; one of the doctors inserted his fingers; and, after feeling about, pulled out of the cut what looked like a portion of the child's liver. This he cut off and gave to the other man, who ate it. The remainder of the liver was crowded back into the hole, and the boy was carried off. Subsequently he was seen about, apparently in good health.

A man representing a bear came into the ring and

was pursued by a number of Indians, who shot arrows at him for some time, without appearing to injure him. At length, however, an arrow pierced him through the bowels, and the wound was plainly seen on each side. The man fell, and appeared to be dying. He was removed to the lodge, and in a short time was entirely recovered.

Major North saw one of these bear performances, in which, the pretended bear having attacked one of his pursuers, the latter slashed him across the abdomen with a large knife, inflicting a cut from which the bowels hung down so that they dragged on the ground. The bear was carried off, and in a short time was healed, and went about as usual.

Major North told me that he saw with his own eyes the doctors make the corn grow. This was in the medicine lodge. In the middle of the lodge, the doctor dug up a piece of the hard trodden floor of the lodge, about as large as a dinner plate, and broke up between his fingers the hard pieces of soil, until the dirt was soft and friable. The ground having thus been prepared, and having been moistened with water, a few kernels of corn were buried in the loose earth. Then the doctor retired a little from the spot and sang, and as the place where the corn was buried was watched, the soil was seen to move, and a tiny green blade came slowly into view. This continued to increase in height and size, until in the course of twenty minutes or half an hour from the time of planting, the stalk of corn was a foot or fifteen inches in height. At this point Major North was obliged to leave the lodge, to take out a white woman who was fainting from the heat, and so did not see the maturing of the corn. All the Indians and white men who remained assured him that the stalks continued to grow until they were of full height, and that they then tasseled out and put forth one or more ears of corn, which grew to full size, and that then the doctor approached the plant, plucked an ear, and passed it to the spectators.

Similar to this was a feat performed with a cedar berry. The berry was passed around among the spectators for examination, and was then planted as the corn had been. Then after a few moments the doctor approached the spot, put his thumb and fore-finger down into the soft dirt, and seemed to lay hold of something. Very slowly he raised his hand and was seen to hold on the tips of his fingers the end of a cedar twig. Slowly his hand was moved from the ground, the twig growing longer and longer. When nine or ten inches high it began to have side branches. The doctor still holding the topmost twig of what was by this time a cedar bush, continued to lift his hand very slowly, until it was about three feet from the ground, and then let go of the bush. Then presently he took hold of the stem close to the ground, and, seeming to exert a good deal of force, pulled up the bush by the roots; and all the people saw the bush and its bunch of fresh and growing roots.

Enough has been said of these mystery ceremonies to indicate that they were very remarkable. The circumstances under which they were performed would seem to remove them from the more common-place tricks of professional jugglers. And I have never found any one who could even suggest an explanation of them.

As might be inferred, these mysterious doings greatly impressed the Pawnees; and the older men among them have a vast store of reminiscences of past dances, which they delight in repeating. In the course of a long talk with Bear Chief one evening, he recounted a number of instances which he had seen. He said:

"A man in our tribe was blind; he could not see.

He could travel in the night as well as we can in the day, but when daylight came he could see nothing. At one time he called together his relations, and told them that, though blind, he wished to lead out a war party. He said, 'I know that I, with my party, will kill an enemy.' They started out, a young man leading him by the hand all day long. After they had been out several days, he told the young men to be ready, that the next morning he was going to kill an enemy. The next morning, while they were traveling along, they saw an enemy, and surrounded and killed him. They took the scalp and brought it home, and he had great credit, because, being blind, he had killed an enemy. They were all surprised that a blind man should have killed an enemy. He sacrificed the scalp to *Ti-ra'-wa*, and was made a warrior, and went to the sacred lodge and told the story of his campaign, and was made a warrior—a blind warrior.

"It was a wonderful thing for a blind person to be able to travel in the night. This must have come from *Ti-ra'-wa*.

"One of the wonderful things done by this man was at a medicine dance. Everybody was there. He stood up with his bearskin over him, and was led out before the people. A cedar branch was given him, and he sharpened the end where it had been cut off, and stuck it in the ground. Everybody was now asked to pull up this branch, and many tried to do so, but the strongest men in the tribe could not move it. He could pull it up, as if it were stuck in the mud. He thrust the pointed end in the ground again, and asked the doctors to pull up the cedar branch. They tried to do so, but could not stir it. The chiefs also were asked to try to do this. They tried, but could not move it. Something seemed to hold it in the ground. After everybody had tried to pull it up, and failed, this blind man went to it, and taking hold of it, pulled with all his strength, and pulled up with it about six feet of roots. There lay the tree with all it roots fresh and growing.

"There was, in my young days, a certain brave man in the tribe. His name was Elk Left Behind. He was so brave that, when the Sioux surrounded him, he would kill so many that he would scare the rest away. In one of the doctors' dances he had the skin of a fawn in his hands. He called out to the people, 'Now, you people, watch me; look close and see what I shall do, and you will find out what my bravery is, and that it all comes from this that you see.' In our presence he shook this fawn skin, and the fawn slipped out of his hands and then stood before him, a living fawn looking at him. 'That is what I mean,' said he. 'If the enemies surround me, that is the way I come out of it. The fawn can run so fast that it can never be caught, nor can it ever be shot.'

"This man was wonderful. He used to imitate the deer and the elk. He could never be driven into timber or brush, or where there were thickets. He said, 'If I am ever wounded, it will be when I go into timber or brush.' He always wanted to be in the open plain where he could be surrounded. He never ran to the timber for shelter.

"If they suspected that the Sioux were coming to attack the village, he would load a gun and shoot it off. If the ball came back to him, there were no Sioux coming. If it did not, then they would be coming. When I was present it always came back to him. There were no Sioux coming.

"At one time in the doctors' dance I saw him driving ten young men, who pretended that they were deer. He had a gun and loaded it, and shot the ten men, one after another, through the side. They fell

down wounded, and then got up and limped off half
dying. He drove them around the ring so that the
people might see their wounds. After they had

SUN CHIEF—KIT-KE-KAHK'-I.

looked at them, he went up to the first and slapped
him on the back, and the ball dropped out of him on
to the ground, and the man straightened up, healed.
So he did to all, up to the tenth man, and they were
all healed. This was wonderful.

"At one time he wanted to show the people that he could stand anything. He and two others were attacked by Sioux. He said, 'I want to be wounded; let us go to the thickets.' They did so, and a Sioux shot him through the back, and the other two were wounded, but he healed them all after they had got away from the Sioux.

"Another man in the doctors' dance had four young men pretend that they were horses. All had manes and tails, and were painted to imitate horses. He had a gun, to which was tied a scalp. He loaded the gun, and while he was doing this the horses ran off, and stood looking back at the man. He cocked the gun and laid it on the ground pointing toward the horses, and placed the scalp near the trigger, and walked some steps away. Then he motioned to the scalp and the gun went off, and one of the horses went down wounded. It seems that the ghost of the scalp obeyed his motion, and shot off the gun. He loaded the gun again, and placed it on the ground as before. The second time he went way off, and as soon as he waved his hand and said, '*wooh*,' the gun went off and another horse went down. This was repeated until all the horses were down. The people examined them and saw that they were really wounded in the breast. The man went up to them and they seemed to be dying and vomited blood, and the young man slapped them, and the balls came out of their mouths, and as soon as the balls came away from them they were healed.

"There were two people, a brother and sister, children of a man who had been helped by a bear. One time when we were having a doctors' dance, the sister and brother came forward, each carrying five cedar branches about three feet long. They rolled a big rock into the middle of the lodge, so that all might see what they were going to do. Then they called ten private men who were not doctors, and told them to thrust the ends of the branches into the stone as if they had grown there, and they sang:

> "'See the trees growing in the rock;
> The cedar tree grows in the rock.'

"These cedar branches were cut square off at the butt, and were set on the stone. They were not big enough to be even and balance, but still they stood upright, as if grown from the rock. The doctors tried to blow them down with their fans made of eagle feathers, but they could not do it. You could not blow them off nor pull them off. At length the

men who put them there were told to take them off
They had hard work to do it, but at last they suc
ceeded.

"The sister (I saw her do it) put her hands up to
the sun, and then putting them on the ground and
scratching and throwing up dust, she would take up
her hands, and have hands like a bear, with hair and
long claws.

"She used to understand how to make plums and
other fruits grow on trees. She supplied the doctors
with choke cherries and plums. The doctors had
trees brought in that had no fruit on them. She
would make the plums grow, and shaking the tree,
they would fall down, and everybody would have a
taste of them. This was at a doctors' dance."

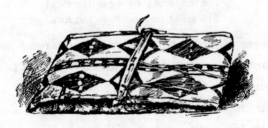

A PARFLECHE.

LATER HISTORY.

I. REMOVAL TO THE INDIAN TERRITORY.

THE project of removing the Pawnees from their reservation on the Loup River in Nebraska appears to have been first heard of in the year 1872. The Pawnee reservation was close to civilization, and the settlers moving west into Nebraska coveted the Indians' lands. It was the old story, the same one that has been heard ever since the rapacious whites first set foot on the shores of this continent.

The Pawnees were strongly attached to their home in Nebraska. They had always lived there, and were used to it. Their forefathers were buried there. Up to the winter of 1873–74 they had no idea of moving. But they were constantly being subjected to annoyances.

Settlers crowded in close to the Pawnee agency,

and even located on it on the south and east, and in
the most matter of fact way drove their teams into
the Pawnee timber, and cut and carried off the Pawnee wood, on which the tribe depended for fuel and
for building materials. This open robbery gave
rise to constant disputes and bickerings between the
Indians and the whites, in which the former were invariably worsted. On the south and east side of the
reservation the crowding and the depredations were
continuous. On the north and west the reservation
was exposed to frequent incursions from the different
bands of Sioux. War parties came down from their
reservations, stole the Pawnees' horses, killed their
women while at work in the fields, and sometimes
even attacked the village. These attacks, though
always successfully repelled by the Pawnees, were a
continual source of annoyance and irritation to them,
while their consistent desire to obey the rules laid
down for their guidance by the Government prevented them from retaliating in kind upon their
enemies.

The first proposition to remove the Pawnees to
the Indian Territory originated with the whites, but
there is some reason to think that an independent
movement with the same object in view was made by

members of the Pawnee tribe. As nearly as I can learn from conversation with Indians who took a leading part in the movement, this project for a removal of a part of the tribe to the south originated with Lone Chief, the Kit-ke-hahk'-i; and was taken up and supported by Left Hand, known also as Spotted Horse, a turbulent spirit, who was killed a few years ago by an United States marshal; and by Frank White, an intelligent soldier of the Chau-i band.

In the summer of 1870, Lone Chief led a visiting party, which is said to have numbered three hundred men, south to the Wichitas. When this party turned back to go north in the fall, many of them were sick with chills and fever—a disease unknown to them until that time—and some died on the way. At this time the notion of the removal had not been suggested, but it is probable that even then Lone Chief was considering the advisability of moving south with his own immediate family, and taking up his residence with the Wichitas. He had not yet spoken of this project, however, but in the winter of 1871–72 he announced his intention of doing this, and even started on his journey, but for some reason turned back.

The next winter—1872–73—while the tribe was

absent on the buffalo hunt, the northern Sioux came down and stole from the Pawnees a number of horses. This made the Pawnees uneasy, and some war parties started out. It was at this time that Lone Chief conceived the idea of increasing the company which should proceed south with him. After some consideration and consultation, Lone Chief, Spotted Horse and Frank White planned that a small party should go south, and visit the different tribes in the Indian Territory, for the purpose of learning how these tribes would regard a general movement of the Pawnees down into their country. The plan was not fully developed until this small party, of which Spotted Horse and Frank White were the leaders, was on its way.

The party visited first the Otoes and Kaws, and then going south came to the Wichitas, Comanches, Kiowas and Apaches, and were everywhere hospitably entertained, and given presents of horses. They asked the chiefs and headmen of the various tribes which they visited to come together at a certain specified time at the Wichita camp, telling them that they had something that they wished to say to them there. The Pawnees then returned to the Wichita village, and awaited the appointed time.

Soon the representatives of the different tribes began to arrive. Day after day they kept coming in, until all were present. When they had assembled in council, Spotted Horse rose to speak. He said, "My brothers, I want you to know one thing—We, the Pawnees, want to be brothers, and to be at peace. I have made up my mind to come down here with my party of Pawnees to live with you."

The chiefs representing the different tribes all expressed their satisfaction at this announcement, and urged him to come as he had intended. They said, "We have good land here, and lots of buffalo. We shall be glad if you decide to come." After all had spoken, Spotted Horse again stood up and said, "Brothers, there is here with me one leading man among the Pawnees. He, also, will tell you what he thinks about this." Frank White then spoke and said that he intended to accompany Spotted Horse when he should move south. The chiefs of the different tribes again expressed the hope that they would carry out their intentions, and arrangements were made with the tribes that they should come down and live with them.

It is stated that just before this visiting party started north toward their home, news came from the

Pawnee agency that the tribe had been attacked and massacred on the Republican River by Sioux, and as they journeyed north they learned the details of the occurrence. On reaching the village, Spotted Horse and Frank White reported to Lone Chief and to their families what they had done, and their action was confirmed. The chiefs of the tribe and the agent were then notified. Soon afterward a general council was held, at which public announcement of their intention was made by these three men. To most of those present the project was wholly new, and there was a good deal of confusion in the council, the people exclaiming at the news and discussing it.

Efforts were made by the chiefs of the bands to dissuade those who proposed to move. The Head Chief, *Pi'ta Le-shar*, tried to persuade Frank White not to leave the tribe, but he said that he had promised, and he should go.

In the autumn of 1873, Lone Chief, Spotted Horse and Frank White, accompanied by their personal following, started south. With them went about two-thirds of the tribe. The three leaders had a pass from the Superintendent of Indian Affairs at the Pawnee agency. The chiefs of the tribe were still bitterly opposed to the notion of the removal, and *Pi'ta Le-shar*, the Head Chief, exerted all his influence to prevent the movement. After the migrating party had gone about fifty miles, messengers from the chiefs overtook them, directing them to return to the village. The march was stopped, and the three leaders, as delegates, returned to the agency to learn the cause of the order. They reached there in the evening, and spent the whole night conferring with the agent (Burgess), to whom they gave presents to persuade him to accede to their request to continue their journey. Lone Chief was the most determined, and insisted that they should be permitted to go on without interference.

At length the authorities yielded, and a new pass having been given them, they returned to the camp. The responsibility of taking away so large a part of the tribe was weighing heavily on these three men, however, and they determined to send back all except their own families. On reaching the camp, therefore, they told the Indians that they all were to go back, but hid their own horses, pretending that they had strayed off, so that the main body would start back without them. After the others had moved out of camp on their return march to the agency, the lost horses were at once found, and the three men with their families went on south.

The following year all the tribe followed, except the Skidi, Lone Chief, and a few personal friends, who still refused to leave the old reservation. This small company remained in their old home one year longer, and then they, too, went south to their present reservation.

Shortly before the removal of the tribe to the Indian Territory in 1874, *Pi'ta Le-shar*, the Head Chief, was shot, and died from his wound. It has been stated, and generally believed, that his death resulted from the accidental discharge of his own pistol, but there are well-informed persons who believe that he was murdered. There is reason to believe that the shot did not come from his own weapon, but that he was shot by a white man in order to get rid of his influence, which was consistently exerted to keep the Pawnees in their northern home. The Chief's wound was not a serious one, and he was doing well under the charge of a white surgeon, when he was induced to put himself in the care of a Pawnee doctor, under whose treatment he died.

Ti-ra'-wa Le-shar, another bitter opponent of removal, had been killed in 1873; and the death of

Pi'ta Le-shar left Lone Chief, Skidi, the only man of strong character to oppose the movement.

The full history of the plot to eject the Pawnees from their northern home may never be recorded, for there are few men alive who know the facts. If it should be written there would be disclosed a carefully planned and successfully carried out conspiracy to rob this people of their lands. This outrage has cost hundreds of lives, and an inconceivable amount of suffering, and is another damning and ineffaceable blot on the record of the American people, and one which ought surely to have had a place in Mrs. Jackson's "Century of Dishonor."

II. PRESENT CONDITION AND PROGRESS.

During the first four years of their sojourn in the Indian Territory the condition of the Pawnees was most miserable.

They had left the high, dry, sandy country of the Loup, and come south into the more fertile, but also more humid country of the Indian Territory, where they found a region entirely different from that to which they had been accustomed. Soon after their settlement on their new reservation, they were attacked by fever and ague, a disease which had been unknown to them in their northern home, and many of them died, while all were so weakened by disease and so discouraged by homesickness that their nature seemed wholly changed. They lost their old spirit and their energy, and were possessed only by a desire to return to their northern home. This was, of course, impossible, since their old reservation had been thrown open to settlement, and in part occupied by the whites. During the first ten years of their sojourn in the Territory more than one of the agents appointed to look after the Pawnees were either incompetent or dishonest, so that the people suffered from lack of food, and some of them even starved to death. They were miserably poor, for they did not know how to work, and no one tried to encourage or help them to do so. The few horses which they had were stolen from them by white horse thieves, and they were now in a country and under conditions where they could not practice their old war methods. The tribes against which their expeditions had once been made were now their neighbors and their friends.

When Major North and his brother Luther visited the agency in 1876, to enlist scouts for General

Crook's northern campaign, they found the Pawnees in a pitiable condition. They were without food, without clothing, without arms and without horses. Their sole covering consisted of cotton sheets, which afforded no protection against cold and wet. It is not strange that under such circumstances the people died off fast. At this time Major North had orders to enlist only one hundred scouts, but he was greatly perplexed in selecting his men, for four hundred wanted to go with him. Every able-bodied man in the tribe, and many who were not able-bodied, tried to get their names on the muster roll. Each man, at any cost, sought to get away from the suffering of his present life; from the fever that made him quake, the chill that caused him to shiver, and above all from the deadly monotony of the reservation life. After Major North had enlisted his quota of men and started with them on his way north, more than a hundred others followed him on foot to Arkansas City, in the hope that he could be persuaded to increase his force, or else that some of those enlisted would drop out through sickness, and there might be room for others.

The wretched condition of the Pawnees continued up to about 1884 or 1885. Before this time the people had become in a measure acclimated in their new home, and had come to realize that it was absolutely necessary for them to go to work if the tribe was to continue to exist. They began to work; at first only a few, but gradually many, of the Skidi, and then the Chau-i and the Kit-ke-hahk'-i. Presently a point was reached where it was no longer necessary to issue them Government rations. They raised enough on their farms to support themselves. Each year of late they have done better and better. A drought one season, and a cyclone another, destroyed their crops, but, undiscouraged and undaunted, they push ahead, striving earnestly to become like white men. The Pita-hau-erats are the least progressive of the four bands, and many of them still live in dirt lodges, and cultivate patches of corn scarcely larger than those tilled in their old villages; but as the other bands advance, and as the results of manual labor are seen and understood by those who are more idle, they, too, will catch the spirit of progress, and will lay hold of the plow.

Last March, as I drove along toward the agency, and as we came in sight of Black Bear Creek, I was surprised to see what looked like good farm houses dotting the distant bottom. A nearer view and a closer investigation showed me that the most well-to-do of the Pawnees live in houses as good as those of many a New England land owner, and very much better than those inhabited by new settlers in the farther West. Many of them have considerable farms under fence, a barn, a garden in which vegetables are raised, and a peach orchard. They realize that as yet they are only beginning, but to me, who knew them in their old barbaric condition, their progress seems a marvel. Nowadays by far the greater number of the Pawnees wear civilized clothing, ride in wagons, and send their children to the agency school. They are making rapid strides toward civilization, just such progress as might be expected from the intelligent and courageous people that they are and always have been.

The Pawnees receive from the Government a perpetual annuity of thirty thousand dollars, of which one-half is paid in money, and one-half in goods. Besides this they have a credit with the Government of about two hundred and eighty thousand dollars (the proceeds of the sale of their old reservation in Nebraska), on which they receive interest; and for some years past they have leased to cattlemen about one hundred and twenty-five thousand acres of their reservation, for which they receive about three thousand eight hundred dollars per annum. It will thus be seen that in addition to the crops which they raise, the tribe is fairly well provided with money. While a considerable part of this is, of course, wasted, being spent for trifles and for luxuries, it is nevertheless the fact that a certain proportion of it is invested by the Indians in tools, farming implements, and in furniture. Three years ago the Indians merely dropped their corn into the furrow, while some planted with a hoe. There was then only one corn-planter on the reservation. Now there are thirteen of these implements of improved pattern, bought by the Indians, and paid for with their own money. Reapers and mowers belong to the Indian Department, and are loaned, not issued, and these pass round from one family to another. Within the last four years one hundred breaking and stirring plows have been issued, and one hundred and five double shovel cultivators. Eighty wagons and one hundred and fifty sets of harness have been issued in the same length of time. Besides these, eight two-horse cultivators are loaned them by the Government.

The Pawnees seem to be saving up their money to put into farming implements, and they are looking ahead. Two-thirds of the houses built in the last three years have been built by the Chau-i, who are pushing the Skidi hard in their advance toward civilization.

The following table, taken from the official papers of the Indian Bureau, gives some statistics as to the progress made by the Pawnees during the last three years:

	1885.	1886.	1887.	1888.
Number of Indians.......	1,045	998	918	869
Number of male Indians..	....	483	414	....
Number of female Indians.	....	515	504	....
Number speaking English.	....	289	....	225
Number can read (youths).	....	100	90	100
Number can read (adults)..	....	58	60	75
Number wearing citizen's dress wholly...........	....	300	350	200
Number wearing citizen's dress in part...........	....	400	450	600
Number doing some farming	....	324	400	* 125
Number having other civilized work.............	....	5	6	* 7
Number of births.........	....	28	45	54
Number of deaths.........	....	77	125	106
Houses occupied by Indians	....	61	82	98
Proportion of Indians self-supporting.............	....	⅔	½	⅔
Farming operations—				
Number of acres cultivated by Indians.............	971	1,360	2,094	2,560
Number of acres broken by Indians................	....	67	310	340

* Families.

	1885.	1886.	1887.	1888.
Number of acres under fence	400	1,597	2,597	5,200
Number of rods fencing put up during year..........	200	4,435	2,181	2,975
Produce raised by Indians—				
Number bushels of wheat..	1,177	1,273	5,000	2,500
Number bushels of corn, estimated	35,000	26,120	30,000	60,000
Number bushels of oats...	969	....	640	2,300
Number bushels of potatoes.	100	100	Est.2,500	....
Number bushels of onions.	10	50	100	150
Number bushels of beans..	300	....	500	750
Number of melons........	5,225	50,000	50,000	....
Number of pumpkins.....	3,000	5,000	....	....
Number tons of hay.......	500	....	600	800
Live stock owned by Indians—				
Horses, estimated.........	....	1,200	1,400	1,500
Mules, estimated..........	15	20	20	25
Cattle, estimated..........	300	380	575	500
Hogs, estimated..........	100	....	200	....
Fowls, estimated....	200	2,500	2,500	3,000

Twelve allotments of land made 1888. Whole number allotments to date (1888), 175. In 1885 Indians sawed 50,050 feet of lumber, and cut 126 cords of wood.

In 1886 the Indians hauled 83,814 pounds of freight, for which they were paid $541.54.

During the year 1888 three Indian apprentices learned a trade.

Besides the crops raised, the Indians during 1888 sawed 50,000 feet of lumber, and cut 300 cords of wood.

In 1886 a severe cyclone and hail storm destroyed the growing crops, and in 1887 a prolonged drought again ruined them. During these two years it was necessary to issue to the Indians half rations and one-third rations respectively. This year (1888–89) no rations have been issued.

As will be seen by these figures, corn is the principal crop raised by the Pawnees, and a large part of
the surplus beyond their own wants is sold at from
twenty-five to fifty cents a bushel to the dealers in
Arkansas City, or to the cattlemen in the neighborhood. The Pawnees have as yet few cattle, their old
meat-eating habits have not yet been overcome, and
there is a tendency among them to eat any cattle they
may obtain rather than to use them for breeding purposes. They ought to be encouraged to keep cattle,
to which they could feed their corn, and in this way
obtain a better return for their labor than is yielded
by the direct sale of the grain. They are fairly well
provided with horses, but most of these are small,
and of the old-fashioned Indian pony type. They
should be encouraged to raise a better class of
horses, and at least two well bred heavy stallions
should be kept by the Government at Pawnee for
Indian use. There is one now at Ponca, thirty-five
miles away, but the Pawnees will not take their mares
so far.

Much of the improvement in the condition of the
Pawnees has taken place within the last three years,
and much of it has been due, as I believe, to the
wisdom and judgment of Major Osborne, their agent,

and to the Messrs. McKenzie, who have for three years or more been the clerks directly in charge of these people. These gentlemen appear to have been honest and firm, and yet helpful in their treatment of the people under their charge, and the results of their administration show for themselves, and are something in which these officials may feel a just pride.

Few and rapidly diminishing in numbers as are the Pawnee people, I have yet confidence that by the innate strength of their character their decline may be checked, and their race may rise again. It can never do so in its old purity. It must take to itself fresh blood from other stocks, and thus renew its vitality. What I hope for the Pawnee, to-day and in the future, is that the native vigor of the race, the strong heart and singleness of purpose, which in ancient times led the wild brave to success on his warpath, and gave his tribe so high a place among the savage warriors of the plains, may now be exercised in the pursuits of peace; and that the same qualities may give to these earnest toilers, as they tread new paths, strength, courage and endurance to hold a front rank among those Indians, who, to-day so far behind, are nevertheless resolutely setting their steps toward a place with civilized people.

But whatever the fate of the Pawnee people—whether, like so many other native stocks, it shall dwindle away and disappear, leaving behind it no reminder of its existence, or whether its native force shall enable it under its new conditions to survive and make some mark—we may remember it always as a race of strong, brave people, whose good qualities are deserving of more than a passing tribute.

*
*   *

It was the last day of my stay at the Pawnee agency. I had seen many an old friend; had laughed and joked with some over incidents of former years, and with others had mourned over brave warriors or wise old men who were no longer with us. My visit had been full of pleasure, and yet full of pain. When I had first known the tribe it numbered more than three thousand people, now there are only a little more than eight hundred of them. The evidences of their progress toward civilization are cheering. They are now self-supporting. They no longer die of hunger. But the character of the people has changed. In the old barbaric days they were light-hearted, merry, makers of jokes, keenly alive to the humorous side of life. Now they are serious, grave, little disposed to laugh. Then they were like children without a care. Now they are like men, on whom the anxieties of life weigh heavily. Civilization, bringing with it some measure of material prosperity, has also brought to these people care, responsibility, repression. No doubt it is best, and it is inevitable, but it is sad, too.

It was my last day, and I was again sitting with Eagle Chief, telling him that the time had come for me to go. He said, "Ah, my son, I like to see you here. I like to sit with you, and to talk over the old times. My heart is sick when I think that you are going away, and that we may never see each other any more. But," he added, solemnly, "It may be that *Ti-ra'-wa* will be good to us, and will let us live a long time until we are very old, and then some day we may meet again."

INDEX.